ALSO BY ANN RULE

Every Breath You Take
. . . And Never Let Her Go
Bitter Harvest
Dead by Sunset
Everything She Ever Wanted
If You Really Loved Me
The Stranger Beside Me
Possession
Small Sacrifices
Without Pity
Last Dance, Last Chance
Empty Promises
A Rage to Kill
The End of the Dream
In the Name of Love
A Fever in the Heart
You Belong to Me
A Rose for Her Grave
The I-5 Killer
The Want-Ad Killer
Lust Killer

Heart Full of Lies

A True Story of Desire and Death

Ann Rule

Free Press
New York · London · Toronto · Sydney · Singapore

***f*P**

FREE PRESS
A Division of Simon & Schuster, Inc.
1230 Avenue of the Americas
New York, NY 10020

The names of some individuals in this book have been changed.
Such names are indicated by an asterisk (*) the first time each appears in the book.

FREE PRESS *and colophon are trademarks*
of Simon & Schuster, Inc.

For information regarding special discounts for bulk purchases,
please contact Simon & Schuster Special Sales:
1-800-456-6798 or business@simonandschuster.com.

Designed by Lauren Simonetti

Photo of Liysa and her attorneys on page 15 of the photo insert by
Elane Dickenson, the Wallowa County Chieftain.

Manufactured in the United States of America

1   3   5   7 ·9   10   8   6   4   2

Library of Congress Cataloging-in-Publication Data is available.

ISBN 0-7432-0298-8

For Chris's little boy
to read
when he can understand

_____ CAST OF CHARACTERS _____

LIYSA NORTHON'S FAMILY

Mother: Sharon Arnhart DeWitt Fisher
Father: Wayland DeWitt, Ph.D.
Brother: Dr. Jon Keith "Tor" DeWitt
Jimmie Rhonda DeWitt, Tor's ex-wife
Gene Arnhart, her maternal grandfather
Lois Arnhart, her maternal grandmother
Barbara "Bobbi" Chitwood, Liysa's maternal aunt
Papakolea "Papako," * her son with Nick Mattson
Bjorn Northon,* her son with Chris Northon
Kurt Moran,* her first husband
Nick Mattson,* her second husband
Lora Lee Mattson,* Nick's current wife
Mary Mattson,* Nick's mother
Tim Sands,* her ex-fiancé
Jane Sands,* Tim's mother
Makimo,* her former lover

"Ray," a former lover
Randall Edwards, her high school date
"Kevin,"* her high school boyfriend
Craig Elliot,* screenwriter, coauthor

LIYSA NORTHON'S FRIENDS

Marni Kelly Clark* and Dr. Ben Clark*, Walla Walla, Washington; Ellen Duveaux,* Dayton, Washington; Betsy Haygood, California; Kit and Cal Minton,* Hawaii and Connecticut; Mia Rose,* Bend, Oregon; Billy Shamir,* Mia's ex-husband; Jane Pultz, Kailua; "The Pool Group," Kailua.

CHRIS NORTHON'S FAMILY

Dick Northon, Chris's father
Jeanne Stevenson Northon, Chris's mother
Mary Hetz, Chris's sister
Phil Hetz, Mary's ex-husband
Sally Byers, Chris's sister
Bjorn Northon, Chris's son with Liysa
Rick Northon, Dick's half brother
Yvonne Brown, Chris's aunt
Steve Brown, Chris's cousin
Ed Brown, Chris's uncle
Tom Brown, Chris's cousin
Jean Topping, Chris's aunt

CHRIS NORTHON'S FRIENDS

Margaret Lefton, landlady in Kailua; Maggie and Joe Rhys-Wilson, (fellow pilot); Randy Ore (pilot), Eva and John Gill,

Bend, Oregon; Arne and Carrie Arnesen,* Bend; Charlene "Maka" Makanani, ex-girlfriend; Sabrina Tedford, ex-girlfriend; Anna Goodrich, ex-girlfriend; Gina Goodrich, Anna's sister; Gay Bradshaw, ex-girlfriend; Sharon Leighty, ex-girlfriend; Don Strain, Bend handyman/carpenter; Buck Zink, boyhood friend, Bend; Rob Ezell, Bend; Dan Jones (pilot), Utah and Hawaii; Dr. David Jones; Debbie and Dave Story (pilot), Kailua; Warren Kitchell (pilot), Kailua; Kris Olson and Becky Jones, Bend.

CRIMINAL INVESTIGATION TEAM/ COURT PERSONNEL

Undersheriff Rich Stein, Wallowa County
Sheriff Ron Jett, Wallowa County
Detective Matt Cross, Wallowa County Sheriff's Office
Jody Williamson, United States Forest Service
Detective Patric Montgomery, Oregon State Police
Detective Jim Van Atta, Oregon State Police
Detective Mike Wilson, Oregon State Police
Detective Rob Ringsage, Oregon State Police
Dan Ousley, District Attorney, Wallowa County
Carol Terry, Assistant to Dan Ousley
Criminal Investigator Dennis Dinsmore, Oregon Attorney General's Office
Steve Briggs, Assistant Attorney General, Oregon
Deputy Kevin Larkin, Columbia County (Washington) Sheriff's Office
Dr. Karen Gunson, Oregon State Medical Examiner
Lieutenant Jeff Dovci, Criminalist, Oregon State Police Lab
Christine Ogilvie, Criminalist, Oregon State Police Lab
Deputy Dick Bobbitt, Umatilla County Sheriff's Office
Judge Philip Mendiguren, Trial Judge

Klista Steinbeck, Tracey Hall, Jary Homan, Court Operations Specialists, Wallowa County
FBI Special Agent Ariel Miller, Computer Expert

FOR THE DEFENSE

Pat Birmingham, Criminal Defense Attorney
Wayne Mackeson, Criminal Defense Attorney
Robin Karnes and Harold Nash, Private Investigators

HEART
FULL OF LIES

FOREWORD

ALMOST EVERY BOOK I have researched has had a beginning, a middle, and an end that were obvious when I began. By the time the defendant went to trial, his—or her—guilt appeared to be well established. There was little question that a sudden death might have been an accident or a suicide. There was no particular mystery about "who-dunnit?" Although loyal family members might have been in one corner or another, the mass of witnesses were testifying *against* the defendant.

In *Heart Full of Lies,* I found instead an emotional tug-of-war with dozens of people pulling on the victim's side and as many fiercely loyal to the accused. To this day, most of their allegiances have remained steadfast. Initially, I was puzzled that anyone could find the deceased so flawed and the defendant so angelic. Few human beings are either all good or all bad. The only way I have managed to deal with this impasse has been to show *both* sides as clearly as possible.

Still, in the end, the truth began to sift out of a morass of statements. I've noted that correspondence sent to me anonymously came from those who praised the defendant. They would give neither their names nor their positions in the defendant's life. On the other hand, the friends of the person who died were ready to step forward and give me their names and their connection to this case.

It is difficult to place your trust in people who hide in the shadows of anonymity. *Did you personally see this happen?* I asked again and again, trying to cut through the curtain that email with its endless choice of screen names affords. *Could this have been an accident?* And the answer was always *No*.

Then how do you know what happened? I pressed.

I just know, they all answered, either because they were absolutely convinced they were right or because they had been charmed and bewitched and manipulated by a brilliant and charismatic sociopath.

CHAPTER ONE

THE MOUNTAINS and high plains of extreme northeastern Oregon are so far from well-traveled freeways that even most Oregonians have never been to this wilderness area where the sky seems close enough to touch. These are the "Oregon Alps." Serious outdoorsmen and those with family ties to Wallowa County follow the thin red lines on the map that promise at most only "paved highways," up and up through the mountains from Pendleton or La Grande. The summits are more than five thousand feet high, and then the roads descend through tiny villages whose buildings are mostly gray shadows of their former incarnations, tumbled with old-fashioned perennials and weeds, fading storefronts and little churches with peeling paint: Adams, Athena, Elgin, Minam, Wallowa, Lostine. Near the end of the road is Enterprise—the county seat—and finally the hamlet called Joseph, named for the great chief of the Nez Percé tribe. All these towns, so far-flung from city lives, have a presence and a feeling of serenity that comes only with long history and time without urgency.

Enterprise and Joseph blossom in the summer as tourists who *have* discovered Wallowa County arrive. Sheltered between the Wallowa Mountains to the west and the Hells Canyon National Recreation Area to the east, Enterprise, population 1,900, is a wonderful place to live, but only if one is self-employed, working for the county or the city, or serving the needs of the residents. It is too distant from the larger Oregon cities along the coast or in the center of the state to make commuting feasible. The only industry of any sort is up the road eight miles, in Joseph. Perched on the shore of Wallowa Lake, Joseph has embraced sculpture and bronze foundries as a very successful economic lifeline; every street corner has a statue that seems to burst with life frozen in mid-movement—maidens and cowboys and eagles in flight—each statue large enough to require a truck to pack it out.

In the summer, Wallowa Lake is a burning hollow in the mountains, with its azure water reflecting the sun and the sky. The water there is cold, but not cold enough to deter boaters and water-skiers, who seem somehow out of place on the waters where Native Americans once fished. The mountains and the soaring trees have always been there and *will* always be there; the humans playing on the lake seem, in contrast, quite temporary.

Deer wander at will in Joseph, strolling along the narrow roads, peering into windows, and mingling with tourists at food stands and riding stables. A lift carries tourists who aren't afraid of heights far up the Wallowa Range. Flowers of every variety burst forth in the short summer season, boldly defiant against winter for their precious few months in the sun.

The center of Wallowa County government is in Enterprise, where a courthouse built in 1909 sits in the center of parklike grounds. Ninety-four years' worth of feet have worn away the interior stairways as generations of citizens went about their business with public records and the laws of Wallowa County.

Bright greenswards and paths crisscross the courthouse square, and baskets of trailing geraniums, ivy, and sweet alyssum make it resemble a set for *The Music Man.* There are concerts in the bandstand on the courthouse lawn, and the melodies floating on a summer's night are nostalgic enough to sting the eye with tears.

In 2000, Dan Ousley was the district attorney of Wallowa County. He was a familiar presence before judges and juries in the courthouse in Enterprise. But he was well into his second term in office before he ever had to deal with a murder that wasn't an open-and-shut case. And when he did have to prosecute a baffling homicide, it was a case that would have challenged prosecutors in Portland or Seattle or San Francisco, a crime that defied all reason, one that could be viewed straight on or through a microscope, and even then failed to reveal all its incredible variables.

Was the victim ultimately answerable for the bloody crime? Or was the accused capable of a meticulously choreographed execution? And perhaps even more important, who was the person who had held the weapon? There seemed to be a dozen different answers, and no way of telling if the personality shown to the world was truly the one almost everyone had perceived. Or was it all a clever masquerade, hiding evil?

* * *

IT ISN'T EASY to get to the camping sites on the Lostine River near the Maxwell Campgrounds trailhead that leads mountain hikers into the Eagle Cap Wilderness. To reach the campgrounds, one has to turn off Route 82 and head south from the town of Lostine. The first six or seven miles are partially paved, but that soon gives way to a gravel road. Even a four-wheel drive vehicle skitters along the washboard road that carves a path through the trees, the road so high-centered that it is a challenge for even the most competent drivers. It isn't a Sunday sight-seeing drive; one misjudged stomp on the brakes and a car or truck can slide and roll over and over.

Twelve miles or so from Lostine, fir forests cluster thickly along the road. On the right, there are a few cabins that were once occupied by the late United States Supreme Court justice William O. Douglas when he craved the solace of deep wilderness. They are spartan and overgrown now with brush. On the same side of the road, there is a forest ranger station—usually the last outpost where a phone of any kind will work. Beyond that, the Wallowas rise up and up, shutting off radio and cell phone transmission. In this tunnel of trees, it is impossible not to think of the danger of forest fires and wonder how quickly this road could be closed off by flames.

Almost twenty miles in, just before the trailhead, thin rutted paths begin to appear, wide enough apart for tires to traverse. They lead to campgrounds, maintained by the U.S. Department of Agriculture Forest Service, that are situated so each camping party has privacy. Much sought after in the warm months, the riverside campgrounds are empty in winter, buried beneath snowdrifts, next to a river as cold and clear as ice.

On a weekday morning in the autumn of 2000, most outdoorsmen who enjoyed hiking had gone back to civilization. More so than in many other places, October brought the empty sense that comes with a season's ending. It would be only a matter of weeks before the road in—or out—would be choked with snow.

If anyone *was* camping in early October, their vehicles parked close to the river campsites were nearly invisible from the road. Campers could drive at least seventy-five feet off the main road before they reached the horizontal tree trunk barriers that delineated parking spots. Trees and shadows hid their rigs, and from there, they had only to walk down an easy slope to the sandy shores of the Lostine River.

The Lostine itself is narrow, not more than forty feet or so across, shallow and crystalline with little ladders of rapids frothed with white. It is an icy cold river, stemming from alpine lakes high in the mountains. A storm runoff from the mountains has occasionally turned the Lostine dangerous, but in October it is usually a tranquil upstart of a river two or three feet deep at the most, surrounded by sentry rows of fir trees standing perfectly straight, their feathered tops piercing the sky hundreds of feet above.

* * *

IT WAS EARLY Monday afternoon, October 9, 2000, and the Shady Campground—one of the closest to the trailhead—appeared to be unoccupied. There were no sounds at all, save for the wind high in the trees and the occasional cry of a bird. For the moment, it was totally silent in the deserted camping area next to the winding Lostine River.

Rich Stein was the undersheriff of Wallowa County. He had been involved in law enforcement for eighteen years, and he had worked in the Wallowa County Sheriff's Office for fourteen and a half of those years. He was hoping to become sheriff the next month through a flourishing write-in campaign. Sheriff Ron Jett didn't plan to run again.

Stein halfway believed that he was on a wild-goose chase as he drove slowly along the gravel road close to the trailhead. He wasn't quite sure what he was looking for, a lost camper or someone who was injured. Sheriff Jett had sent him up to the campgrounds after Jett received a couple of phone calls from outside the county.

"I want you to go on up to the trailhead—maybe check things out along the river, see if anybody is there," Jett had said. "I'm not sure what you might find. . . ."

Stein wasn't really familiar with the campgrounds. His primary job was to oversee the deputies and run the patrol, but in Wallowa County, even the undersheriff had to pull shifts and work patrol. Sheriff Jett had told him to check out all of the overnight campgrounds. Stein thought there were about a dozen of them nestled down by the river. The one he thought was the last campsite was the Williamson Campground, and he drove in, parked, and walked down to the sandy beach but found no one there.

Stein estimated that the area he was searching was about eighteen miles from the town of Lostine. He couldn't raise anyone on his sheriff's radio, so he drove back along the forest road until he came to a high spot where his radio worked. He thought that maybe if he could get a little better idea of what he was looking for, he could be more effective. He called the Sheriff's Office, and Jett said that the latest information indicated that it was probably the Shady Campground he should check out. "It's the last one down the line."

This time, Jett's voice was more serious. It was possible that Stein was looking for a person who was critically wounded. He passed a campground and saw a lone car parked there. He checked that and found nobody in or near it. Now he could see there *was* another campsite. He glanced toward the sign marking it as SHADY CAMPGROUND and saw a newer model white Chevy Suburban parked against the log barrier.

Stein pulled his pickup close to that vehicle. Like a lot of cops who have ridden patrol cars for years, he had a bad back, and he winced a little as he eased out of his truck and crossed the uneven ground to look into the Suburban. He could see that the locks were pushed down. Inside, there was camping gear and other items, the usual stuff that people brought up to the wilderness—but there was no sign of a driver.

The Forest Service's picnic table just beyond the Suburban had camping equipment on it, too. It looked as though a family had enjoyed a picnic. "I walked over there and called out—announcing that I was a deputy sheriff," Stein recalled. "And I was shouting, 'Is there anyone around?' But there was no response."

There was a tent pitched nearby, but there was no movement inside, and no answer to his calls.

Two trails led down to the river, one shorter and steeper than the other, although neither demanded that a hiker be in good condition. Stein took the shorter trail that went straight down. Even though he knew there was probably a simple explanation for his feeling of dread, he acknowledged the eerie sensation. He shook it off; the people who had come here in the Suburban were probably just taking a short hike from the trailhead. An empty vehicle wasn't unusual.

And then he glanced to the south and caught a glimpse of bright blue fabric spread out down by the river. It was a sleeping bag.

"I yelled again," Stein recalled. "No response."

Gingerly, Stein walked down toward the river, his boots sinking and skidding a little in the sand.

The sun was high in the sky and it cut through the mist in the treetops, casting a glow over the sleeping bag. It was bright enough to awaken even the heaviest sleeper. The mummy-style bag lay at right angles to the river, with the "head" part almost touching a log the Forest Service had placed there just where the sandy beach began. The shallow edges of the Lostine lapped softly against its shoreline. Otherwise, it was completely quiet.

Stein called out again, more softly now, "Anybody here? Sheriff's office . . ."

Nobody answered. As he got closer, Stein could tell that there was somebody in the sleeping bag. "I approached it very cautiously," he said. He wasn't afraid. And it wasn't as if he hadn't investigated reports of a possible body before; it was more that this was one of the loneliest places he had ever been.

The form zipped into the sleeping bag was as motionless as the scattered boulders on the shore. Stein saw tufts of hair just above the one ear that showed. Either it was reddish blond naturally or something had stained it pale mahogany. He thought it was probably blood or some other dark liquid, although the sleeping bag wasn't stained as far as Stein could see.

At this altitude, in October even the glaring sun wouldn't warm the air in the shadows enough to make a sleeper perspire and peel down the confining layers. But maybe the person who lay there was no longer able to unzip the sleeping bag and crawl out. Maybe the person had fallen and sustained a head injury. Or maybe someone had struck the still form on the head while the camper was sleeping—or passed out.

Had someone abandoned the sleeper and the camp in the scenic wilderness deliberately? Or had the camper come alone to this small cleared area high in the mountains to get away from the problems of the world, possibly never intending to go back? Was it an accident—or a homicide? It was so isolated in the Shady Campground that it would have been a long time before hunters chanced on the scene and discovered whatever had happened here. And if a sudden early blizzard came—as it often did in Wallowa County—it might have been spring before anyone came in.

Except for the blond hair stiff with blood, and a folding chair tilted at an odd angle in the river, the campsite had an almost benign air.

Stein slipped his hand carefully into the sleeping bag, still hoping that he'd discovered only a drunk sleeping it off. He touched skin and found it cold as marble. He pressed against the flesh just below the ear, searching for the reassuring beat of blood pulsing through the carotid artery.

But there was none.

Stein chose the gently sloping trail back to the picnic area and returned to his pickup truck. He couldn't take the steep route back because he didn't want to walk through the death scene again. It was only when he slid into the driver's seat that he realized he didn't know if it was a man or a woman who lay dead in the sleeping bag.

The undersheriff hadn't touched anything beyond the cold flesh of the neck, and he wasn't going to, not until the sheriff had a complete crew on the scene. Assuming that his radio wouldn't work, Stein drove a mile south to the trailhead. There was an open spot there where he thought he might be able to get through to the Sheriff's Office, but his radio wouldn't work there either. Once more he drove two miles north past the Shady Campground and tried again.

This time he got through.

"Sheriff," Stein said hurriedly, "I need you up here. We do have a body. We need the medical examiner and a lot of help up here."

* * *

THE CALLS THAT HAD originally sent Rich Stein up to the Shady Campground had come in to Sheriff Ron Jett from two law enforcement officers who were some distance away from Wallowa County—one in Washington State and another in Umatilla, Oregon, on the Oregon-Washington state line. The details were blurry, but the callers said they had been in contact with a woman who suggested that someone should check the Maxwell Campgrounds. Either the woman had been there or she knew something about what had happened there.

At the moment, she was far away, at least a four-hour drive from the shore of the Lostine River. She was in the little town of Dayton, Washington, thirty miles north of Walla Walla, the site of Washington's oldest penitentiary. Barely holding herself together, she had told a number of people about how she had driven through the night, fleeing desperately to save the life of her three-year-old son.

Her story was still coming out in staccato bursts and vague

ramblings. Clearly, the woman was upset, although she wasn't hysterical. The drive north from the Lostine River would have been perilous from the beginning. Just getting down to the town of Lostine in the middle of the night without spinning out was a feat. After that, there was no way out of the Oregon Alps without crossing mountain passes where the air was thin and the roads pitch-dark and lonely. For a woman afraid and in shock, it would have been a nightmare. If she had gone by way of Pendleton on 204, she would have had to cross "Dead Man's Pass," with an altitude of 4,200 feet. But it was likely that she had taken a more direct route through Weston and Milton-Freewater, and then crossed the state line into Washington and up to Walla Walla.

State Route 204 was more than a mile high at the summit, an unbelievably beautiful vista in daylight in October. But the woman had fled in the middle of the night. She would have seen nothing alongside the road, only a black void that, depending on where she was, could be either a forest or a deadly precipice.

It was all the more treacherous because she had had her small son with her as she hurtled through the night. Her damp clothing—or perhaps something else—must have made her shiver. Her young son was safe, but she told Washington lawmen that she had been determined to get to her other son, who was nine years old, to be sure he was safe, too. If she had allowed herself to think about the horror she had left behind, she wouldn't have been able to keep her SUV on the road.

If any woman could have managed it, *she* could. She was a slender woman with strong muscles and a body as sleek as any model's, an athlete who worked out and practiced yoga. She was very determined and unafraid of anything when it came to her boys. She would have died for them without even considering any threat to herself. Her friends, scattered from Hawaii to Oregon to the East Coast, considered her a kind of super-woman—perfect mother, exceptional athlete, talented writer, and a friend they could always count on. But now it was she who would have to depend on her friends.

Her name was Liysa Ann DeWitt Moran* Mattson* Northon. Thirty-eight years old, she had already lived an adventurous and remarkable life.

* * *

THE PEOPLE LIYSA TRUSTED the most lived in Washington State, and it wasn't surprising she had run to them. Sometime in the early hours of Monday, October 9, 2000, she had headed north, crossed over the Oregon-Washington border between 6:30 and 7:00 A.M., and driven to her brother's house in Walla Walla.

Dr. Jon Keith "Tor" DeWitt was a chiropractor, specializing in sports medicine. Short and stocky, he was a bodybuilder, probably more fit than most of the athletes he worked on. He was Liysa's only sibling, a few years younger than she was. Divorced and living with his children in a house that was three blocks off the main route to Dayton through Walla Walla, DeWitt was a man of careful habits. He usually got up at 6:00 A.M., and he was in the kitchen, just beginning to swallow his morning regimen of vitamins, when he was surprised to hear the unlocked sliding door open. He turned, startled, and saw that his sister, Liysa, had come into the dark kitchen.

"We talked for a few minutes before I saw her face," he recalled. It appeared to him that she had been "beat up." Looking at Liysa closely, he saw a cut on one finger and a bruise on her "third thoracic vertebra." She was wearing sweatpants and a shirt, and they were damp. Her hair was wet, too.

DeWitt urged his sister to go to the emergency room at St. Mary's Hospital, but she declined, saying she would rather have Dr. Ben Clark,* the husband of Marni Clark*—one of her best friends—examine her. For some reason, her brother didn't think it was a good idea to involve the Clarks. "Just go to St. Mary's," he suggested again.

Liysa didn't seem to be that badly hurt, and DeWitt had to get to work. He had seen her with bruises before and heard through a third party that her husband, Chris, had put them there. But when he said he wanted to confront Chris about it, Liysa had begged him not to. Now he assumed that Chris was the one who had hit her. She had told him another time that Chris was sometimes violent with her.

Almost offhandedly, Liysa murmured something about "taking a shot" at Chris.

"Did you hit him?" DeWitt asked, alarmed.

"I don't know," she said vaguely.

Liysa told her brother that she had to hurry to pick up Papako*—her nine-year-old son—from Ellen Duveaux's* house. "Bjorn's* sleeping in my Explorer," she said. "I have to get to Ellen's."

Somewhat bemused, DeWitt said good-bye to his sister, but urged her to call him and let him know how she was. She had been with him for only a few minutes, and he wondered if she hadn't been exaggerating when she said she'd taken a shot at Chris. He left for work, concerned, but not really anxious. Liysa could wax very dramatic about things that wouldn't disturb most people.

It was so early in the morning; the sun had barely risen when Liysa had pulled up at his place. It wasn't seven o'clock yet and now she was gone, headed for the Duveaux farm in Dayton.

* * *

ELLEN DUVEAUX and Liysa had been friends in Walla Walla since Liysa DeWitt was only sixteen and still in high school. Ellen was eleven years older than Liysa, but they'd always gotten along well. Much of Walla Walla County was fertile farmland, known worldwide for its "Walla Walla Sweets," gourmet onions, but also a major source of other crops and fine wine. Liysa and Ellen had spent summers bringing in the mature produce, mostly peas. Liysa had driven the swather, wrestling the heavy vehicle as easily as any man, while Ellen drove the pea combine.

Ellen was married to Francois-Louis Duveaux,* whose name sounded like a romantic French actor's, but who was a really down-to-earth man who loved the verdant soil of Walla Walla County. They had a wheat ranch and a good life in the tiny town of Dayton, Washington, even though it wasn't the most exciting spot on earth.

Liysa had wanted another life after she left Walla Walla High School. She planned to be a world traveler and adventuress, but she had deferred to her father's wish that she go to college first.

Ellen loved Liysa and sometimes felt protective toward her; Liysa longed for so much that she seemed to take terrible chances with her heart. The twenty-three years they'd known each other had gone by swiftly, but the two women had remained friends. Even though years might pass when they were out of touch, they always picked up right where they'd left off.

After a long time apart, they'd gotten back together in the early nineties and saw each other once a year or so. Liysa always had some amazing story to tell. Sometimes it was about a doomed romance or a close escape she had had, but more often it was about various wonderful new plans she'd made.

Ellen often lost track of Liysa, but she knew that she'd hear from her eventually. She didn't know all the details of her past. She wasn't really sure just how many times Liysa had been married.

But she had always found Liysa to be tough and strong yet very warm and caring at the same time. Petite as she was, Liysa could compete with any man in what was considered "man's work." Ellen was an artist, using stained glass as her medium, and she was very good, working in her home studio and teaching talented students. Liysa was a constant traveler, and to Ellen, she seemed remarkably brave—no matter what life handed her. Ellen wasn't aware of everything Liysa had done while they were apart but she suspected she didn't know half of her accomplishments.

It was about 7:30 on that smoky-bright Monday October morning in Dayton, and Francois-Louis Duveaux was about to leave for work when he called to Ellen that Liysa had just parked her SUV and it was blocking his car. Ellen had expected her—but not this early.

At Liysa's request, Papako Mattson, who was Liysa's son by an earlier marriage, had spent Friday night, Saturday, and Sunday with the Duveauxs. Liysa had called Ellen to tell her that she and her present husband, Chris Northon, and their three-year-old son, Bjorn, would be camping on the Lostine River down in Oregon that weekend. But Papako loved working with Ellen. Very talented artistically, he had chosen to come to Dayton to have some glass lessons from Ellen rather than go on the camping trip. Ellen agreed at once; Papako, nine, was a delightful child, and he was welcome at the Duveaux house anytime.

Liysa had driven all the way from Bend, Oregon, where she and Chris had a home, to deliver Papako to Ellen on Friday night. It was a *very* long drive, more than three hundred miles one way. She had spent the night, and then she and Bjorn left on Saturday morning to join Chris at the campsite on the Lostine River. She said she would be back on Monday to get Papako.

Now it *was* Monday and Liysa had returned. She moved her Ford Explorer and then walked slowly up to the back entrance of the house. Ellen was horrified when she saw her standing there, "wet and beaten up."

When Ellen sensed that Liysa was in deep distress, she rushed to help her. As she would recall later, Liysa's hair looked as though she'd just toweled it dry after a shower, but her clothes were so wet that when Ellen hugged her, she got wet, too. "She was pretty messed up, vacant, glazed eyes, spacey—in shock," Ellen recalled.

"Why are you all wet?" she asked, but she didn't really get an answer. It seemed to her that Liysa's arm was hanging at a funny angle.

"I need help getting Bjorn out of the Explorer," Liysa pleaded. "My shoulder's injured and I can't seem to lift him out."

Ellen hurried behind Liysa to the SUV and lifted the sleeping toddler easily out of his car seat. Liysa looked as though she was hypothermic, and her teeth were chattering. That wasn't unusual for her; Liysa was always cold, even in Hawaii, where she lived half the time. She had Raynaud's disease, too, and her fingers turned bluish purple with the least drop in temperature.

Ellen's eyes searched Liysa's face. Her friend seemed so distraught, so injured. She had a swollen cheek, a slight bruise near her eye, and an arm or shoulder that appeared to be broken.

"Chris tried to kill me," Liysa burst out. "Chris tried to kill me. . . ."

Chapter Two

WHATEVER HAD HAPPENED at that beautiful mountain campsite, no one who was acquainted with the couple who had set out for the Lostine River three days before would believe it. Visualizing Chris Northon as a killer was virtually impossible for his friends and family. Picturing Liysa Northon in either role was just as preposterous to *her* friends. They were the perfect couple with the perfect life. More accurately, an almost perfect life; like any viable marriage, theirs was sometimes marked by dissension.

But at this point, the detectives who responded to Rich Stein's call for crime scene investigators knew nothing at all about the Northons. Chris and Liysa didn't live in Wallowa County. They spent part of their time in Kailua, Hawaii, and the other part in Bend, Oregon. They not only lived in one paradise—they had the best of *two* paradises.

* * *

LISA ANN DEWITT was born in Silver City, New Mexico, on March 10, 1962, to Sharon Irene Arnhart DeWitt and Wayland DeWitt. (Lisa would change her name in high school to "Liysa," which she found more exotic.) Her birth occurred eighteen days after astronaut John Glenn became the first American to orbit the earth. John F. Kennedy was at the peak of his popularity, exceeded, perhaps, only by his wife Jackie's. Nineteen sixty-two was a time of prosperity, and there was more public fascination with an English group of young musicians known as the Beatles, the scandal of Elizabeth Taylor and Richard Burton in the making of *Cleopatra,* and the suicide of Marilyn Monroe than there was with the expanding war in Vietnam.

The DeWitts moved to Warrensburg, Missouri, when Liysa was about six months old. Her second child, Jon Keith, called "Tor," was born on November 7, 1963. Liysa's mother, Sharon, was sometimes the only parent at home caring for two babies who were just eighteen months apart. Wayland DeWitt was an educator and traveled a great deal. He was a kind-faced man who resembled George Gobel, a wildly popular TV comedian in the fifties and sixties. Wayland even sounded like Gobel. But he was highly intelligent and would eventually get his doctorate and rise to the higher echelons of college administration.

When Liysa was five, her family moved to Walla Walla, Washington, a city of 30,000. The DeWitts lived in a newer large white house in a private cul de sac, and they became prominent in the community and in the congregation of St. Paul's Episcopal Church. Liysa attended the church's summer camp—Camp Cross—in Coeur d'Alene, Idaho.

At Prospect Point Elementary School, she became friends with Marni Kelly, a close friendship that would span twenty-five years. Both girls' fathers were educators, but it was more than that. From the age of ten on, Marni and Liysa just got along. They went to gymnastics classes together and they both had ambitions to become cheerleaders. Liysa had a freckled face and reddish tones to her brown hair, and Marni was a brunette with huge brown eyes and an impish look. The best friends went on to Garrison Junior High and then to the only high school in town: Walla Walla High School. For decades, students have referred to it as Wa-Hi. Throughout their school years, the bond between Liysa and Marni never faltered.

When she was a child, Liysa Ann DeWitt spent a lot of her time near Joseph, Oregon, long before it became a haven for talented artists in bronze and a tourist magnet. Her grandparents lived there, as did her maternal aunt, Barbara—"Bobbi." Liysa was always an outdoor girl, and the area near Hells Canyon was rife with opportunities. She skied, both downhill and cross-country, swam like a fish, floated down the rivers in drift boats, and hiked into the mountains. Although she was petite, she was very strong.

Sharon DeWitt, née Arnhart, was raised in Joseph, in the Oregon territory where Chief Joseph once walked. Her family had had ties with Wallowa County for generations. Sharon was an attractive woman who had once been a pretty girl with thick dark hair—so pretty that she had been chosen queen of "Chief Joseph Days" in Wallowa County when she was only fifteen, the youngest Chief Joseph Days queen ever. Beauty counted but not as much as riding ability and public speaking. Wearing light green western shirts and pants, white hats with light green bands, and white boots adorned with gold eagles, the girls who vied for queen of the Chief Joseph Days celebration were much admired by their peers. They spoke twice—once at the rodeo grounds and again at the civic center. Sharon was the best rider and the most eloquent speaker.

Her days as queen were heady. She was deeply embarrassed, though, when she danced with one of the contest chaperons—Vern Russell. "He turned me one way, my feet went another, and I grabbed his shirt and ripped it down the back!" she remembered. Six years later Sharon was married and gave birth to Liysa Ann. She became a mother at twenty-one to a daughter who would resent her almost from the time she could walk.

Even Ellen Duveaux didn't know all the details of Liysa's childhood. But to other friends and lovers she would later recall that she had been routinely reviled and beaten by her mother. Her memories were that she suffered horribly as a child at Sharon DeWitt's hands. She said that her mother had chased her with a knife, screamed at her, and had broken twenty-six bones in her body before she was sixteen, and finally old enough to flee and live on her own.

Liysa said that she had to kneel naked in the bathtub when she was nine years old so her mother could be sure she wouldn't urinate on the floor in response to the pain of the beatings. Liysa would rarely criticize her father or fault him for choosing his career over everything else, but she suggested that it was apparently Wayland who had looked away, leaving her helpless to face her mother's rage.

Also, according to Liysa, when she was eleven and approaching puberty, almost everything she did irritated her mother. She remembered being slapped in the face and struck with belts and vases until her back was bloody. Her vivid recall was that the only inside door that locked in their house was the bathroom door. In her attempt to escape her mother, Liysa held the doorknob with its flimsy lock and wedged her feet against the wall to get a better grip. As an adult, she told intimates that her mother became so furious with her that she picked the bathroom door lock with a knife. She even recalled that her mother held her head underwater and she was afraid she would drown. Liysa said she tried to stay in the bathroom until her father came home, when both his wife and his daughter would demand that he mediate their differences.

Later on, Liysa spoke of her mother with more compassion, acknowledging that the woman she once considered "an agent of hell . . . who should be put to death for her irrational outbursts" had probably been insecure after a horrendous childhood of her own. Even so, Liysa couldn't have found her grandparents too terrible because she spent so much time visiting with them. Wallowa County residents recall that Gene Arnhart, Liysa's grandfather, had hauled some of the logs that were used to build the original Chief Joseph Day rodeo stadium in Joseph way back in 1947. His wife, Lois, was said to be a sweet and caring woman.

But as an adult, Liysa would recall that her mother was a woman who had been left on her own, ill equipped to cope with the intellectuals Wayland met as a college administrator, and having to care for two children. Sometimes, Liysa said that she had suffered from epilepsy when she was a child.

She did not mention that her mother was a personnel staffer, who had been instrumental in the development of two community colleges from the ground up—Walla Walla, Washington Community College and Northeast Texas Community College in Mount Pleasant.

If she vilified her mother, Liysa apparently idolized her father as brilliant and kind. She gave credit to Wayland DeWitt for teaching her that prejudice was wrong and that she should treat everyone she met with respect, even going so far as to urge her not to turn down dates with any of the boys who asked. "Don't judge a book by its cover," her father said.

She thought it was amusing that many of the guys Wayland approved of were wildly dangerous. She was serious when she thought of a man for whom her father saw no future, and how she had broken their engagement. Years later, she wrote that she realized that *he* was the man she should have married. But, of course, then it was too late.

Only rarely did Liysa view her father as someone who might *not* always be right. She speculated later that his reliance on platitudes and "doing the right thing" eventually helped to bring down his successful career as a college president.

Early on, Liysa had a sense of fantasy and a talent for story-telling. One day, she would become a writer of no little talent, and her imagination was always full of "what-ifs?"

All children wonder at times if they are adopted, or imagine a father or mother other than the ones they've been told they belong to. Liysa's daydreams went further. She sometimes thought Wayland wasn't her biological father. She didn't look like him—she was thin and he tended to put on weight. But she *wanted* Wayland to be her father, the genetic source of her intelligence. They were almost bizarrely close, while she was at war with her mother, whom she found evasive and "uptight."

It wasn't just her father that Liysa wondered about. She was convinced that her mother and aunt were not her grandfather's biological children. She envisioned a strong brown-eyed Indian lover in Joseph for her grandmother, positive that two blue-eyed parents could not have produced a brown-eyed child. Her belief in that Mendelian theory was wrong, of course, but it supported Liysa's fantasy.

Liysa's magical thinking might simply have been part of her creative personality. She showed more talent than most children and teenagers and she was far more introspective than any of her peers. She lived inside her head. But whatever had happened to her as a child and as a teenager—whether it was brought on by parental abuse or something genetically predetermined—she developed a tremendous hunger for security. That, however, was virtually impossible to feed because she also craved adventure, recognition for her many talents, and absolute, continual, unconditional love and romance. Sexually, she seemed insatiable, which, for the men she encountered in her life, was not necessarily a negative trait. She often bragged that she had to have sex every day.

* * *

LIYSA WAS POPULAR at Wa-Hi in Walla Walla, but she wasn't one of the blond, blue-eyed teenage beauties that other girls envy. She was attractive in an athletic, healthy way. She had lovely eyes and perfect teeth, and she wore her hair in the then-in-vogue "Farrah Fawcett" shag cut, which tended to accentuate her rather broad face. The bone structure she would have one day didn't yet show; she still had a slight overbite. Her figure was ordinary, too—neither too heavy nor too thin, but despite her athleticism, she had very poor posture, tending to duck her head and slump her shoulders.

A onetime classmate recalled, "Liysa *was* attractive and popular—but in such a small school and community, everyone knew everyone else. She never stood out that much in the crowd; she was just another student." Another fellow graduate disagreed, noting, "Liysa was pretty popular by senior year—she was into a lot of activities."

Walla Walla's main "industries" are farming and maintaining the Washington State Penitentiary. Most students at Wa-Hi had family members working in one or the other. The prison was a shadowy presence to the residents who were so used to its being there that they paid attention only when there was a high-profile escape.

"Even then," one resident commented, "we didn't worry too much—the escaped cons wanted to get as far away from Walla Walla as they could. Most of the time we didn't lock our homes and we left our keys in our cars. In the seventies, we had only two radio stations—both A.M.—and when they broadcast a prison break alarm, we'd bring in our keys and lock our doors, but then we'd go back to our old habits."

Some of the state prison's trustees were allowed to participate in work programs like washing dishes or busing tables in local restaurants. Many of them attended classes at Walla Walla Community College, and regular students watched them as they sat together in the commons, accompanied by guards. "We never really thought about them," one of Liysa's classmates said. "They never scared us. They were more scared of us, I think."

Liysa's father sometimes went into the prison as a lay religious counselor. He often talked of being a psychologist who worked with prisoners. He was extremely affable, intelligent, and charming, a man who most people liked immediately.

Walla Walla in the 1970s was as all-American as any small town in the Midwest, boring to some teenagers, comforting to others. There wasn't much to do beyond going to dances or watching Wa-Hi's sports teams—the Blue Devils—play and their mascot perform. Sports were *very* important.

And they "Bombed the Gut" every weekend—their term for driving the loop from Isaacs Street to Main Street and back again, honking and waving at friends. They would "convoy," forming a train of cars, and meet late in the evening for a kegger, drinking beer in the middle of a wheat field. Sometimes they smoked homegrown marijuana. Liysa participated in those forbidden activities.

As a junior, she was on the district champions' tennis team, but it was Wa-Hi's Allison Bingham who took first in the tournament and came in seventh in the state. Liysa was a mainstay on the tennis team in her senior year, too. She *did* become a cheerleader and really blossomed in her senior year. Liysa and Marni were both picked to be members of the Homecoming Court. Liysa also dressed up as a Little League baseball player for the "Play-Day" high jinks of homecoming weekend. She was Key Club Sweetheart and on the ASB—student council. She was on the rally squad, and she and Marni were both on the varsity gymnastics team, although it was Marni who won state honors on the balance beam, vaulting, and free exercise competitions.

Still, the most important social accomplishment at Wa-Hi was to be accepted by one of the school's "service clubs," which were actually more like exclusive sororities or fraternities. Out of a typical class population of 250 to 300, only 20 girls could hope to be chosen by each of the three elite clubs in a year. Kappa Chi, Jeune Fille, and Phi Mista began to rush all the incoming sophomores with parties during the summer, and then blackballed most because their parents' income and social standing and their own reputations didn't measure up. The few girls who were accepted were subjected to hazing initiations, dressed in clothes that made them look ridiculous, and publicly embarrassed. And then, thrilled beyond measure to belong, they were formally initiated in solemn ceremonies. Despite her parents' social status, Liysa didn't make it until she was a junior, when Jeune Fille chose her. She was finally able to wear the special club sweatshirt and attend semisecret meetings at 7:30 on Wednesday nights.

She wasn't an extraordinary student, and her remarkable intelligence didn't shine through at Wa-Hi. She didn't date a lot, but the one boyfriend that most people remember was Randall Edwards, a tall, blond student with a crooked smile and superior grades. He was on the boys' tennis team and was the best friend of Chuck Stonecipher, who was dating Marni Kelly. Later, Liysa and Randall would both, in their own ways, make headlines.

Randall was Liysa's escort as her name was announced for the homecoming court, and they went to the senior prom together, disco dancing along with the crowd. Later, Liysa recalled that she got drunk that night and was grounded for a whole year. If she wasn't completely grounded, her activities were severely restricted for a long time.

Of all the girls on the rally squad or the cheerleading team or in the homecoming court, Liysa Ann DeWitt would seem to be the least likely to have a chaotic life. She looked so wholesome, and when she was elected to the homecoming court, she wore old, ragged jeans and didn't even sit up straight in her chair. The long-stemmed red rose in her hands looked out of place.

It's quite possible that Liysa always had secrets, repressed memories, or soaring ambitions, crushing disappointments or impossible dreams. Her personality in high school seems to have been barely formed, or submerged so deeply that no one really knew her.

Perhaps even Liysa didn't know then how many things she wanted—how many she *needed* to feel happy.

CHAPTER THREE

LIYSA GRADUATED from high school in 1979 and headed off to Oregon State University in Corvallis. Marni Kelly entered prelaw studies. Liysa stayed at Oregon State for about two years. There, she apparently had a passionate and satisfying love affair—her first orgasm as she recalled it—with a star football player for the Oregon State Beavers. The man—or boy— was named Ray, but none of Liysa's friends now recalls hearing about him, and they certainly don't know his last name. According to Liysa, they were engaged to be married when Ray was killed in a car accident between Corvallis and the Oregon coast two months before their wedding, and she was inconsolable.

Many years later, she would write about the first time Ray made love to her. Ray may have been Samoan or Hawaiian.

In the 1980's, with their two children virtually grown, Sharon and Wayland DeWitt drifted toward divorce, which Liysa attributed to their disagreements about what was acceptable discipline and what was "child abuse." She continued to remain closer to her father than to her mother.

LIYSA DID NOT GRADUATE from Oregon State. She married Kurt Moran* on almost the first day of summer—June 20— 1981, not long after they were introduced by a mutual friend. She was just nineteen. Marni, who was in the wedding party, and her friend Ellen Duveaux were among those celebrating with her. Liysa would later say that there was nothing to celebrate—that her first marriage was only a sham. And as with so many friends after marriage, both Ellen and Marni would lose track of Liysa for a decade.

Kurt Moran, twenty, was from Santa Barbara, and he was the physical type that Liysa would always be drawn to. He was very tall, probably over six feet four, and had a slender build. He was quiet and Liysa would describe him as "shy." He was a musician—a talented flutist. After their wedding in the Walla Walla Amphitheater, the couple moved to Ithaca, New York, where Kurt continued his studies at Cornell University. The water sprite in Liysa may have enjoyed Cayuga Lake, but she was never an East Coast girl. She wasn't happy there.

Liysa would relate many different versions of their marriage. In years to come, she told one lover that she had married Kurt simply to appease her parents after they found out she had slept with him, and that the marriage was in name only. She said it hadn't even lasted the weekend and she had gone to Mexico immediately to get a divorce.

That simply wasn't true. Liysa actually lived with Kurt for four years—until January 1985. And they were *legally* married for six years. After a few years in Ithaca, they moved to Hawaii at Liysa's request. By that time, a very disturbing pattern began to emerge, and Kurt had come to realize that Liysa was lying to him about any number of things. "She was very manipulative," he recalled. "She *couldn't* tell the truth. She would lie about who she was working for, about where she was last night, personal things. . . ."

Early on, Kurt had had trouble believing her sometimes bizarre stories, but although they had arguments, their marriage was anything but violent; they never hit each other. Indeed, Kurt could remember only one or two occasions when their arguments escalated to yelling.

They had occasionally used marijuana, but rarely, and as far as Kurt could tell, Liysa had no problems with alcohol or drug use. She told him that she had taken "something like Ritalin or Dilantin" when she was a child because she had "something psychological" wrong with her that manifested itself in seizures. She was never more specific than that, and she had apparently outgrown her seizures. Her symptoms suggest epilepsy, for which Dilantin is the drug of choice. Ritalin, similar to methamphetamine, is given to hyperactive children, in whom it has an opposite effect.

"She was a bright, secretive person," Kurt remembered. "[But] she could twist information in the complete opposite direction from reality. She would say *anything* to convince you her story was true."

One of Liysa's constant complaints as a young wife in the early eighties was that "no one loves me." Kurt concluded she had very low self-esteem because of all the stories she told him about how she had been used by men, some of them *after* her marriage to him. Moving to Hawaii hadn't made her any happier, and the marriage was doomed.

Kurt met Wayland DeWitt and admired his father-in-law, whom he characterized as a very outgoing and highly educated man. Liysa clearly respected her father, but her relationship with her mother was not good. Things between Liysa and Sharon were "very strained." It seemed to Kurt that the two women were constantly competing for Wayland's attention and approval. But, oddly, Liysa didn't say anything to her husband about being abused as a child. He never heard even one story about Sharon beating Liysa.

When Liysa told Kurt that she was having "blackouts," he doubted it. It seemed contrived. Then he discovered that she had been unfaithful to him with a number of different men, and for him that was the end of their marriage. "I had to get out—our relationship wasn't true," he recalled.

It was January 1983, when Liysa and Kurt moved to Hawaii from Ithaca. At the time, of course, Liysa was still a married woman. And yet she soon met a man whose name would appear continually in her life story. He was a tall Hawaiian lifeguard named Makimo*. Muscular and darkly tanned, Makimo sat atop a steel lifeguard tower as his eyes swept the water beyond the beach at Hanauma Bay, a wondrous, protected near-circle of everchanging blue and green sea off the island of Oahu. Hanauma Bay plays a huge role in ancient Hawaiian mythology and soon became magical to Liysa, too.

She came to the beach at Hanauma Bay with several other young women who were dedicated lifeguard groupies. They often hung out with the handsome guards after they finished their shifts. Makimo was well aware that the other girls worked as exotic dancers and some were prostitutes, but he wasn't sure what Liysa's job was. She simply appeared with the group of pretty girls in their bikini bathing suits. And she had dramatically changed from the bland, freckled girl who had graduated from Wa-Hi back in eastern Washington just four years earlier. She was extremely attractive and she stood out from the crowd.

Liysa's early days in Hawaii are hard to track. She may have lived for a time on the Big Island, part of the fringe culture of the early eighties. Her first husband said that she refused to tell him what she did when they were apart.

On the beach at Hanauma Bay, it quickly became apparent to Makimo that Liysa had singled him out. She was very seductive toward him, and, at first, he flirted back casually. He had no idea that she was married—and he would *never* know the full truth about Kurt.

Makimo wasn't married, but he was in a committed relationship and he had a child with his lover. Nevertheless, he and Liysa had a short, intense physical affair. It meant far more to Liysa than it did to Makimo; her fascination with him bordered on obsession and would color the rest of her life.

Years afterward, Makimo would refer to his sexual encounter with Liysa as a "one-night stand." Liysa would tell subsequent lovers a different story. She claimed that she and Makimo were officially engaged from January to May of 1983. Whatever the truth was, Makimo would always be the model with which Liysa compared all the men who came into her life. "Oh yeah, Makimo was the *perfect* man," one of the men Liysa was engaged to said. "I got tired of hearing about him."

Perhaps she fixated on Makimo because he was one of the few men she couldn't have. Liysa's romance with the muscular lifeguard—whether it was one night or several months in duration—*was* over by May 1983. Devastated, she flew to the mainland for a few months. Her father was president of Walla Walla

Community College in her hometown, and he was always a comfort to her.

In 1984, Wayland DeWitt left Walla Walla Community College to become the president of Northeast Texas Community College in Mount Pleasant, Texas. Liysa kept in touch with her father and promised to visit him there. In many ways, he was her lifeline. But it would be difficult for her to leave Hawaii. Liysa had found a spot on earth that suited her perfectly: the lush flowers, the lifestyle, and the soft tropical air. She quickly mastered Hawaiian phrases and learned the ancient folktales.

It wasn't just Hawaii that enchanted her; it was the ocean. The girl who had gloried in her brief summers in Joseph and Enterprise in the high plains of eastern Oregon felt as if she had come home when she saw the ocean in Hawaii. She was energized and inspired by the sea. The curling waves with their translucent green, shading to blue and silver and finally to white froth, embraced her and made her feel totally alive. Her first lovemaking with the elusive man called "Ray" had taken place in a pool, and ever after she preferred to have intercourse in or near the ocean.

Perhaps she had accepted that she could not have Makimo, but she couldn't stay away from where he was. And that was on the beach at Hanauma Bay. Liysa now had a flawless body, and her long brown hair with blond strands bleached by the sun fell to her waist. Bikinis became her. If she wasn't really beautiful— nor viewed from some angles even pretty—she was unquestionably striking, all sculpted with defined cheekbones and a high forehead, her eyes light against her bronzed tan, with a spray of faint freckles. Twenty years hence, her constant sun worship would probably leave a web of fine lines on her face, but for the moment, she was everything most twenty-two-year-old women wanted to be, and everything most men wanted.

In 1984, Liysa was still technically living with Kurt, although their paths had grown farther and farther apart. She enrolled at the University of Hawaii, where she concentrated on journalism and video technology. Liysa had always kept journals and written almost compulsively. She had a natural talent for fiction. A career as a writer wasn't her sole ambition—she had many—but it was high on the list.

It becomes even more difficult to trace Liysa's movements after 1984. She worked one summer as a research diver for the University of Hawaii in the Northwest Hawaiian Island chain. She may have had a relationship with a man named John Laurance* on that trip. She told some of her friends that the captain of the boat she worked on had sexually abused her, possibly in Caribbean waters. She told others that she was raped by her boss when she worked a few months later for a videographer.

Liysa seemed to be a constant target for sexual harassment. She said that she was the only woman to pass the test to be a Navy Seal, but she was disgusted by the officer who had tested her for swimming and diving skills. According to her, he deliberately put his hands on her breasts and pelvic area when she knew the swimming test didn't call for that. She laughed as she said she'd kicked him in the testicles.

She was still married to Kurt, and somehow, she was able to keep all of her stories in the air, deftly juggling one and managing to catch another just before it crashed to earth. Kurt had most certainly become suspicious, but they remained together—at least legally.

CHAPTER FOUR

AS 1985 BEGAN, Kurt officially parted from Liysa. He moved first to the island of Maui, and after 1985, he never again initiated any contact with Liysa. A year later, in July 1986, he moved back to the mainland, settling in Santa Barbara. There, in April 1987, he finally filed for divorce. When she was served with divorce papers, Liysa didn't contest the action, and their decree was granted six months later.

Given his choice, Kurt would have preferred to sever all ties with Liysa. His initial attraction to the charming nineteen-year-old girl had long since been erased by her infidelities and problems with the truth. He moved on, although he would be surprised to hear from her many years later.

Liysa always had to have a man in her life, and it wouldn't be long before she began another romance. In truth, many of her liaisons tended to overlap. She rarely leapt blindly into single life, as she had invariably chosen the next man. Although her obsession with Makimo was always with her, he had told her that they could never be more than close friends. He meant it; even a woman with Liysa's power of persuasion couldn't shake his loyalty to the woman who had borne his child.

Liysa was always drawn to men of a certain physical type. She was only five feet four, but she liked her men a foot taller, lean and muscular and—except for Makimo—blond and blue-eyed. High intelligence was also a quality she looked for. She met lots of men and she herself was on display frequently in her latest job, at Sea Life Park on the windward side of Oahu, about a twenty-minute drive from the town of Kailua. She swam with dolphins, her long hair streaming behind her, and dove into a large viewing aquarium to feed tropical fish. She was so at one with that water world, she might as well have been a mermaid, but one with beautiful legs.

TIM SANDS* REMEMBERS the night he met Liysa. "It was July thirteenth, 1985. We were at a friend's party in Lanakai." Twenty-four then to Liysa's twenty-three, Tim found her fun and attractive and "a little different." He was a very handsome man, almost six feet four, in perfect shape, and he had light hair and blue-green eyes. He didn't realize until much later that he fit perfectly within the parameters of her preferences.

Liysa told Tim that she had just received her bachelor's degree from the University of Hawaii—either in journalism or marine biology. He wasn't sure which. She also confided that she had a genius IQ. Tim didn't quite believe that at first, but it didn't matter; he was drawn to her because she was lovely and vibrant, not because she was superintelligent. When he introduced Liysa to his mother, Jane, she was impressed. "She seemed like a fine person—a fine 'charmer,' " Jane Sands would remember. "She was a beautiful girl and there was no question that she was absolutely brilliant."

Tim met Kurt Moran about a month after he and Liysa started dating, but he had no idea that Kurt was Liysa's estranged husband, and that she was still legally married to him. He assumed Kurt was just someone she had once dated.

"A week or two later, she told me she had been married to Kurt, but only very briefly," Tim said. Liysa explained that she had dated Kurt back in Washington State when she was very young and they had had intercourse. She said her parents were shocked and upset when they found out she had slept with him. "So she said she had married Kurt Moran, just to satisfy them," Tim recalled. "But she assured me that they got divorced the next day . . . so it wasn't really a marriage."

It was early in their relationship and Tim believed what Liysa told him. He had no reason not to. A lot of people made dumb mistakes in their teens, and he wasn't going to blame Liysa for a marriage that didn't really exist. He was *ready* to believe her; he was enthralled by her and it wasn't long before they were essentially living together. However, Liysa insisted on keeping her own place. It seemed important to her to maintain control. With Tim, she was never a helpless woman. Indeed, she was very strong.

Tim had grown up on Lanipo Street* in Kailua on the other side of the island of Oahu from Honolulu. His mother still lived there and so did a lot of people he had known since he was a boy, including peers he'd gone to Punaho High School with. Lanipo was a friendly street, built around a cul de sac, and was a steep walk up from the beach with an incredible view of the ocean. Its houses were set on a bluff above the beach, and those who lived there looked down upon coconut palm trees and Norfolk and Cook Island pines which grew so thickly that most of the rooftops below were hidden. Lanipo Street seemed to be suffused in a shimmery green cloud, with flowers that came and went, the sun shining and the temperature moderate.

The ocean changed continually, its color dependent on the weather and the sky. Sometimes it was light turquoise at the beach and deep purple as it headed toward the open sea. It could be dark and threatening or as clear and pristine as pale green glass. The Mokolua Islands were half a mile from shore, lush and beautiful, serving as benign and luxuriant protectors as they caught the surging waves and gentled them.

Lanipo Street was populated by longtime residents and newcomers alike. Most of them would be involved to some extent in an intricate web of friendships and relationships that were more bizarre than anything a fiction writer could imagine. And yet they somehow managed to maintain a civility that could never be workable in a big city on the mainland.

Tim Sands had graduated from the University of Hawaii-Hilo on the Big Island with a degree in math. "When I met Liysa," he recalled, "I was out of college, but I was kind of not going anywhere."

Living in Hawaii didn't demand intense ambition and progress toward some career goal. There was time to just live. Tim and Liysa got along very well, sharing cooking and cleaning duties at his place. They might argue occasionally, but they never had physical conflicts. Their attraction for each other was strong, but Tim admits that he grew tired of hearing about how magnificent Makimo was. "Liysa said he was the love of her life, and she made him out to be almost a demigod. She said they ended their relationship in 1983, but I think she was always in love with him. I never met Makimo, though I heard a *lot* about him—to the point where I was thinking, 'Enough already!' "

Now Liysa's main obsession was neither Makimo nor Tim. "Her interest was the ocean," Tim said. "She loved to bodysurf and dive and swim, and just be in the ocean."

Tim knew very little about Liysa's past. Although he never met Wayland DeWitt, he met her mother, Sharon, who seemed pleasant enough. That surprised him because Liysa told him that her mother had beaten her and broken a number of her bones when she was a little girl. "I never saw any evidence of that, though," he said. Liysa was so healthy and active and she had no marks or scars that would indicate she'd been severely beaten. She was such an enthusiastic surfer that she often had *fresh* bruises and scratches from being tumbled around by the waves, but Tim saw no old scars.

Liysa had another obsession—writing in her journals. "She went up in the mountains to do her writing," Tim's mother, Jane, recalled. "She said she needed to have her 'space' so she could write in her journals, and she *never* allowed anyone to see what she had written. She wrote so much that she had whole boxes full of her journals."

In 1985, Liysa went to visit her father in Pittsburg, Texas. Once when Tim called her, she told him that her father had hired an African American woman as his secretary and the townspeople were angry about that. She said her admiration for her father had increased even more. She was proud of him be-cause he would not allow any minority to be discriminated against.

During another call, Liysa sounded tense to Tim. Then, suddenly, she told Tim that she heard a crowd gathering outside and she had to put down the phone. "I'll be back in a minute," she said breathlessly. To his horror, Tim heard the report of several gunshots. He wasn't sure what to do: hang up and call the police or wait until Liysa picked up the phone again.

He waited and Liysa came back on the line, saying, "I had to go outside and fire several shots in the air to scare them away."

There was certainly more drama in Liysa's life than in any other woman's he'd ever known.

Tim didn't care that Liysa demanded privacy or that she was very independent. At first, he was just happy to be with her. But, like Kurt Moran before him, he came to a place where he had to admit to himself that Liysa didn't always tell him the truth.

"I think she is such an adept liar that she actually believes her lies," he remembered. "That's why she was so convincing later. She lied about numerous little things. I have a real good memory, so I'd always catch her contradicting herself. The fact that some of the stories were so preposterous made me think that she lied regularly."

Still, Liysa's little wars with the truth didn't bother Tim that much; her lies didn't interfere with their relationship—not for many months. They only made him wary. As a couple, they were compatible and life was good. If they were drifting without any real destination, they were young and it was endless summer on Oahu. As far as Tim knew, Liysa was happy being with him.

But one day in May 1986, he saw a side of Liysa that totally shocked him. He was driving her to the airport to catch a flight to another island when she suddenly told him there was "something wrong" with their relationship and they had to talk about it. He looked over at her, surprised. They had been getting along very well. Without any preamble, she suddenly burst into hysterical sobs.

"She clutched the bag that she was going to take with her on the flight," Tim remembered. "She repeatedly grabbed the strap of the bag and pulled on it—it seemed to be an obsessive-compulsive type of act. I kept trying to communicate with her, but there was absolutely no response from her. Her eyes were blank and without any sign of recognition. . . ."

Realizing that Liysa was in no shape to get on an airplane, even for a short hop to another island, Tim turned his car around and headed home. There, he put her to bed and she fell asleep. She seemed almost "catatonic," Tim remembered.

"She woke up in the middle of the night asking for *Makimo*," he said. "I finally figured out that she wasn't living in the present. I asked her what year it was, and she said '1983.' "

Somewhere, Liysa had lost three years. Or at least she was claiming that she had. When Tim told her it was really 1986, she looked at him as if *he* were the crazy one.

She was so adamant that it was 1983, the year she began her abortive romance with Makimo, that Tim struggled to think of some way to bring her back into real time. Finally, he came up with an idea that might work. "It was about two A.M. and I took her to the nearest 7-Eleven so she could see a newspaper and know that it really was 1986."

Tim was almost persuaded that Liysa *did* have amnesia and that she didn't recognize him at all. But, in retrospect, he realized that it was her way of ending their affair. "It *was* a very convincing act," he said. "I think she may have convinced herself that it really happened—but later I found out that she planned it."

Liysa seemed to be in such a fragile emotional state that Tim didn't know what to do. He called his mother and she suggested that Liysa should see a psychiatrist or psychologist. She *did* go to the HMO she belonged to for a short time, but physicians there could make only a tentative diagnosis. They thought she might be suffering from post-traumatic stress disorder, and they felt she would slowly get better.

Liysa didn't snap back from her "amnesia" for some time. She continued to say she didn't know Tim or his mother. Jane Sands suggested that Tim bring Liysa over to her house near Kailua and she could stay there for a while. "Just bring her home to me and we'll figure it out," she'd said.

"She didn't seem to remember anything," Jane recalled. "She had a number of friends over on our side of Oahu, and it was so strange. I watched as her girlfriends had to reintroduce themselves to her as if she was meeting them for the first time. She didn't recognize any of them."

Liysa was quite convincing. Even though she was no longer going to be with Tim, Jane didn't want to see her wandering around, confused by her amnesia. In October 1986, with great kindness, Jane invited Liysa to stay on in her house for a while, rent-free. Jane's husband—Tim's father—was moving to Hong Kong, and Jane was going with him.

Liysa stayed for more than two months. The Sands had mainland friends arriving to spend Christmas vacation in their house, and they let Liysa know that she would have to find another place to live by then.

Some time after she moved out, a cousin of Tim's found one of Liysa's journals half buried under a cabin the family owned. Curious, he read it. Liysa had outlined her very detailed plot to fake amnesia so that she could break up with Tim without any recriminations. She had written it all down as if it were a play or a novel, and then she had followed her own plan—right up to her hysterical acting-out as Tim drove her to the airport.

Tim's friends had already become very suspicious of the "whole amnesia thing" even before the journal showed up. And many of the older women who lived along Lanipo Street and watched the young woman living in Jane's house had also begun to doubt her story of complete memory failure. She seemed too cheerful and she was having too good a time living as the guest of Tim's parents in a spot that was wonderful and private.

Tim was understandably a little bitter that Liysa could not have just talked to him about her desire to break up. She could have given him a chance to work things out—or, if she didn't want to be with him any longer, she should have been honest about that. Instead, she had faked a histrionic attack of amnesia, like something right out of a soap opera.

Later, Liysa told Tim that the epilepsy she had had as a child might have caused her "amnesia." That was news to him. It was the first time he'd heard of her history of epilepsy. So often, she had come up with pat explanations out of the blue. She was the "woman who cried wolf" and had become impossible to believe. But Tim and Liysa's time together was over. He was hurt when it ended the way it did, but he wasn't crushed. He moved to Boulder, Colorado, and started graduate school. "But I wasn't into it and I dropped out after taking a couple of classes."

Still stung from dealing with the bizarre aspects of Liysa's personality, Tim wasn't ready to go back to Hawaii yet. He went to Singapore instead, where he worked as a hotel and real estate consultant for his father for three years.

It would take some time for Tim to sort it all out, and then he remembered one of the oddest conversations he had ever had with Liysa. "She asked me once what my *touchstone* was," he recalled. "In my infinite wisdom, I answered, 'Huh?'"

"Liysa said, 'You know—how do *you* tell reality from fantasy or from a dream?'"

"I'd never had that problem," Tim said, his voice still incredulous. "But apparently she *had*."

He finally concluded that he had been living with a woman who had to have something tangible to help her discern the difference between what was real and what was only a dream. Although accepting that eccentric truth eventually enabled Tim to completely write off their ten months of pseudoparadise together, it also frightened him. There was something indefinably dangerous about Liysa.

Chapter Five

IN 1987 OR 1988—a year or so after Liysa had the hysterical "amnesia attack" that signaled the end of her affair with Tim Sands—she married the man who would remain in her life the longest. Nick Mattson* was tall, slender, and in good shape; physically, he was Liysa's type. Like Tim, he had broad shoulders. One neighbor described him as "the Adonis type."

Those who knew Liysa in the late eighties said she was already involved with Nick when she left Tim; she just wanted to avoid the messiness of telling Tim the truth. Nick was a little older than Liysa, and he had carved out a solid career as a surf photographer. In fact, he was something of a legend in the Hawaiian Islands. At the pinnacle of his career as a surf and underwater photographer, he was one of perhaps a half-dozen men whose daring and skill with a camera let them capture the tremendous power and beauty of the gigantic waves that burst forth from the ocean. His images were both calm and savage. Or awesome. An artist in a very specialized field, Nick always had more work than he could handle—some of it still photos and some of it shooting backgrounds and stunts for Hollywood movies on location. And he didn't film only in Hawaii. He often spent months on Fiji or Tahiti.

Nick was a "Haole," as Caucasians are called in Hawaii. Those who knew him praised his camera skills first and then invariably added, "You'd like him. Nick's a really nice guy."

It was true. Nick was a gentleman and a gentle man, sensitive and concerned about other people. Liysa had no real career when she met him. She told some people that her college majors were in journalism and video technology. Her father believed that she had a degree in marine biology. Regardless, she wasn't working in any of those fields. In reality, she had only two years of college, mostly elective courses at Oregon State and the University of Hawaii.

Liysa was given a tremendous opportunity when she became an apprentice to Nick. He was a generous teacher and she was an apt student. She had always loved the sea and she was a natural. Soon, Liysa was accompanying Nick on his trips and beginning to gain her own reputation as a surf photographer. They became lovers and planned to marry.

IN 1989, LIYSA FLEW BACK to the mainland to attend the tenth anniversary of her graduating class from Wa-Hi. She seemed very different from the open-faced cheerleader she had been a decade earlier. "She was wild!" one of the women who'd gone to school with Liysa recalled. "Ready to party all night long." Liysa was also drinking quite a bit, which was out of character for the girl they remembered.

It's likely that she had a brief reunion with a man in Walla Walla, someone she had also been with in high school. It may have been only a meeting over the punch bowl at the reunion dance, but in Liysa's mind, it became a defining moment of truth. More likely, she had seen him in the mid-eighties because she had written a very long letter then to the man she called Kevin*, blaming her mother for aborting what they might have had together. She told Kevin that she had written him a letter just before she married her ex-husband, Kurt Moran. Liysa wrote that she strongly suspected that her mother had deliberately taken her letter to Kevin from the DeWitt mailbox. Otherwise, he would have received it. She reminded him of the secrets she'd shared with him on their last night together, when she told him how desperate she was to escape her mother. Still, she explained that she hadn't had the strength to do it alone—and so she had married Kurt Moran "temporarily" as an escape hatch until she could set up a stable life. "Then we could work things out," Liysa wrote to Kevin. "I said that I was desperate and that if you *really* meant it when you asked me to marry you, to come and get me. When I never heard from you—and I waited until I walked down the aisle. I was upset."

She had, perhaps, imagined a scene right out of *The Graduate,* because Liysa recalled being broken-hearted that Kevin hadn't rushed in, stopped the ceremony and taken her for *his* bride.

Seeing Kevin again had renewed Liysa's interest in him. But he was happily married, and she was about to marry Nick Mattson. He did not respond to her letter as she had hoped. There was no indication at all that he was ready to leave his wife and stop Liysa from going down the aisle with Nick.

Indeed, the whole incident sounded like the plot from a romance novel.

When Kevin failed again to intervene, Liysa and Nick got married in 1987. And they would stay together for nine years, the longest relationship she ever had—with the possible exception of her obsession with Makimo. Liysa told Nick about her affair with Tim Sands and explained to him about her attack of amnesia that ended it. She told Nick, too, that she had suffered from epilepsy when she was a child, and that had probably caused her temporary amnesia. They didn't discuss it much. Nick accepted it as part of Liysa's past.

Liysa also told Nick about her long-drawn-out divorce proceedings with Kurt Moran, and about how emotional and difficult it had been for her. She assured him that she'd had no intention of marrying him while she was still married to Kurt. She had thought her divorce from her first husband had been final for years and said she was horrified to find that wasn't true.

They quickly straightened out the legal tangle.

Nick taught Liysa how to use a camera and shoot the magnificent surf photos that approached his own in perfection. Married to Nick, Liysa became a kind of celebrity. It suited her and she loved being the center of attention on shoots. She was a quick study, enthusiastic about catching the surfers on film as they raced toward shore, great plumes of spray behind them. At the O.P. Classic surfing tournament, the waves were fifteen feet high, and a hundred photographers angled for good shots. But only two of them actually waded into the roaring surf with their cameras, and one of the daring photographers was Liysa. She was fearless. From her photographs, it's clear that she had to be almost as consumed by the towering waves as those who rode the boards.

In 1990, Liysa and Nick collaborated on a book, a pictorial really, about Hanauma Bay. Liysa wrote the narrative, and Nick took the enchanting photographs. It sold briskly for years in Hawaiian airports. Liysa dedicated the book to "those who know the secrets of the sea," and acknowledged Nick, her new in-laws, Makimo and his wife, and even her ex-boyfriend Tim Sands and his mother.

Many of Liysa's surfing photographs are still listed for sale on the Internet and they are breathtaking. They don't match Nick's work; he is a master, but hers are certainly well beyond amateur status.

* * *

LIYSA'S YEARS WITH NICK were satisfying to her for a long time. She would talk later about the houses they had literally built by themselves, "using only a bubble level." She boasted that she had once found an error in a foundation that saved them $14,000, and she was very proud of her ability to design homes even though she had no particular architectural training.

The Mattsons made a good team in terms of what they accomplished together. But there were reasons why Liysa may not have been the best of wives. She was less adept at, and far less interested in, homemaking than she was at surf photography and carpentry. She loved the cleanness of the ocean, with its salt spray that scoured everything it coursed over. She cared little about cleaning house or doing laundry or cooking. The houses where she lived with Nick were in constant disarray. He put up with it because he loved her.

In almost every other way, Nick and Liysa got along. Still, according to mutual friends, she nagged him a lot. Even on the morning of their wedding, Nick's friends had been troubled to hear her henpecking him, although it all seemed to slide off his back. Apparently, Nick was so used to being nagged that he unconsciously shut out the sound of her voice.

Liysa was insistent that Nick drop his old friends when they got married. "She told him she never wanted him to see them again," a friend of his said. "And she had him get a tattoo of her name on his arm to remind him."

Nick himself would acknowledge only that they argued occasionally, "just about the normal things in a relationship." Whatever the argument, usually Liysa prevailed because Nick wanted peace in their household, and she just didn't quit when she had fixated on what she wanted.

Nick already knew Makimo when he met Liysa and didn't find her admiration for him as annoying as Tim Sands had. Nick had always felt the handsome Hawaiian was a "person of high integrity." Beyond that, Makimo had long since married the mother of his daughter and appeared to be loyal to her.

Liysa seemed at ease with that. If she felt any jealousy toward Makimo's wife, Nick certainly wasn't aware of it. He and

Liysa socialized occasionally with Makimo, who now worked as a firefighter, and the two men fished together.

The truth was that Liysa's mind was always full of real or imagined romance. Her craving for someone who would love her as dramatically and as passionately as scenes she saw in movies or read in novels was profound. She secretly believed that Makimo yearned for her, and she often wrote in her journals about two other men who had been tremendously important to her. There was, of course, Kevin back in Washington State, with whom she hoped to reconnect. And there was Ray, whose last name she never wrote down for anyone to see. Ray— if he had existed at all—was dead, and Makimo and Kevin were married to other women.

Liysa wrote almost compulsively. She saved copies of letters, filled voluminous notebooks, and experimented with fiction—both books and screenplays. She alternately used real names and made-up names for her characters—perhaps deliberately, so that no one could ever identify what was real and what was her own creation. Again, she herself may not have been able to tell the difference.

It wasn't Liysa's imagination that caused the most trouble in her second marriage. She had always come across as something of a risk-taker, and physically she was remarkably strong for a woman. But she wasn't quite as unafraid as she seemed. Her tendency to embellish her stories was easier to spot than her almost obsessive need for some physical place that belonged to her where she might feel safe and create a haven for others whose lives were haunted.

No one could be sure what Liysa feared. It might have been homelessness, or abandonment; it might have been that her childhood *was* as cruel as she often said it was. Whatever the reason, she seemed consumed with owning real estate. She longed to have houses to run to and property that would ensure her financial stability. And she certainly had that with Nick—at least as much property as most people could need. He cooperated with her on the purchase of several houses she wanted. He was making a solid living and soon so was she.

"She was a good photographer, good enough to earn eight to ten thousand dollars a month—and sometimes more," an acquaintance recalled.

When Liysa became pregnant in 1991, her adventures in surf photography were of necessity curtailed. In November, she and Nick had their first—and only—child together. He was a beautiful boy, fair like his father. They named him Papakolea*, a rare Hawaiian term for "breaking wave," a sight that meant a great deal to both parents.

Liysa gave Papakolea four middle names, too. Papakolea Moonbeam Puana Aquarius Antonio Mattson was a much loved child. The baby was nicknamed "Papako."

Liysa had reveled in her pregnancy, and she delighted in the childbirth education classes and the support groups for nursing mothers that she joined. She was determined to be the best mother she could be. She saw that Papako was a child who was supremely gifted and special, and it wasn't just a fond mother's opinion; he *was* so enchanting that strangers commented on it. Liysa vowed never to let anything hurt him or turn him away from the path she planned for him. Other pregnant women in her classes found Liysa a woman to be emulated, and a mentor in motherhood. They loved her and found her brave and wonderful.

Liysa was twenty-nine when Papako was born, and it seemed to her that she had waited all of her life to love this child. She took him everywhere she went, and taught him about the sea and fish and what the wind was saying. He was an adorable baby who grew to be a handsome, tanned little boy with a tumble of sun-bleached curls, so handsome that people stopped to stare at him and his lovely mother.

When Nick had to be away for six weeks at a time on a shoot, Liysa wasn't lonesome—because she had Papako.

It would have been hard for any man not to notice Liysa as she strolled to the beach in her bikini, almost always with Papako in tow. She combined both sensuality and the glow of motherhood. She watched over him near the ocean, although it wasn't long before he was as fearless in the waves as she was.

A bond formed between Liysa and Papako, even stronger than the usual linkage between a mother and a young child. It was only natural because they were alone together so much, but their closeness was enhanced by Liysa's total focus on her little boy. She would teach him everything he needed to know, or she would find artists and dancers and musicians to teach him so every budding skill would be developed. She would breast-feed him as long as he needed to nurse. She planned to homeschool him so he wouldn't be infected with the negative ideas of bad teachers.

If her own childhood hadn't been smooth or neat or particularly happy, she would make up for it in her child's world. She wrote in her journal that Papako had been conceived on the beach at low tide, as zephyr winds blew and the sea glowed with magical phosphorescence. And that was as it should be.

He was the perfect child.

In Liysa's mind, there still continued to be two worlds, one that she lived in and another that was lovely and muted and serendipitous. It was a world that existed only in her imagination. And that may have been why she asked Tim Sands what *his* touchstone was when he needed something to distinguish reality from his dreams.

Liysa clearly believed that she could bring Papako into the lovely side of her world and make him strong and safe.

She also wanted him to keep the sweetness that he had as a little boy, and she wanted to hold the "soulless, industrialized world" far away from him. They lived in a natural paradise, and

Liysa often wrote that she wanted to instill values in Papako that would let him appreciate the glory of sea and sky and the earth around them as he grew to manhood. She knew there would be "brighter, easier neon and plastic" beckoning to him with "tantalizing temptations at every turn."

Liysa lamented that "honor has no place in the modern world. Yet I can't give up my belief in it."

Her dreams for Papako were to somehow raise him in the old ways of Hawaii, with few modern conveniences or fast-food joints. Papako would eat vine-ripened tomatoes, and eschew McDonald's. When he was old enough, Liysa would urge her son to save sex "as an expression of commitment of love rather than squandering it on emotionally empty recreational encounters. . . ."

She loved Papako fiercely, and she and Nick were getting along well, possibly because he *was* away a lot. He had almost always given her what she asked for and gone along with her plans. But perhaps he was *too* good to her, and *too* dependable. Liysa wanted both security and fireworks from a man, and very few could have given her enough of either—and certainly not enough of both.

Nick certainly tried. He was a good man, but he was shocked by Liysa's seemingly insatiable craving—not for other men—but for more real estate. She begged and argued and pleaded with him to buy more and more and more property. Nick had already acquiesced on a number of houses and apartments, although it had become necessary for him to go to his parents as cosigners on the last round of purchases. Finally, he had agreed to buy Liysa an older house on Lanipo Street, a house that was, coincidentally, next door to Jane Sands's home, where Liysa had once been given shelter after her memory loss.

"To a point, we had the same goals," Nick recalled. "But [her need to buy more real estate] was putting a strain on our marriage. She wanted an Oregon ranch and wanted to sell our property in Hawaii. I didn't want to sell. I didn't want to move to the mainland. I liked to own property, too, but we couldn't afford what she wanted."

Liysa was full of altruistic dreams and goals that may have come about because of her own scattered fears. She longed for a constant feeling of complete peace and harmony, something most humans attain only rarely in their lifetimes. Now she was determined to have enough land to build a school or a camp or a spa that focused on "healing" all who came there.

When she and Nick bought the property she called "Paauilo," she foresaw the metamorphoses that could take place there and, later, in its Oregon counterpart. Liysa's goal was to eventually have two retreats—one in the mountains and the other by the sea. There, emotionally bruised women could swim, wander, and gather their thoughts in beautiful settings. They could choose to be alone or commune with others, receive therapeutic massages, wholesome meals, and restful sleep. Liysa's sanctuary would be welcoming and perfectly designed so that it would flow. "There would be yoga and group discussion, candlelight and bell meditation. Good food. Peace . . ."

She planned to call one of her spas "Chrysalis," the last stage in the development of a butterfly. It was a wonderful concept.

Yet Liysa's dreams outstripped all realities but her own. Although Nick was an extraordinarily patient and caring man, his wife's soaring plans had begun to make him wary. He wondered where it would end. His parents were still connected to a few of their real estate loans, and he wanted them to be off the hook as soon as possible. Liysa was always promising that she would make bank payments, pay taxes and maintenance bills—but after Papako was born, it was much more difficult for her to work at surf photography. They clearly were not in a position to invest in anything else. Nick had thought the house on Lanipo

Street would satisfy her. It didn't, and as Nick packed for a long shoot in Tahiti, she came to him with still another project.

"Liysa had a ranch picked out in Oregon," he said, shaking his head. "Three to five hundred acres! The ranch had cattle on it. I'm not a rancher. Her ideal was to winter in Hawaii and be in Oregon in the summer. She talked about raising llamas, alpacas, or bison and about having a guest ranch."

One of the last land purchases that Nick agreed to was a six-acre spread in the Tumalo area of Bend, Oregon. They bought the land for $119,000 and sold it for $160,000 not long after. It hadn't been a bad business deal, but, for Liysa, it was a disappointment. It didn't come close to the huge ranch she wanted.

The watershed point of their marriage came when Nick finally threw his hands up and asked Liysa to write down all the properties she planned to buy. When she handed him an extensive list, he was stunned. She wanted too much. And he knew she would nag and plead until she got everything on the list. For a man with a solid photography business in Hawaii, it made no sense at all to buy five hundred acres for a ranch/spa on the mainland in Oregon.

There would be no end to it. At that point, Nick finally accepted that their marriage wasn't going to work any longer. He knew he couldn't begin to keep up with Liysa's land-hunger. Even so, he never spoke harshly about her. "I was responsible for paying the bills and I believe that Liysa actually thought we had more money than we did."

CHAPTER SIX

THERE WERE OTHER REASONS for the end of their marriage. By late 1993, Liysa had become bored with Nick. Now she thought about Tim Sands, and with the blurring that comes with the passage of time, she began to believe that she had had more sexual fulfillment with him than she had with Nick. But Liysa and Nick had been married for a half-dozen years. Few couples are able to continue the blazing passion of a honeymoon or an affair forever. She resented Nick and felt that the real unfolding of her life was blocked by his stubbornness.

Once again Liysa began to long for Ray and for Kevin and for Makimo. In her view, Nick developed more and more flaws. He didn't have "spiritual quality" or "vision." He was negative, and his negativity made her explode. She blamed all of her unhappy emotions and her temper tantrums on him. She felt trapped.

Liysa began to mouth a silent mantra that she noted in her journals, "I hate my husband. I hate my husband. I hate my husband. . . ."

She believed that Nick was deliberately trying to sabotage her with criticism and thoughtlessness. One time, he'd forgotten her 300-mm camera on a shoot, and she was sure he'd done it on purpose to keep her from getting great shots. She was so furious with him that, for a few moments, she actually wanted to kill him.

Liysa daydreamed about other men the way teenage girls do. She seemed to need unconditional love, and now she felt she had probably had that with Tim. Now she wanted to reunite with him. But Tim wasn't at all interested in starting up again with Liysa.

When Nick was home, Liysa forced herself into a "catatonic state," and thought more about Kevin and Makimo and attempted to arrange liaisons with them while Nick was away in Indonesia. Disappointed and frustrated when they weren't responsive, she fell into a state of depression. She became convinced that she had cervical cancer, a disease sometimes caused by venereal warts, a virus transmitted by the penis.

Papako was about two when Liysa wrote again to Kevin in Oregon. It was an extremely convoluted letter. She had apparently elicited a promise from him earlier that he would give Papako a job when he was a teenager, and suggested they should meet to discuss that. She explained that she was now writing from a hospital where she was being treated for cancer. She didn't know how long she might live.

Liysa thanked Kevin for agreeing to hire Papako fifteen years hence, but scolded him for refusing to see her.

"I was *shocked*," she wrote, "that you are worried about getting together." Liysa pushed a few guilt buttons, saying that Kevin was the *only* person whom she trusted to keep his word, and reminding him that he had promised to be there for her "no matter what." How could she be sure Kevin would help Papako in fifteen years, when he had sworn falsely to her ten years earlier that they would meet again?

It was a long, long letter. Liysa confessed to Kevin that she had sacrificed her own chance for happiness with him because she didn't feel worthy of him. But he had "haunted" her. She actually compared herself to Humphrey Bogart's character as he said good-bye to Ingrid Bergman's character in *Casablanca*. She reminded Kevin again that she had forced herself to turn and walk away from him when everything in her wanted to stay.

Because she had cancer and was on morphine, she told him that she was at last uninhibited enough to tell him the truth. Her "cancer counselor" had explained to her that repressed emotions can cause malignancy. And she had hidden her love for Kevin so long. Was it cause and effect?

"You were my one true friend," Liysa wrote, "that I opened up to. To everyone else, I'm as tough as a cactus. In the rain of your tears, I was a rare cactus blossom."

However poignant Liysa's rhetoric was, she failed to convince Kevin to meet with her. For a time, she turned her attention instead to caring for Papako and filming with Nick. Nick's career was burgeoning and some of the projects they worked on were the *Endless Summer* films that proved to be surprising box-office smashes, with audiences flocking to see surfers follow the sun to ride the crests of magnificent waves. Nick had also been approached to work on *Castaway,* starring Tom Hanks as the onetime executive lost for years on a Pacific island.

It still wasn't enough stimulation for Liysa. She continued to enjoy the beach and devour mystery stories avidly, but she was discontented. With alarming regularity, she began to ask Nick for a divorce. For a long time, he didn't think she really meant it.

But she did. Liysa had found someone else, a man who seemed to embody exactly what she was looking for in a life mate. His name was Chris Northon.

Chapter Seven

IN NOVEMBER 1993, three Hawaiian Airline pilots—Joe Wilson, Randy Ore, and Chris Northon—who were based in Honolulu, regretfully had to leave the waterfront rental house on Kaneohe Bay where they had lived for years. It had been sold. Things were changing, anyway. Joe had met a wonderful, freckle-faced flight attendant named Maggie in September, and he was more than ready to leave bachelorhood behind.

"I knew from the moment I met her that it was all over," he said, grinning. Joe was forty-two to Chris's thirty-seven, and told Chris that it was up to him to find the next house. And Chris did find a place for them, fully aware that Joe would probably be getting married, and that he would need to find a new roommate soon.

It wasn't really a house this time, but instead the upper floor of a shared dwelling at 319 Lanipo Street. Their landlady, Margaret Lefton, whom Joe Wilson recalled as a "lovely lady," lived in the daylight basement of the house while the ever-changing group of pilots occupied the upstairs. A couple of them were always gone on a flight, and the new place continued as an open house for a while, but they weren't rowdy. Margaret Lefton remembered them as good tenants. She especially remembered Chris.

"The day was always better from a smile and a few words from Chris," she said. "He was a wonderful man, always cheerful with such a sunny smile. . . . The neighbors all liked Chris."

They laughed as they recalled his loud voice. "He would 'chat' with us from his front yard," one said. "Chris had such a booming voice that he would shout to someone down the street, and you could hear him all over the neighborhood. But it was always friendly conversation."

Chris was doing very well at Hawaiian Airlines. Chief Pilot Al Dixon had recommended him to the Federal Aviation Administration's Honolulu district office as a good candidate for the job of Proficiency Check Pilot: "His day-to-day performance of duties exemplifies what we are seeking from all of our pilots and [I] believe therefore that he will make an excellent instructor and role model," Dixon wrote.

Chris had 4,500 hours of flight time under his belt in multiengine, turboprop, and jet aircrafts. He was happy living his life in two very disparate states: Hawaii and Oregon. Between Bend, Oregon, where he had grown up, and Kailua, he had the best of both worlds. He could stay close to his family and the mountains he loved in Oregon, and he could hang out with his longtime pilot friends in Hawaii and surf in the warm waters off "one of the ten most beautiful beaches in the world." He could experience almost every kind of weather there was and enjoy beaches and mountains, rivers and forests.

Chris had a lot of friends in Bend, too, and decided to buy a house there. John Gill and Arne Arnesen were probably his best friends. Chris and Arne went way back. They had been as close as brothers for a long time, ever since Arne dated Mary, Chris's sister, for a few years. Arne and Mary's relationship ended, but the two men stayed fast friends. They got together often to ride bikes or hike when Chris was in Oregon.

Arne was pleased when Chris bought his own place in Bend and started to renovate it. It wasn't lavish. When it was built twenty years earlier, it had been a typical two-bedroom, one-bath house, which a previous owner had remodeled into a three-bedroom, two-bath place. After Chris bought it, he had a new roof put on and hired professionals to completely paint the interior and landscape the grounds. That gave him a spot in Bend of his own. Most men wouldn't dream of commuting such long distances, but that was Chris's lifestyle and his career. He could fly from Honolulu to Portland, Oregon, and then drive to Bend as easily as someone might drive thirty miles to a job every day.

In Oregon, Chris could hike with his father, Dick Northon, or with John Gill. John and Chris had grown up together and they both loved hiking and fishing. John's life was vastly different from Chris's. He was married to Eva, who was a steady "earth mother" type of woman, and they had adorable daughters. The Gills owned the Rock House Inn and Guest Resort on Tumalo Falls Road north of Bend. Arne Arnesen was a rancher. He grew alfalfa and did custom farming for people who didn't have their own equipment to till their land and bale their hay. But John, Arne, and Chris all gloried in sports and the outdoor life Oregon offered.

Chris was bouncing back from his breakup with a Hawaiian woman named Maka, and he had returned to a woman whom he'd dated in 1989: Sabrina Tedford. They had begun to date again six years after their first romantic relationship. Sabrina, who owned a boutique in Portland, really cared for Chris, but she was a single mother and it was difficult for her to keep up with a man so accustomed to spontaneous adventures.

"Chris liked Sabrina a lot," Dick Northon said. "She was very nice and bright, and I think she loved him, but the timing was never right for them." "Sabrina would have been great for Chris," his mother, Jeanne remarked. "And then Liysa entered the picture."

FATE OR SYNCHRONICITY or sheer chance was about to bring Chris Northon and Liysa DeWitt Mattson within shouting distance of each other. Their life paths had been nearly parallel before, but they had never met. While Chris had been flying in the Gulf War, Liysa was on Oahu giving birth to Papako. She had come to Kailua on the eastern coast of Oahu by a circuitous route, just as he had. Both had roots in Oregon, but they'd never met each other there. And Chris would live on Lanipo Street for months before he first glimpsed Liysa. When he did, she had been married to Nick Mattson for almost a decade.

After Chris and Joe Wilson first moved into Margaret Lefton's upper floor, they'd noticed a ramshackle house across the street. "Some poor old woman had just died there," Joe remembered. "It was a dump. Just imagine how it had been for a few years—a dilapidated house, all run-down, and the sole occupant just waiting to die."

The old place remained empty for a while, and no one even bothered to put up a FOR SALE sign, but one day Joe and Chris noticed a real estate agent showing it to a couple. Neither of them remembered what the couple had looked like, and it wasn't a memorable occasion for the pilots.

"But later I realized that it must have been Liysa and Nick because they bought it," Joe said. "Nick grew up in the neighborhood, so he would have known the potential in the place. It was location, of course. Close to such a great beach and one of the few properties still left on the block. The land was what mattered."

Soon, Joe and Chris began to see a slender woman with long silky hair walking to the beach with a little boy twice a day. The man they had assumed was her husband wasn't around. Like many sun lovers, the woman wore the tiniest of bikini bathing suits, with just enough cloth to keep her from nakedness. In time, they learned she was Liysa Mattson. She and her husband had bought the old place just before Nick left for an extended shoot in Tahiti.

For a few months in 1986, Liysa had lived right next door to the house she and Nick bought. That was during her "amnesia" period after her breakup with Tim Sands. His mother, Jane, still lived in the house she'd let Liysa stay in more than eight years before. As a mother whose son had been hurt by Liysa's histrionics, Jane admittedly disliked her. She watched warily as Liysa returned to Lanipo Street. "Her brain was always working," Jane said of her new neighbor.

Joe Wilson was easing his way out of Hawaii. His fiancée, Maggie, was stationed back east, flying out of Newark, New Jersey, and he wanted to be close to her. That meant he would no longer be based in Honolulu and would be leaving his beloved Kailua behind. Around this time, Chris mentioned to Joe that he had met the woman across the street, describing her as a "surfer girl/photographer." It was a kind of throwaway remark, and Joe didn't realize what a sea change was about to come into his old friend's life.

Chris laughed when he spoke to Arne Arnesen about meeting Liysa. "She told me she thought I was gay at first," he said. "She saw all the guys coming and going from our apartment and just assumed we were all gay. When she found out we were pilots, she realized we were straight."

Chris proved that rapidly to Liysa. In 1994, she recalled her first evening with Chris in capital letters in her journal. "CHRIS CAME TO DINNER—TALKED 4–5 HOURS!" She described him as a "huge new element in my life."

The feeling was mutual; Chris was certainly attracted to Liysa, and impressed by her independence. Since he was an avid athlete, the fact that she was, too, meant a lot to him. She would often swim out to the little Mokolua Islands, a half-mile distance few men would have challenged without a companion boat. Her very self-sufficiency suited Chris. She clearly didn't *need* him for anything, but liked him for himself.

"Chris told me that she'd been married for about eight years," Joe Wilson said, "but her marriage was on the rocks and her husband was gone on a long assignment."

Maggie was based on the East Coast, but she had layovers in Honolulu. "She'd come straight to our house," Joe recalled, "and she would just barely get to say 'hi' to Chris before he'd tell her he was busy that night, and then he'd point over at Liysa's house and say, 'I'm going up to the big house.'"

That wasn't like Chris. He was very fond of Maggie and normally would stay an hour or so and visit with her and Joe when she was in town. Actually, Chris liked most of his married pilot friends and their wives, and never minded being the fifth wheel. There were many couples who enjoyed spending time with Chris and who happily set another place at the table when he showed up. But they were all seeing less and less of him. He was spending every minute he could with Liysa and Papako.

Rapidly, Chris had become besotted with the woman across the street, although he looked away when Joe questioned him about her. He didn't want to talk about Liysa. He had never talked much about the women he dated and certainly didn't share intimate details; he had been raised to believe that men didn't comment on sexual conquests. He was especially discreet about Liysa—who was, after all, still married.

An old friend, Dr. David Jones, cautioned Chris to be careful because he might be getting into trouble with Liysa's husband. "He listened to me," David recalled, "but he said it was hard to stay away from her. She was coming over at night and crawling through his window, and he couldn't seem to say no. I think her husband must have known, but he never confronted Chris."

As she had been with all of her previous lovers and husbands, Liysa was now obsessed with having Chris on a permanent basis. The fact that he was almost forty and had never been married only made him more desirable. The challenge appealed to her. They had a very strong physical relationship, one that Liysa compared favorably with her lovemaking with Ray and Makimo.

Chris was the first man she had *ever* allowed to approach the status of the dead football star and the lifeguard she'd idolized for years. Her journals were full of her delight with Chris as a sexual partner. Sex was very important to her and she wrote of it continually, just as she wrote about nature and the idyllic world in her imagination.

She reveled in the knowledge that she and Chris had practically everything in common. He was athletic and health-conscious and appreciated the simple diet that she preferred. They watched old movies together and made love, and Chris liked Papako. It seemed to Liysa that that was more than enough to make him want to marry her.

CHAPTER EIGHT

IT WAS 2:00 P.M. on Monday afternoon, October 9, 2000, when the first Wallowa County investigators arrived at the Shady Campground site where Undersheriff Rich Stein was waiting. The scene in the shadows of the tall fir trees would soon be cast into darkness.

Although they still didn't know exactly what they were dealing with, the Wallowa County Sheriff's Office and its District Attorney's Office were certainly not geared up to launch a major death investigation. The county itself was wide and sprawling, but much of it was taken up with mountains and forests and the national recreation area known as Hells Canyon on the Idaho border. There weren't that many people living in Wallowa County, only about 7,100. There were probably as many horses and deer in the county as humans.

If someone unfamiliar with the justice system in the state of Oregon were to deliberately choose a place to get away with a crime, they could not have done better than the Maxwell Campgrounds in Wallowa County. To the layman, the laid-back ambiance of the little town of Enterprise might seem something like Mayberry, where Sheriff Andy Taylor and Deputy Barney Fife protected citizens. This wasn't Portland or Eugene, or even Sweet Home, Oregon. However, Wallowa County had some top investigators, a highly intelligent district attorney, and backup from the Oregon State Police detectives and criminalists if they needed it.

Matt Cross was a young detective with the Wallowa County Sheriff's Office, who had wanted to be a cop for as far back as he could remember. Tall and athletic with a dark crew cut, Cross grew up in Klamath Falls, Oregon. He'd been an Explorer Scout who helped in police searches and participated in their "Ride-Along" program, through which, as a teenager, he had watched *real* police officers in action. He then spent four years in the navy, where he was assigned to the Presidential Support Unit guarding President George Bush.

By the time Cross was mustered out of the service, his goals were focused on becoming either a commercial pilot or a police officer. There wasn't much of a tug-of-war between the two. He went to Lane Community College in Eugene to study law enforcement. And then he joined the Wallowa County Sheriff's Office in late 1996, assigned as almost all new hires are to the Patrol Division. He also had training in narcotics investigation and in using K-9 dogs that could sniff out drugs. And that was fortunate because Wallowa County provided any number of hidden locations where marijuana thrived.

Members of his department had to wear several hats, and Matt Cross was no different. He had been a narc for the Wallowa County Drug Task Force and made many arrests for burglary and car theft. He had not, however, worked a baffling death investigation yet.

Now he was about to do just that. He would be the case officer for Wallowa County in this probe at the Shady Campground site.

Sheriff Ron Jett was already there, when Matt Cross arrived at the scene at 3:30 in the afternoon. The body in the bright blue sleeping bag hadn't been moved. There was no hurry any longer; perhaps there had never been a need to rush the victim to a hospital or a doctor. A pathologist would determine that later.

Cross walked past the white Chevy Suburban and noted the license number—VRS673—then past the picnic table and the tent. Except for several empty bottles that had once contained alcohol, the Shady Campground looked as if an average family had been camping there.

Jody Williamson, the U.S. Forest Service law enforcement officer, had already begun to wind yellow crime scene tape around trees and shrubs to protect the site all the way from the road down to the beach where the body rested.

They set up a log to chart the arrival of various investigators and officials. Dr. Lowell Euhus, 57, was one of only five doctors practicing in the county. In his Winding Waters Clinic and at the Wallowa Memorial Hospital just across the street in

Enterprise, Euhus had been serving Wallowa County's sick for thirty years, and he'd seen injuries completely alien to city physicians: "Horse wrecks galore—even chain saw injuries to every part of the body."

Euhus had fought hard to bring better medical care to the wilds of eastern Oregon, and somehow he'd managed to fit his own interests into the seventy to ninety hours a week he worked as a physician. He was a private pilot and a mountain climber who had made 260 climbs, including 31 ascents of the towering 9,716-foot Chief Joseph Mountain.

Lowell Euhus was also the medical examiner of Wallowa County. Ironically, he would soon have next-door neighbors who shared many of his interests: Dick and Jeanne Northon. Sadly, he was about to have another connection to them.

The sheriff's investigators led him to the spot about twenty-five feet beyond the picnic table where the body lay zipped up in the cocoon-style down sleeping bag. Once inside, any room to move would be extremely limited. There was a foam pad beneath the sleeping bag, and a blue tarp under that. Only the hair and the top part of the body's head were visible.

The body was clearly that of a tall person. The investigators could see now that it was a man who lay mostly on his back. Rigor mortis was complete; the man had been dead for a long time, probably more than twelve to fourteen hours.

He appeared to be about forty years old, in good shape, with thick dark blond hair. The investigators at the scene suspected that the dead man was Christopher Northon. They knew from talking to Umatilla County and Washington State authorities that Northon, his wife, and young son had been camping here for the weekend just past, and they'd apparently had a violent altercation. The wife had fled the scene. The wife was talking to police up in Umatilla, saying she'd fired a warning shot as she ran to her vehicle, aiming blindly in the darkness of night. If that were true, her wild shot had been tragically on target.

One thing was certain: Whatever had happened, the Wallowa County investigators were going to need help from the Oregon State Police's homicide experts. The closest OSP office was in La Grande, sixty miles away. Detective Patric A. Montgomery, who was stationed in La Grande, was an experienced investigator in the Criminal Division of the Oregon State Police. He had almost thirty years in law enforcement with the OSP. As a member of the Major Crime Team, he was called to the Lostine River site, arriving at 5:20 that Monday afternoon, as the pale sun was hovering on the horizon beyond the mountain peaks. The sky was lowering and it was going to rain, so everything beyond the yellow tape barrier looked muted to him, almost as if it were a black-and-white movie.

From the moment he left his car, Montgomery's trained eyes noted everything close to the campground.

There was a black Volkswagen parked near the trailhead with the driver standing behind it. When Montgomery questioned him, he gave his name and said he was retired and lived between Joseph and Enterprise. He'd arrived at the Eagle Cap Wilderness Area just after noon, parked, and left on a five-hour hike to Maxwell Lake and back.

"I saw the white Suburban parked down there," he said, "but I didn't see anybody around the campsite."

"You hear anything unusual?" Montgomery asked.

"Not really. As I was walking the trail, I heard some rifle shots by the meadow near Maxwell Lake—but I figured it was deer hunters. They couldn't have come up from the campground though; there weren't any rigs parked there, except for the Suburban. I noticed some fresh horse tracks and manure on the path. Somebody must have ridden their horses in there a couple of hours before I got there, but I never saw any horses."

The witness said he hadn't gone near the Shady Campground spot and had no idea what might have happened down there.

Pat Montgomery saw the white Chevy SUV where it was backed against a log and noticed it was locked. He could see a small child's car seat in the back, a baby bottle in the drink holder, and an Oregon map fanned out on the passenger seat.

There was a public picnic table and a fire pit nearby, and two green totes with food and camping supplies rested on the picnic table's bench. A new green plastic flashlight and a comb were on top of the table. There was a tackle box with fishing lures under the table, along with a fishing reel, a sack with a sleeping pad, and a propane cylinder.

So far, the scene looked like a normal setup for an outing in the woods. Montgomery saw that two trails led down to the river, one steep and short, the other a more gentle slope. He followed the latter and the river came into view, but the sandy beach area wasn't visible until he was almost on top of it. The Lostine River was shallow but running swiftly, with little rivulets frothing white as they encountered rocks and tree limbs. There was another small camp set up on the beach itself—a camp chair and two fold-up tables. The tables had pots and pans sitting on them and a little sack that contained a child's toothpaste and medicine. There was an empty Rapala knife sheath there, too, but no knife. Someone had hooked a Coleman stove and a lantern to a propane gas bottle.

Now Montgomery could see the first indications of a struggle. A half-full bottle of Kahlúa, a partial bottle of 100-proof Kentucky bourbon, and an empty wine bottle were scattered on the beach as if they had been knocked off the table.

Between the tables and the river, the OSP detective saw a chair with sopping wet clothing slung over it and waterlogged men's shoes nearby. As he moved closer, he had an eerie sense that something violent had happened here. One of the camp chairs was next to the table with a blanket draped on it, but another was lying on its side farther down in the shallow river. Another blanket and a jacket were snagged on a log a short distance downstream. Montgomery studied the ground be-tween the tables and the water and detected several deep gouges and shoe or foot tracks in the sand. It looked as if someone had wrestled there.

Rich Stein and Pat Montgomery made their way carefully through the campsite so that Montgomery could get as many photographs as possible while there was still available light. Dr. Euhus hadn't touched the body; no one had—so Montgomery was able to get clear photographs of the dead man just as he must have appeared the moment he died.

He seemed to have been sleeping on his left side before a bullet whirled his head back with such force that he stared blindly at the sky. There was dried blood on his forehead and a bullet hole on the right side of his head. It appeared to be a through-and-through wound. They could see now that blood had pooled inside the sleeping bag and on the layers beneath. It had also seeped from both ears, and crisscrossed the prominent ridge above his eyes and the bridge of his nose.

The body in the blue sleeping bag was between twenty-five and thirty feet north of the camp table. Although the investiga-tors couldn't see the face because the sleeping bag was still zipped all the way up over the bridge of the nose, the exposed part of the forehead was dusted with river sand. At some point, the body had either been moved slightly from where it had lain on its left side to its present supine position. More likely, it was the power of the bullet itself that made the victim toss his head when it struck.

"A lot of things happen when someone gets shot," Mont-gomery said later. "Even with 'instant death,' the head whips around from the impact."

At 6:49 P.M., crime scene technicians from the Oregon State Police Lab arrived to join the probe: Lieutenant Jeff Dovci and criminalist Christine Ogilvie walked toward the beach. They could not hope to do a thorough investigation at night, but they began their meticulous search of the campsite with high-powered portable lights.

Near the steeper trail just above the body, on the opposite side of the two logs that separated the shore from the trail, they found a small miner's light attached to a blue elastic headband. Its batteries were dead.

They would log into evidence every item that had apparently been brought there by the Northons when they came to camp in the wilderness. Most of it was innocuous, things that most campers would take. Some of the cooking utensils on the table near the river contained tiny tufts of lichen moss and pine or fir needles. Maybe items knocked on the ground could indicate a struggle; maybe they had nothing to do with the dead man.

There was a small gray tent set up in the trees above the beach. Pat Montgomery peered in and saw three sleeping bags, and a small child's shoes and jacket. There was no adult clothing in the tent.

The sleeping bag had only one bullet hole visible from the top—but when the body was lifted up, the investigators saw an exit bullet hole in the bag where a tuft of goose down protruded. The path of the slug through the sleeping pad and the tarp beneath lined up perfectly, and feathers from the mummy bag had been sucked up behind the bullet. Dovci, Ogilvie, and Montgomery probed carefully in the sand, and even there they found feathers driven by the force of the bullet. A copper-jacketed 38-caliber bullet was buried there. It had penetrated the ground in a nearly vertical line.

The investigators stood peering down at the still form, the only sounds the river and the buzzing of flies. *The poor sucker probably never saw the bullet coming. . . .*

At last, the victim's body was removed from where it lay on the cold sand, still encased in the too accurately termed "mummy" sleeping bag. It was taken to Bollman's Funeral Home in Enterprise.

Now investigators who had never known the victim or his wife moved over the area, looking for something—anything— that might explain not only the manner of his death but the reason. They couldn't know that this was a man who had survived bucking horses, mountain climbs, fast ski runs, automobile wrecks, war, and thousands of miles in the air, only to die suddenly on a peaceful beach.

Matt Cross collected physical evidence from the campground along with the Oregon State Police criminalists: the Petzel miner's flashlight, a small black-handled steak knife, the empty knife sheath for a much larger knife, the partially consumed bottle of Kahlúa, a Knob Creek whiskey bottle found almost empty in a blue plastic tote, a small amount of brown flaky substance that appeared to be marijuana, cigarette papers, and tweezers found in a red backpack. There was plenty of identification in the dead man's slightly damp wallet. As they had suspected, it *was* Chris Northon, and the wallet had $17 in cash, an FAA pilot's license, an FAA medical certificate, both Hawaii and Oregon driver's licenses, a MasterCard, a Chevron card, a Visa card, a Costco card, a Safeway card, and photographs of his family.

Jeff Dovci and Christine Ogilvie tried to reconstruct the events of Sunday night by examining patterns in the sugary sand of the beach. They worked their way toward the riverbank onto the sandbar at the water's edge, looking for footprints. It was an almost perfect medium for preserving those prints.

They photographed the toddler-sized tennis shoe patterns there. A second set of prints looked as if they had been made by a woman or a man with small feet. The tread was of a hiking-type shoe. Still a third set of footprints had clearly been made by a large man's shoes—and they matched the soles of the sopping wet size-12 L. L. Bean low hiking shoes the detectives had found near the camp table.

Checking the sand carefully around the cooking area, Dovci and Ogilvie found that it was compacted as if someone had stood there, perhaps preparing a meal. But ten or twelve feet to the south of the camp tables, they discovered a series of impressions in the sand that looked as if someone had been in a kneeling position with palms down and toes pointed into the sand. The knee impression was in line with a thumb mark (from the right hand), and the left hand had made a clear palm print. There were even impressions left by wrinkles in the clothing.

The knee impression was about four feet from the river's edge. The handprints were small. Ogilvie carefully placed her own hand into the print. It fit. It appeared that the person on top in the kneeling position near the river's edge had been either a woman or a man with small hands.

A fold-up camp chair with the jumble of wet and sandy clothing flung over it held man-sized blue flannel long johns, gray shorts, ski pants, a man's long-sleeved fleece jacket, a blue quilted vest, and a gray knit stocking cap. The pockets of the vest were filled with wet sand.

All the evidence was bagged and tagged and loaded into Chris Northon's Chevrolet. It was half an hour before midnight when the campsite was secured. Wallowa County Reserve Deputy Mike Robinson was left behind to guard the perimeters marked off by the yellow tape.

It was a lonely assignment.

CHAPTER NINE

JEANNE AND DICK NORTHON had had a really good time that Monday night. They'd gone to the movies to see the comedy *Meet the Parents* with Robert De Niro and Ben Stiller and laughed heartily. They were having their own "in-law" problems. They had come home to their house on Scandia Loop in Bend and were getting ready for bed when there was a knock on the door.

"There were two young Bend policemen standing there," Jeanne recalled, the memory as clear as if it had happened only yesterday. "They said, 'Your son is dead.' I was in shock. I guess I thought Chris's plane must have crashed—because we always lived with that fear in our subconscious minds. But they said, 'No,' and then my mind raced to thinking it must have been a car accident and I asked, 'The children? Are the children all right?'

"They said it wasn't the children. It was Chris, and then they said, 'I'm sorry—he's been shot . . . by his wife.'

"I didn't cry. I kept thinking that I had to tell his sisters— Mary and Sally—and I wanted to get in my car and go to them. The police didn't let me go. They drove us themselves."

The bottom had fallen out of the Northons' world. Losing Chris in the way they did was more than they could possibly fathom. It would be a long time before Dick Northon could re-member Chris's saying, "I've had a wonderful life. If I died to-morrow, I wouldn't feel as though I'd missed anything," and take some comfort from it.

* * *

"I ALWAYS THOUGHT we led a charmed life," Jeanne Northon said as she sat in her lodgelike home in Joseph, Oregon. "Until what happened happened, I believed that we would all be all right."

Married almost fifty years, a grandmother many times over, Jeanne was still slender and petite with delicate features and fine blond hair. Unlike Liysa's spare attractiveness, Jeanne *did* look like the prom queens and the cheerleaders who went to California colleges in the 1950s. Tragedy had barely marked her lovely face, but it made her seem fragile and anxious. With the memory of something terrible that had visited her family, she no longer had any trust in the future for the rest of them.

Until October 2000, the Northons' lives had been as normal as anyone they knew. With three children, they had problems and worries from time to time. But like most couples who married in the fifties, it seemed to Jeanne that she and her husband, Dick, were headed for a comfortable and happy retirement. She had kept piles of scrapbooks documenting their years of marriage and child raising.

Jeanne Stevenson and Dick Northon met for the first time in the ski hut at Camp Richardson Resort in Lake Tahoe. It wasn't a particularly auspicious meeting, but Dick didn't forget Jeanne; it was just that the timing of their initial encounter wasn't right. She was younger than he was, dating someone else, and he was about to go into the army air force. Still, they were destined to meet again. Jeanne and her sister, Yvonne, always spent part of the summer at Lake Tahoe, and a few years later, Jeanne tagged along with her sister, who was engaged to Ed Brown.

"Ed fixed me up with a date," Jeanne recalled, "and it turned out to be Dick Northon."

They came from different worlds, except that they shared a Swedish heritage, and they each had only one sibling—a sister. Dick's sister, Jean, was three years older than he was, and their mother, Genevieve, had to raise both of them alone after her husband walked out in the midst of the Great Depression when Dick was only four. Without anyone to support them, they had to accept the hospitality of a cousin, a crowded and tenuous arrangement at best. And then Dick was sent to stay with friends on a farm in Willits, California, for several years. His sister stayed with their mother, who felt lucky to have a job as a salesclerk at the H.C. Capwell's store in Oakland. Working ten hours a day, six days a week, she made $15 a week. Eventually, she became the manager of her department, which was unusual for a woman in that era.

"My mother even managed to save our house, but we couldn't live there," Dick recalled. "We couldn't afford to; my mother rented it out, and we had to live in a little one-bedroom apartment in Oakland. We didn't see my father again for eleven years. He was just gone. He might have been dead, for all we knew. But after all those years, my dad came back when I was fifteen. He wanted me to spend a summer working for him. A year later, that's what I did."

Through the hard years, Genevieve had never bad-mouthed her missing husband; she didn't want her children to resent their father. Naturally curious about the man who had fathered him, Dick wanted to see how he lived. He worked as an apprentice carpenter for his father, who was a construction foreman in the Permanente plant in the Santa Cruz mountains. Dick was plunged into a different world from what he had known. "My dad remarried later and he had another son. He named him Rick. My mother asked me if I wanted to invite my father to Jeanne's and my wedding, and I said no."

Jeanne's family was a close one, and they hadn't suffered the financial hardship that Dick's had. Her father, Hugo Stevenson, was a hard worker who was fortunate enough to be employed throughout the thirties. "He had a machine shop," Jeanne said, "and he made equipment and tools to build dams and bridges."

It was a decade dedicated to massive construction. Boulder, Hoover, and Grand Coulee Dams were in various stages of completion in the 1930s. They were essential to America's emergence from the Great Depression and then to the war effort in World War II.

Jeanne's dad also worked on the Golden Gate Bridge in San Francisco, which was finished in 1937. "That's what I took to school for show-and-tell," she said, smiling, "little pieces of samples from the Golden Gate Bridge."

Jeanne was in high school when her family moved to Walnut Creek, California, and her father realized his dream of owning a walnut ranch, buying seventy acres east of San Francisco. He was hiring workers, and Dick Northon was out of the service and needed money for college. Now the time seemed right for Jeanne and Dick, and they were soon dating steadily.

"Ed Brown and I were 'monkeys,' climbing in the walnut trees," Dick said. "We did that for two summers, and we had fun." Dick slept on a cot out in the garage. Both future sons-in-law had loftier career ambitions, but they enjoyed their time harvesting the crop.

Jeanne and Dick dated for a year, but Jeanne was a few years younger, and when they both went to Cal State, they drifted apart. "Neither of us had a broken heart over that," Jeanne remembered. "I think I was young for my age—"

"And I was having a good time," Dick interjected, grinning. He joined the Phi Gamma Delta fraternity, but he wasn't one of the rich kids whose fathers were paying for their college educations. "I couldn't afford to live in the house, but it was a place to eat lunch and go to parties."

Jeanne and Dick saw each other at parties on campus, but they weren't dating. "Then one of my fraternity brothers brought Jeanne to one of our dances, and I got very jealous," Dick said. Inevitably, they started dating again. And when Dick was a junior, he and Jeanne were married at the Park Boulevard Presbyterian Church in Oakland. It was April 20, 1951. After two and a half years of college, Jeanne dropped out and found a job working for a dentist whose office was just off campus. She was now following a different curriculum. In the fifties, it was called PHT: "Putting Husband Through [college]." Dick graduated from Cal State University that year with a degree in public health.

Jeanne was making $80 a month in her dental office job, and Dick worked temporarily in a gas station. "My brother-in-law, Ed Brown, was a teacher," Dick said, "and he really liked his job. He said they were looking for men teachers—especially those with a background in science and health and math. I took the job. They didn't pay much—thirty-two hundred dollars a year . . . gross. We bought a little house on the GI Bill for nine thousand dollars at three percent interest."

It was a tract house in Concord, California, with three bedrooms and one bathroom. Their lot had nine pear trees in the yard, and they were thrilled to own their own place. Jeanne's sister, Yvonne, and her husband, Ed, bought the house next door.

Dick had three jobs. In addition to teaching, he also coached and sold encyclopedias door-to-door to be able to make their mortgage payments. Jeanne worked in a little shop in Walnut Creek. More than most couples, they looked forward to being parents, and they were putting money away for the time Jeanne would stay home with their children.

But their dream of having a family didn't materialize. They were childless for almost six years, and it was agonizing for Jeanne. "I tried so hard to get pregnant," she said. "Everyone we knew had children or they were pregnant and I never was. In our neighborhood, there were babies and little children everywhere I looked. We finally decided to adopt and we were on the waiting list for a baby when I realized that I *was* pregnant at last."

Christopher James Northon was born in Oakland on September 12, 1956. Mary Northon was born on May 29, 1958, and Sally Northon on September 15, 1959, all by cesarean section. After waiting so long, Jeanne and Dick finally had what they had longed for—three children in exactly three years—and they were delighted.

"My doctor laughed," Jeanne said. "He said, 'We couldn't get you started and now we can't get you *stopped!*' "

But they were finished with having babies; they had their family. Dick had never had a real childhood with a family, and he vowed that his children would feel secure. They were a close family, typical of the "togetherness" era. Young Chris loved his grandfather Hugo Stevenson. Although the old man died when Chris was only five, he told his mother that when he had a little boy, he was going to name him Hugo.

When the Northon children were in grade school, Dick vested his retirement in California to get enough money for the family to move from Concord to Bend, Oregon. In the fall of 1968, they bought a huge old house on an eighty-acre ranch, and they would eventually add another forty acres.

"It cost $52,500," Jeanne said. "And that was a lot of money then. We moved to Bend with three horses, three kids, two dogs, and three cats. Dick drove one car and I drove the other."

"We never took vacations without the kids," Dick said. "And I sometimes took hiking vacations with Chris." The whole Northon family skied, rode horses, climbed mountains, and hiked.

Dick received a grant to study for his master's degree. For the next year, he commuted each week to Oregon State University in Corvallis. It was a long drive over the Cascade Mountain Range, and he had to leave home on Sunday and return on Friday nights. When the weather was warm, Dick would occasionally stay over Sunday night and then get up Monday at

4:00 A.M. to make the trip. But in the winter, the mountain passes were socked in with snowdrifts on some Friday nights and he couldn't get home at all.

Chris was twelve or thirteen and the girls were eleven and ten during this time. "Jeanne handled the kids *and* the farm," Dick said. "She did a great job."

With his new master's degree, Dick got a job teaching science at Cascade Junior High School in Bend. Theirs was a working ranch and the whole family pitched in. Chris, Mary, and Sally each had their own horse, and they loved to ride.

Chris learned to twirl a lariat and bring down heifers in the 4-H rodeo. He rode bulls and horses bareback. He was in the Boys' Club and the Boy Scouts. Bend was a much smaller town in the fifties and sixties than it is now. Over the decades since, new residents have been drawn to Bend, and the city now has a population nearing 40,000. Almost due east of Eugene across McKenzie Pass, Bend is surrounded by mountains, forests, and high plains and located on the shores of the Deschutes River. Skiers flock to Mt. Bachelor and golfers to the lodge and velvet green golf courses of the Sunriver Resort. During the summer, Bend smells of baking pinecones and clean rivers. Chris, a natural athlete who played football and ran track in high school, told his father years later, "Dad, I have to thank you so much for bringing me up in Bend."

Dick had worked since he was eight because he had no choice, and even though he didn't have to, Chris had the same work ethic. He wasn't yet nine when he had a job with George Barrett, who owned a neighboring ranch. Chris changed irrigation pipes in the mornings and the evenings.

"He was a good guy," his father said with a sigh, remembering how Chris had labored hard since he was in the third grade. "He worked out George's horses, and he worked for me—bailing hay, running the equipment, cleaning out the stalls. He worked right along beside me on our ranch."

But Chris was born fearless and he had any number of accidents from the time he was a little boy. Usually he emerged unscathed, but 1963 was a bad year. He was seven when he broke his leg skiing, and then his arm in a riding accident. Later, he broke his wrist falling off the bucking barrel.

The young Northon family seemed like something right out of "How America Lives" in the *Ladies' Home Journal,* and mostly it was. Chris, Mary, and Sally loved the ranch and their life in Bend. Jeanne didn't work outside the home when her children were growing up, but she made skirts and vests out of material she'd sewn together into patchwork. She had a brisk business, and once she even designed and sewed a whole patchwork wedding.

Chris was a tall kid early on, his Swedish genes apparent in his corn yellow hair and blue eyes. It would be easy to describe him in retrospect as a perfect kid—but he wasn't. He was an outrageous practical joker, freethinker, chance-taker, who would grow into a unique man, with his own quota of flaws. Chris demanded a great deal from life—freedom, adventure, good times—and he appreciated girls and, later, women.

"No," Jeanne said, laughing as she thought of her teenage son, "Chris wasn't perfect. I remember one time we were mortified when we got a call from the principal at Pilot Butte, Chris's junior high. It seemed that he and his friend Buck Zink barred the door when all the teachers were in their meeting room. Those boys wedged it shut from the outside. And then they turned on the fire alarm! I asked Chris why on earth they did that, and he didn't lie—he never lied. He told me with a straight face, 'We just wanted to see all those teachers crawling out of the windows in a panic.' "

At fourteen, that stunt brought Chris the first spanking of his life. At least his father didn't teach at the junior high school Chris attended, but Dick Northon was embarrassed.

That wasn't the last time Chris tested his parents. "He

streaked at a football game in high school," Dick reported, laughing. "He was a very good student—especially in math and science—but he would do things to shock people."

Chris's high jinks got so bad one time when Dick was away that Jeanne threatened to transfer him to another junior high school. Chris went out to the tack room in the barn and hid under the bed so she couldn't find him. But his disobedience always had to do with something that he considered hilarious. It was his sense of humor that turned his parents' hair gray. Chris was never involved in a fight at school, or in any kind of violence for that matter.

His sister Sally recalled other adventures she and Chris had shared. Thirty years afterward, when it didn't matter anymore, she told her parents for the first time about what they'd been up to. And Jeanne and Dick turned pale.

Sally said that she, Chris, and Mary would sneak the tractor out of the barn and hook snow disks on behind. "We put the tractor in gear," Sally said, "and then we'd all jump on the disks—and ride them across eighty acres of pasture. When it finally got too hot on our bottoms, we would jump off and race to the feeder on the back of the tractor. From there, we could climb up to the seat and stop the tractor.

"It was terribly dangerous, but we made it every time."

Almost every time. Once, Chris revved up the tractor speed a notch too fast and it crashed into a fence before they could clamber up and stop it. Still, they only got shaken up and nobody noticed the slight damage to the tractor.

Sally was Chris's little sidekick who would go along with any wild idea he came up with. Mary was "the good girl," who had to be coaxed into participating.

Sally recalled that she and Chris were always delighted when everyone else in the family went skiing. "We'd tell them, 'We're going to go riding,' " Sally said, "but then we'd crawl out an upstairs window onto the roof. It was very steep and the chimney was way up there. Chris was a great roper, and he'd rope the chimney and we'd climb up that steep roof and sit up there on top of the world. One time, we heard our parents driving up the road and we scrambled down that rope as fast as we could. It flew over the other side and was hanging right down in the driveway where they could see it if they looked up. Chris and I were going, 'Oh nooooooooo!' And of course they looked up and figured out what we'd been up to."

Unlike a lot of parents, Jeanne and Dick had relatively few problems when their three children were in their teens. Those they did have usually involved Chris's danger gene. Once, he decided to teach Sally rodeoing. "He started me out riding rams and then he moved me up to calves," she remembered.

Finally, Chris suggested that he and Sally ride their horses bareback, flying free across fifty acres. "But Chris always made sure I was okay," Sally said, her voice catching a little. "He was my big brother."

Chris was a paradox. He was both a good student and a prankster, a daredevil and a caring older brother. He read voraciously and sometimes bored his friends as he ponderously explained concepts he'd read about. He never had music lessons, but sometime in his mid-teens, he just sat down at a piano and taught himself to play by ear. And like everything else he attempted, he was very good at it; he could play anything—jazz or classical.

CHAPTER TEN

AFTER GRADUATING from high school in 1974, Chris had no particular goals beyond traveling. College didn't interest him. He cared more about sailing, swimming, scuba diving, mountain biking, tennis, and paddleboarding. He moved to

Monterey, California, and spent time there and in nearby Carmel. He worked when he needed to at various odd jobs. A relative taught at the prestigious Robert Louis Stevenson School, and Chris got a job as a groundskeeper there for a while, but he didn't want to do anything that would tie him to one spot for very long.

Chris dated Gay Bradshaw in California. Later, his friend Dave Jones—who was a medical student—went out with her, too, but there were no hard feelings. They were more like the Three Musketeers than a love triangle. The three of them even took a long trip to Mexico together.

When Chris finally came back to Bend, he still wasn't sure what he wanted to do with his life beyond living it to his fullest capacity. Chris swallowed life in big gulps.

He enrolled at Central Oregon Community College, with a vague idea of majoring in music. "He called us one day and invited us to a concert he was playing in," Jeanne said. "We expected that he'd be on the piano, and we were surprised to see him playing the violin in the string section. We didn't even know he could play the violin."

* * *

IT TOOK A WHILE for Chris to decide on any career goals. His father had earned his pilot's license in Reno when he was only seventeen, had flown in the air force, and had gloried in it. And in 1980, when Chris was twenty-four, he finally knew what he was meant to do. *Fly.* Chris would discover that he had an even greater obsession with flying—if that was possible—than his father had had. He found he was most alive when he was in the air.

It would be a long haul, though, before Chris could make a career as a pilot. First, he worked at Roberts Field, an airport in

Redmond, a town fourteen miles from Bend. He pumped gas, cleaned planes—did anything he could to pay for flying lessons. He was over six feet two, but he happily squeezed his large frame into a cramped plane for every hour of instruction he could afford. Chris Conant, his instructor, realized that his student was in a tearing hurry to learn everything there was to know about flying. Once he fixed on what he wanted to do with his life, there was no stopping him.

He got his student pilot's license in March 1980, and his private pilot's license two months later. He called Jeanne and Dick and said, "Meet me at the airport and I'll take you up!" And so his parents were his first passengers.

While Chris practiced for his instrument rating, he towed gliders at Roberts Field. By the end of 1981, he had his instrument rating and his commercial flying license, and he was a flight instructor himself. Dan Jones, who came from Utah and is now a commercial airline pilot, was Chris's first student and became a lifelong friend.

In 1982 and 1983, Chris's first real job as a pilot was as an instructor working out of Roberts Field. Then he flew charters for Resort Air at the Sunriver Resort in Bend. His ultimate ambition was to be a captain for a major airline, but he knew that most pilots got by flying charters initially. For Chris, smaller planes soon became bigger ones and shorter flights gave way to long distances.

There was a girl during those early years, although it never could have worked. Anna Goodrich was eight years younger than Chris. That wouldn't have mattered if he had been forty and she thirty-two, but he met her when he was twenty-four and she was only sixteen—mature-looking, but still only sixteen.

They met at a wedding in Eugene while Chris was still flying for Resort Air. It was perhaps the first instance where a woman was right for Chris, but too many other things were wrong. As much as he loved her, Chris forced himself to walk away from Anna. Maybe one day in the future, things would be different and they would meet again, but in 1980, the timing wasn't right. Their relationship was never physical, but it left an indelible impression on Chris.

He remained friends with Anna and with her family. In fact, many years later, when her sister Gina had marital problems, Chris invited Gina to stay in Hawaii with him and some of his fellow pilots. It was a purely platonic situation; it was always Chris's habit to take in any friend—male or female—who needed a place to stay for a while. Gina lived with Chris, Joe Wilson, and Randy Ore from May through August 1988. Chris often talked to her about how he had cared for Anna, but about how hopeless it had been, too.

"I was sorry that Anna was so young when they met," Gina recalled, "because he would have been good to her. He was a gentle soul. Yes, he brought women home (when I lived with him and the guys) and he slept with a lot of them, but he was always very kind and gentle to them. He placed his mom on a pedestal, and he treated every woman with respect."

Although Chris never had a physical affair with Anna, most of his friends would agree that she was the one true love of his life. Maybe it was easy to say that because their love was never consummated and never tested in a day-to-day living situation.

He felt deeply for her, but Chris accepted that Anna was just too young to be with him and didn't pursue her. A year later, he was twenty-five, and a woman named Sharon Leighty moved to Bend just after New Year's, 1981. She met Mary and Sally Northon first. "It wasn't long, though," she remembered, "before their family became my family."

Sharon and Chris moved in together in the summer of 1982, and she soon realized that he would never fit into any normal work mode. "He was totally nontraditional," she said, but she didn't consider that a negative thing. "He just had a passion to live life at a higher level—with his music and his reading."

And, of course, with his *flying,* which promised adventures yet uncharted.

Chris and Sharon's three years together were memorable, even though she knew instinctively that their relationship would never last. Someday, he would probably get married because family relationships were very important to him, but not soon. And not to her. He was a man who walked by himself and could spend long stretches of time alone.

Chris was the first man Sharon had ever known who was not only totally masculine but sensitive and unafraid to cry. When something touched him, his eyes brimmed with tears. At first, it seemed incongruous that such a large man could be un-abashedly emotional, but she learned that that was Chris.

They got along, although they had disagreements like any couple. Later, when investigators asked her about Chris's anger, she looked at them, confused. "Chris didn't *have* any anger," she said softly. "No hostility . . ."

"Was he abusive?"

"*No!*" she answered. "Not at all—ever. I've worked with domestic violence situations and I know the symptoms. *Chris?* No way. I can't even remember his raising his voice. We always worked things out by talking. Chris never walked away mad."

Their time together wound down, and Sharon and Chris went their separate ways without recriminations on either side. "I went to Europe on a trip when I was twenty-eight," Sharon recalled. "And when I came back, Chris had moved to New Zealand."

Chris had planned to spend six months in New Zealand. But once there, he was hired by South Pacific Island Airlines in Pago Pago in American Samoa. He was a captain there, although it wasn't like being a captain on a major airline. He flew with them for two and a half years before the mostly charter airline went bankrupt.

Chris loved the tropics and wasn't ready to go back to Bend yet. His next job was with Princeville Air, where he was again a captain and flew small planes in Hawaii between Kauai and Oahu. It was a natural progression for him to move on up to Hawaiian Airlines when they announced they were hiring.

Chris's Hawaiian Air pilot class was scheduled to graduate in March 1987. He joined Jimmy Crockett, Mike Saul, Peter Anderson, Gary Kissinger, Kevin Ching, Jamie Cheng, Jay Thompson, Mary Scott, and Joe Wilson. Joe and Chris became close friends almost from the moment they met in January, and they shared the house on Kaneohe Bay on the island of Oahu, along with Randy Ore and other pilots, with the roll call changing from time to time as the bachelor pilots relocated or got married.

Chris, Joe, and Randy were contented bachelors, living the life that half the men in America probably fantasize about. They had sailboats, surfboards, and kayaks when they were home, and they had planes to fly. They would live in their "bachelor pad" for seven years, and none of the three was tempted to get married. They were flying into exotic countries, dating, throwing parties, and playing music as loud as they wanted. Maybe they would think about marriage . . . someday.

Randy Ore always gave his close friends nicknames. For his own reasons, he dubbed Chris "C-Sting," and Joe was "Joey," while Randy himself was "Seymour." Randy characterized their place on Kaneohe Bay as a kind of postcollege fraternity. They all knew it had to end someday, but for the time being, their lives were great.

Chris vowed to himself that if he should ever marry, it would be for the rest of his life. As for having children, he didn't really think about that. His parents knew that Chris lived a free-wheeling bachelor's life and didn't see any reason to settle down in the foreseeable future. Jeanne and Dick were happy to meet the women he introduced to them, but they didn't get excited about it or expect it to last; they knew that he dated dozens of women in Hawaii and in the exotic places he flew into. Chris enjoyed women unabashedly, but he respected them and he never kissed and told if a woman stayed over.

"The thing was," Dick said, assessing his son's single status as he approached forty, "he didn't want to be responsible for other people. He had seen his sisters' marriages fail, and he'd seen most of his friends go through divorces. He told me once, 'I'm having such a wonderful time on my own. I like to go and fish and camp, hunt and bike ride, and when I'm not flying or being on reserve, I really like to be out in the wilderness.' "

That was true. He loved to cross-country ski and climb the mountains around Bend, sometimes alone in the wilderness and sometimes with his friend John Gill or with his father. It was essential to Chris that he had enough time to enjoy the sports he loved, and that didn't change as he grew older. He showed no signs at all of settling into a comfortable middle age where sitting at home growing a little paunch was the norm.

Chris had lots of "best" friends, although Joe Wilson and John Gill were probably closest to him as he hit forty. "Chris was always more of a man's man than a ladies' man," Joe said. "If someone was in a bind, Chris wouldn't hesitate to step up, and risk his life if he had to." One year, Randy Ore hurt his back and could hardly move. Chris dropped everything to take care of him.

Injuries among the "fraternity" weren't unusual, but it was Chris who took the most chances. Joe Wilson noted that "Chris had this so-called recklessness, but it was always within his control." He recalled that Chris enjoyed pushing himself to the limit. "Those Mount Everest climber types had nothing on Chris."

During the Gulf War in 1991, Operation Desert Storm took Chris on a different kind of flight pattern. The military mobilized airlines to move troops in a program called CRAF (Civilian Reserve Aircraft Fleet). The flight crews chosen to fly troops were interviewed by military intelligence teams and preapproved before they were accepted for CRAF. Chris became a First Officer on a four-engine DC-8, which had an exceptionally long range.

He flew first to Guam and Cubi Point in the west and then was ordered to the east, where he flew to Sicily, Athens, Riyadh, Diego Garcia—or wherever troops were needed in a hurry.

The crews usually stayed together for a month or so, pooled their per diem pay, and used the extra money to take side tours. Chris loved it. He had always felt wanderlust for faraway places, and he added dozens of exotic ports of call to his memory bank. He was awarded the Air Medal for his service to America, although he played it down, explaining that the duty was more a boon for him than the other way around.

About this time, Chris fell in love for the second or third time in his life. Her name was Charlene Makanani, and everyone called her "Maka." Though at first acquaintance Maka appeared to be a rather mild-mannered local girl from Kauai, she was anything but that. She was the daughter of a career army man and was very well educated, cultured, and worldly. She was six years older than Chris but that made no difference to him.

"Maybe it was Maka who came the closest to being Chris's 'soul mate,' of any woman he knew," his friend Joe Wilson said.

Everyone who knew the couple expected that they would marry, but it wasn't to be. Chris was still the ultimate bachelor, and Maka was sometimes jealous. They drifted apart and Maka eventually married someone else.

Ironically, although Chris had always been a daredevil,

challenging the ocean on his surfboard, and flying over enemy territory in the Gulf War, his most painful injury came in an accident near the Mojave Desert. He was riding in a twelve-seat hotel airport courtesy shuttle with two other pilots, headed for Los Angeles, when the van driver suddenly changed lanes. Either he clipped another car or a car behind them hit the van. At any rate, it rolled several times. When paramedics responded, they tagged the driver and Chris as the most critically wounded. True to form, Chris was the only man in the van who hadn't bothered to put his seat belt on.

The driver *was* in critical condition. When Chris pulled him from the overturned van, he was drenched with the driver's blood. But, when medics wiped off the blood, they found Chris's only apparent injury was a broken left ring finger.

Chris got emergency treatment and made his flight. However, the doctors hadn't found the profound whiplash damage to the soft tissues in his neck. The nagging pain in his neck lasted for almost two years, but it never occurred to him to file a claim against the hotel's insurance company. He was surprised months after the crash on California's Highway 14 to receive a settlement check for $10,000—but not too surprised to keep the money. He would have preferred to be able to turn his head without pain.

That didn't change his personality. One of the things that people recalled about Chris was his constant broad smile. He seemed the happiest man in every group.

CHAPTER ELEVEN

JOE AND MAGGIE WILSON were married in Greenwich, Connecticut, in April 1995, and lived for almost a year in an apartment on West Seventy-second Street in New York City. By the time, Joe and Chris really got to talk with each other again, Joe was shocked to discover how entrenched Liysa Mattson had become in his best friend's life.

When Joe was so focused on moving to the East Coast to be with Maggie, he hadn't asked many questions of Chris. "I could see they were getting closer," he said. "They had books and water sports and eating simple food in common. But she was still married, and Chris seemed almost embarrassed to admit he was into this girl. He really hadn't lived with a woman since his college days. It was funny; he convinced me and the other guys that he wasn't going to be living with Liysa in her house."

Although an intense sexual relationship was very important to Liysa, Chris told Joe that she had insisted he go through careful testing to be sure he had no venereal disease. As much as she was attracted to him, she wouldn't sleep with him on a regular basis until she was sure he was "safe." Because it was so important to her, Chris had agreed. When he got a clean bill of health, they began to join their lives in earnest.

"He built a kind of bachelor's pad in her backyard—kind of an 'ohana,' " Joe said. "As I recall, he took out a thirty-thousand-dollar loan with the Hawaiian Airlines Credit Union, and he put together a real nice place."

Actually, Chris remodeled an older structure that sat behind Liysa's house. Its charm was that it had a wonderful view of the ocean. With Joe gone, Chris had moved to the little basement apartment where Margaret Lefton had once lived while he worked on the one-room structure on stilts in Liysa's backyard. It was about four hundred square feet and spartan. It had a bed, a little bathroom, a hot plate, room for his piano, and an outside shower. It also had a "killer" view, according to Joe.

Chris took great pleasure in working on the small structure behind Liysa's house. He was something of a perfectionist when it came to his home, and for a bachelor, he was a neat housekeeper. Joe and Randy Ore teased him about his little house and called it "The Berchtesgaden" after Hitler's onetime eagle's nest hideout.

It may have been the best-built structure on the street; most of the homes dated back to the late 1940s and were of single-wall construction. The weather was so mild that thick insulation wasn't necessary. The houses weren't grand at all, but the land was. Something was always blooming or bursting with life along Lanipo Street: the orange African tulip trees, plumeria, Kaiwe or "Mesquite trees," monkey pod trees, and the feathery Norfolk pines. It was, indeed, a wondrous place to live.

Joe Wilson still had reservations about Liysa, but he didn't bother lecturing Chris. The man was thirty-nine and fully capable of handling his own affairs. And while marriage wasn't breaking up the old gang completely, the young pilots of a decade earlier were easing into middle age and beginning to settle down.

THROUGH HER ALMOST COMPULSIVE journaling, Liysa had become a very adept writer. A career as an author or playwright was yet another goal she sometimes focused on, and she certainly had the native talent to do that. She had written a few tentative screenplays. Nick had read them and found them pretty good. One was an historical saga that dealt with leprosy and the banning of its sufferers to Molokai. Another had to do with diving.

As far as Nick knew, Liysa hadn't actually sold any of her screenplays, although she'd been commissioned to do an outline for a movie about a surfer on the north shore. "She was paid some money for a romantic comedy, I think," he said, "but it was never produced."

When Liysa had complained that she couldn't have the

ranch she wanted, Nick suggested gently that she try to sell her
screenplays to make the extra money that it would take.

"Not right now," she said positively, "but I will someday.
It's one of my goals."

UNTIL 1995, NICK HAD BELIEVED they had a very good marriage. "There was no defining end to it," he would recall quietly.
"Not until the last year. It was just a gradual erosion. I think it
was over in her mind before *I* gave up on us."

He would have done almost anything to please her and to
save their marriage. If she needed more freedom, he was willing
to give it to her. But their relationship was so worn down that
nothing could reconstruct it. A year before Liysa met Chris, she
and Nick had begun to sleep in separate bedrooms.

Liysa had finally accepted that Nick wouldn't jeopardize
their financial stability to buy whatever she wanted. He'd
agreed to buy her the house on Lanipo—but that was all. And
right after they signed the papers on that property, Nick had left
to go to a Tahiti shoot for a few months.

By the time he returned, Liysa was virtually living with
Chris Northon and their marriage was over for good. He accepted that. Nick never moved back in with Liysa and Papako;
he stepped out of her life without challenging her.

Despite the money that Chris put into the eagle's nest, Liysa
charged him $1,000 a month rent, and asked him to pay her for
groceries for food he ate. He didn't mind; it still seemed like a
bargain.

* * *

BY THE MID-NINETIES, Lanipo Street in Kailua was crowded
with Liysa's present, past, and future. Jane Sands remembered
Liysa all too well. Jane had a great dog named Splash who

adored Chris, and Jane liked him, too. She was not at all fond of Liysa; she had never forgotten how Liysa had hurt her son and wasn't particularly happy to have her as a neighbor.

Tim Sands and Nick knew each other, too; they had gone to Punaho High School together. They had no ill feelings toward each other. Like most men who had been with Liysa for any length of time, any regret they might have had about losing her was mitigated by the relief they felt to be free of her histrionics and demands. Given the close proximity of their lives, Tim and Nick would both come to know Chris Northon. Tim liked him well enough and sometimes was tempted to warn him that life with Liysa wasn't always predictable.

But he didn't. Men don't usually do that. Sometimes women warn other women not to plunge into relationships with men *they* know too well—but it never seems to do much good anyway, given the wariness of the new woman toward any female in a lover's past.

Understandably, Nick was less fond of Chris. He and Liysa had been married for almost ten years and they had a son. Although Nick didn't blame Chris entirely for the breakup of his marriage, he was somewhat cautious around him. Whatever had killed it, Nick's marriage was over and he was ready to work out property and divorce settlements with Liysa. She wanted very much to be free of her second husband so she could concentrate on persuading Chris to become her third.

"She must have moved verr-ry fast," Joe Wilson said regretfully. "I never saw any 'courting.' I'm not sure how she convinced Chris to marry her. . . ."

Joe had approved of all of Chris's girlfriends before, but there was something about Liysa that set his teeth on edge and filled him with concern. "I did not like her," he said. "But it wasn't because of anything concrete. She just wasn't likable and she wasn't meant for Chris, and she and I didn't do or have anything in common."

Joe's reaction to Liysa was alien to him. He liked most people and he wasn't a snob, yet all his instincts told him that this woman would be a disaster for Chris. He kept questioning himself about why he felt so uneasy about her.

Randy Ore disagreed with Joe. He liked Liysa. "She made a great first impression," he recalled. "Several of us thought she was perfect for Chris. She was friendly and attractive and fun to be around. She was in good shape and she was very mellow."

One of Chris's closest friends in Kailua was another Hawaiian Airlines pilot named Dave Story. Dave and his wife, Debbie, had a school-age son and daughter, and Dave also had credentials as a minister in the Universal Life Church. Wearing that hat, he had married two dozen couples.

Chris and Dave had known each other casually as fellow HAL pilots, but after they were paired in flights in 1993, their friendship really developed. With Joe Wilson living in New York City, Dave Story became another of Chris's *best* friends in Hawaii. They both had dozens of friends among the pilots who flew with Hawaiian Airlines. Often the HAL pilots would recognize one another's voices on the radio as they flew. It was a tight fraternity.

Chris was usually assigned to Hawaiian Airlines Flight 25 from Portland to Honolulu, or he "dead-headed" home on this flight. As a pilot, after leaving the Portland flight control zone, he would call San Francisco radio: "ANELE two one-zero-five, flight level three-five-zero, estimating APACK two-one-two-zero, next MAGGIE, fuel two-four decimal three, minus four-eight, two-four-zero diagonal five-five, light chop: go ahead."

As Chris's plane passed ANELE, he hooked up with the Honolulu center to be cleared to fly direct to BAMBO. The air chatter was as familiar to him as breathing, but he was always alert to the unexpected as Flight 25 cruised 350 miles from Honolulu. The skies were invariably a soft baby blue with puffy white clouds ten to fifteen thousand feet beneath them and they could see the navy blue of the Pacific Ocean seven miles down. Flying at fourteen thousand feet above sea level, the crew of Flight 25 began to see the peaks of the Mauna Kea and Mauna Loa volcanoes off their left wing as they rose from the Big Island of Hawaii. Two hundred miles from Honolulu, Maui and its Haleakala volcano appeared.

Chris never tired of the majesty of it. A hundred miles from the Honolulu airport, cliffs on the north shore of Molokai rose two thousand feet from the sea. Even as the millennium approached, hundreds of leprosy patients, once sheltered by Father Damien, still live there on the Kalaupapa Peninsula.

Flight 25 was close to home. When Chris and Dave Story flew together, they could look down at their hometown of Kailua on the windward side of Oahu. They could see from Makapuu Point to the northernmost tip of Oahu: Kahuku Point. On the right was Kaneohe Bay where Chris and Joe Wilson and Randy Ore once lived. Ten miles farther, they saw the six-mile stretch of white sand beaches of Waimanolo, Lanikai, and Kailua. Just offshore, the familiar Mokolua Islands and Flat Island. Close to landing, Flight 25 flew over the Koolau mountain range that divides the windward side of Oahu from the congested side with bustling Honolulu and Waikiki. They could almost reach out and touch Koko crater, Koko Head, and Diamond Head crater. On the town side of the Koolau Range, houses crept up all its ridgelines. And then, as Honolulu International Airport and Pearl Harbor came into their line of sight on the right, they gradually descended, approaching Waikiki Beach, downtown Honolulu, the Aloha Tower.

"Hawaiian 25," the tower operator says, "Maintain 2500 feet until the shoreline and one-eight-zero knots until EWABE, cleared for visual approach runway eight, left . . . Hawaiian 25, cleared to land eight left, hold short of four left . . . Honolulu, ground Delta. Taxi to Gate 31."

"Roger." Chris and Dave grabbed their flight bags. They were home.

Chris loved everything about his job, and reveled in the thought that he would soon be swimming or paddleboarding to the Mokolua Islands he had just flown over. His life in Hawaii was a constant source of joy for him.

Chris and Dave played a lot of tennis at the Kailua Tennis Club; his membership there was one of Chris's few extravagances. The club looked like something right out of a movie set, with swaying palm trees, profuse tropical flowers, and more than a dozen tennis courts. It even had beautiful female tennis champions from the University of Hawaii to give neophytes private lessons. Chris was in his element there, and Dave's son was a spectacular Punaho High School tennis champion who would soon win a scholarship to Northwestern University.

Dave was about six years older than Chris and a great tennis partner, full of hilarious remarks during a game but also very empathetic and self-effacing. Although Chris towered over him, Dave had a calm confidence that Chris admired.

The two men played tennis, surfed, and went paddleboarding. Chris was so strong, he left Dave panting. He could use one arm to propel their twelve-foot paddleboard toward the Mokolua Islands and still carry on a conversation. Afterward, the men climbed the steep hill to Chris's house carrying the paddleboard. "I'd be trotting along behind him," Dave recalled, "all out of breath, but Chris was in perfect shape."

Chris introduced Liysa to Dave and Debbie Story, and they liked her a lot. For the first five or six months that the Storys knew Liysa, she was very nice to them. Chris really liked their family lifestyle, and Liysa noted that. "I guess you could say she wooed us," Dave recalled, "because she could see how close Chris was to us. But that faded after she was sure of Chris."

Liysa made between $5,000 and $12,000 a month, and Chris had always thought it would be great to be with a woman who was financially independent. Liysa came across that way, and Dave could tell that Chris—who had always shied away from marriage—felt he was moving toward a loving partnership.

But, gradually, Liysa stopped going over to the Storys' house; Chris went alone. Dave saw Liysa only when he and Chris came back from some sports activity; while Chris would be putting things away, Dave would sit talking to Liysa in her living room, but there was something in her manner that disturbed him.

"It's hard to explain. She was quite cordial, but I told Debbie, 'She gives me the creeps because she's not really *there*. It's an eerie feeling that she's not really connecting with me, and doesn't care to.' "

Dave Story was a man of the nineties who believed that women have rights and should never be abused. He'd seen women who had been abused—emotionally and physically—but Liysa wasn't like them. She was never tentative or worried that something she said would make Chris angry. Rather, she was very confident.

Now Dave and Debbie saw Chris almost as often as they had before he and Liysa were together, but Dave accepted that Liysa mostly avoided them. Debbie was a little closer to Liysa. A massage therapist, Debbie often gave Liysa massages, and they talked about their children.

The elder Northons had had a similar experience as their relationship with Liysa progressed. With their children grown, Jeanne and Dick built their dream house near Tumalo Falls, not far from the Gills' resort and in the very area where Nick and Liysa had bought and sold their acreage. The Northons traded their living quarters with Chris for their vacation time in 1994. He was still living in Margaret Lefton's apartment then, and for a week or two, they stayed there and enjoyed Oahu. Later, he'd spent time on Tumalo Road. They'd done the house exchange before and it worked out well. They even used each other's cars during their vacations.

"There was a knock on Chris's door in Kailua," Jeanne recalled. "When I answered, this pretty lady was standing there. I remember I said, 'Oh, you look just like my daughter Sally.'

"It was Liysa. She was so nice. She couldn't do enough for us. She and Chris were just dating then, and Liysa was, of course, living in the house she had bought with her estranged husband." This was the first time they met Liysa, and the Northons liked her a lot. She impressed them as sweet and intelligent, and her little boy was wonderful.

LIYSA WANTED TO MARRY Chris Northon. Those critical of her would remark later that "Liysa always married up," suggesting that she used men as stepping-stones to attain what she needed and wanted out of life. Nick Mattson was a celebrity in the islands and made an excellent living. But she left him when she felt he didn't believe in her dreams any longer.

She may have seen Chris as a man with more potential. He was qualified on a Dash 7 and a twin-engine Otter, and sometimes worked as a flight engineer and copilot on DC-8s and DC-10s. He was just about to qualify as a captain on the DC-10s. Chris listened to her plans for her retreat, Chrysalis, and she felt he was impressed. She misjudged, assuming that his sexual attraction to her meant he was fascinated with everything she talked about.

That could not have been further from the truth, but reality had never been Liysa's forte. She saw great sexual potential in Chris, too, and she simply pasted the traits she wanted in her third husband over his real self. And she told him exactly what he had always wanted to hear from a potential wife. In fact, they were not meant for each other in any way beyond specifications listed in a personal ad.

It was a recipe for disaster.

Liysa had seduced Chris, although no one could argue that he was not a most willing subject. But getting him to commit to a long-term relationship, much less marriage, wasn't going to be easy. Chris could be aloof and shut off. He was still a loner and, in some ways, happiest out in his "Berchtesgaden." Most women say they're looking for a strong, sexy man who is also sensitive. And yet many have to conclude that these attributes rarely coexist and make adjustments to their *own* attitudes. Liysa wanted it all, and she shut her eyes to Chris's need to be a lone eagle—more often than most men.

She was completely focused on marrying him. Now it was Chris who received her masterful letters that were meant to make him feel alternately enchanted, guilty, beloved, pressured, passionate, and wary. Liysa was immensely talented at evoking strong feelings with her words. Of all the writing she did, her letters were, perhaps, her best work.

She also wrote letters to Nick, but with no hint of romance. She was the one who dictated how their property would be divided, warning him that it was vital that his parents continued to like her. "It will be up to you to try to convince your parents to remain friendly to me. They should know that it's in their best interest to do so, since I will have custody of Papako, but you know how they can be. . . ."

Papako, loved by both his parents and his grandparents, was a pawn in Liysa's property strategy. She assured Nick that she had "no animosity" toward him but that *she* had to be the one to make any final decisions about Papako's care. She typed out her list of "mediation issues" with Nick. She wanted sole physical and legal custody of Papako, and she would work out a "formula" for child support from Nick. She estimated that the costs of Papako's education would be shared equally, but could vary according to their incomes. She would allow Nick visitation with his son, but would not permit his parents to see him unless Nick was there. However, they would have to remain as debtors on the loans for property she had wanted. If she couldn't make the payments, Nick would have to do that.

"PROPERTIES . . . Prenuptial agreement(s) with future spouses setting these properties off-limits. To remain unencumbered for Papako . . .

LANIKAI HOUSE: Liysa

MAKAHA APARTMENT: Liysa

PAAUILO HOUSE: Nick

BEND LAND: Liysa

VOLCANO LAND: Liysa

WAIKII LAND: (To be sold; equity, if any, to be used on Bend House or other use by Liysa.)"

She suggested that they divide their business and equipment, but that she would receive all royalties from her photographs and be the only one who had the authority to negotiate or sign contracts. Liysa would get the royalties on the Hanauma Bay books, although she hoped they would work together on a "project by project basis."

She wanted alimony. If the royalties from all the surf photography that Nick had taught her to do didn't come to $4,000 a month, then he was to guarantee to pay her the difference. He was also to pay her $600 a month in child support for Papako and adhere to very strict visitation guidelines. His child support would end only upon his death, and, even then, if Nick didn't have an insurance policy worth $100,000 with Papako as the beneficiary, his estate would be responsible for paying his son $100,000. Nick had no problem with that; he loved Papako.

He was a complete gentleman about their divorce. Liysa was free to remarry on February 16, 1996. It may have been a bad omen that that particular February was not a propitious month for romance: two weeks later, Princess Diana agreed to divorce Prince Charles.

Liysa's past relationships with men had invariably overlapped, and she always had her next man picked out. This time, she had been careful not to find herself married to two men at the same time again. But now, even though she was legally free to wed, she was stunned that Chris wasn't as eager to rush into marriage as she was. Instead, the fact that she was single tended to make him back off.

It had been relatively easy for her to convince Chris that he should remodel the little living quarters behind her house on Lanipo Street. With his longtime roommates leaving, the timing was right for Chris to be—if not actually *live*—with her. But getting him to *commit* wasn't as simple as Liysa had hoped. He had a stubborn streak that surprised her. Not since Makimo had a man been so reluctant to do what she wanted.

Marrying Chris made complete sense to Liysa—both romantically and pragmatically. With him at her side, she believed that she could buy the ranch she wanted, and his position with Hawaiian Airlines would mean that *she* could fly almost anywhere at no cost.

In one letter she wrote to Chris during a temporary breakup, she explained her disappointment: "You may not think the monetary gain to be able to 'fly for free' means much, but for *me*, it was *huge*. Being able to go on those Maui overnighters with you, the weekends, outer islands, visiting my mom and dad, skiing in April, shooting in Tahiti. It could help my . . . business *so* much!"

Perhaps Liysa had read the tale of Scheherazade and the stories that saved her life night after night. In her journals, she fantasized about keeping a man captive by satisfying him physically in inventive ways that would bind him to her forever and keep him from harming her, all out of fear that he would lose the best sex he'd ever known.

Liysa certainly intrigued Chris sexually, but he had reservations. Their intimate life satisfied both of them. And it maddened Liysa that he would come close to giving in only to pull away. But despite their powerful physical connection, Chris saw little of the sweetness in Liysa that he had found in his affairs with Maka or the other women he'd been with for a long time. Still, their lives became more and more entangled until finally one night Chris proudly announced to Joe and Maggie Wilson that Liysa *was* his girlfriend.

The two couples had gone out to Fast Eddie's in Kailua-town. Maggie, who was always gracious, made an effort to find something she and Liysa might have in common, but Joe still felt a sinking sensation. This woman wasn't right for Chris. She was attractive enough and intelligent, but she seemed totally heedless of what people thought about her. She apparently didn't own any clothes beyond a bathing suit and a saronglike wrap. She didn't wear shoes, not even now as they went out to dinner.

Chris had always been drawn to well-groomed women, and Joe expected him to be embarrassed by Liysa's bare feet. But he didn't seem to be. Chris was too infatuated.

Liysa laughed as she told them about the time she tried to board a Hawaiian Airlines plane—long before she met Chris— in her bare feet. "They turned her away," Joe recalled. "It's a federal regulation that you have to wear shoes to board a plane."

Liysa explained that she had solved the problem by stepping out of line and using a marking pen to *draw* flip-flops on her dusty feet. Then she'd demanded that they let her board.

And they had.

——— CHAPTER TWELVE ———

LIYSA MADE HER OWN RULES, and Chris didn't seem troubled by her creativity, although he might have been if he had been the pilot on that plane and had known her at the time.

Gina, Anna Goodrich's sister, came for another visit and met Liysa. When Liysa realized that Gina and Chris were only platonic friends, the women got along well. Months later, when Gina visited again, she learned that Liysa had suffered a miscarriage and had lost Chris's baby. Sometime in 1995, Liysa *had* become pregnant, and she hadn't been intimate with Nick Mattson for a year. There was no question that Chris was the father.

Chris had confided in Joe Wilson that Liysa was expecting a girl whom she had already named Mikala. He wasn't happy about the unplanned pregnancy that had come as a complete surprise to him, but he had accepted it as a fact. Liysa had often told Chris that she'd had complications with Papako's birth and was unlikely to conceive again. He had believed her and failed to use birth control.

However, she never had the baby she carried in late 1995. According to what Chris told Joe, there were "problems" as she approached the last months of her pregnancy. She flew to Seattle to have a "procedure" and returned without a baby.

It couldn't have been an early-term abortion because Liysa had put on a great deal of bulk around the middle of her normally slim figure. It was possible that she had borne the child and put it up for adoption, but that wasn't like Liysa, who treasured the child she did have—and it would have been almost a certainty that Chris would have married her. No one but Chris and Liysa would ever know for sure, although Chris confided in Maggie Wilson that he thought the baby might have died in Liysa's womb in Hawaii—that she had been to a doctor who confirmed that.

At any rate, Liysa flew to Seattle and was there for several weeks. Chris arrived later and found her hysterical in a recovery room.

Joe Wilson was playing tennis with Chris when Chris told him of "the problems" with Liysa's pregnancy, and that it was over.

"Well, Chris," Joe said awkwardly, "you lucked out and you're off the hook now."

Chris looked away, his thoughts unreadable. He had been raised to believe in family and to take responsibility for his own actions. He was a man who had never wanted to hurt anyone.

Joe was surprised when Chris didn't move out of his relationship with Liysa; instead, after a short separation, they got a marriage license.

But they didn't use it. Still, Chris remembered the promise that Liysa had wrung from him in the Seattle hospital—that he would give her another baby. He admitted to Maggie that he had no intention of doing that, that he'd promised Liysa just to calm her down. He didn't think she *really* wanted another baby and believed she was just hysterical with grief.

As for Liysa's earlier "cancer," Chris didn't mention it. Not then or ever. Apparently, she had never told him about it, if, indeed, she ever had surgery for a malignancy.

Chris took Liysa to Bend with him to meet his friends Arne and Carrie Arnesen. They liked her. As Arne recalled, "She seemed like a neat person. She was very intent on buying a farm or a ranch and we took her around. She was interesting—a jetsetter who was here one day and in Tahiti or someplace else the next. She was tan and she had a cute little body when she wore her bikini into our hot tub. She had a big smile and kind of stringy blond hair that looked fine with her tan."

Carrie, however, was a little taken aback because Liysa spent "about eighty percent" of her time talking about Chris—or rather, about the wonderful sex life she had with him. Liysa talked more about sex than any woman Carrie ever knew, and she was very specific when she shared extremely intimate details. She complained that she got upset with Chris if he was too tired to have sex with her.

"She said she had to have sex *every day*," Carrie recalled.

Chris's friends were somewhat surprised that his affair with Liysa continued. He was a bachelor at heart, a man who enjoyed time by himself and hated being nagged.

Dave Story was at the tennis club one day when Pete Kneer, who was also a friend of Tim Sands's, took him aside and urged him to warn Chris about Liysa. "She's bad news," he said. "Somebody's got to tell Chris." Kneer told Dave about the amnesia incident with Tim. "She's kind of weird, too—she went to a kahuna once, trying to get a hex put on somebody she was mad at."

Dave knew by this time that Liysa had a different kind of energy than most women, and he was disturbed by the amnesia incident, but he also knew it wouldn't do any good to warn Chris. Chris did what he wanted, and he seemed to want Liysa—a lot.

Liysa and Chris seemed to be getting along well, except that she was trying to put a tight leash on him. And he was a man used to planning his own days. When he came in from a long flight with his muscles cramped from fitting his tall frame into the confines of the cockpit, he wanted nothing more than to surf in Hawaii for an hour or so, or—in Bend—to go for a bike ride. He would call Dave Story or Arne Arnesen from the air as he headed for Kailua or Bend and say, "Hey, man—what's happening?"

"I never said no to him about bike rides," Arne recalled. "We'd start up in a meadow near Mount Bachelor and ride for two or three hours, and half the time we got lost because Chris loved to take chances."

Liysa resented Chris's need for exercise after flights; she expected him to come straight to see her when he landed. And she was determined to have a baby with him. He liked children well enough, but he had never had an overwhelming wish to have his own. He thought he would . . . someday. At forty, he was a nomad who had seen much of the world, and planned to see the rest of it before he died. But he was also a man who shouldered responsibility, both for his passengers and in his personal life.

In truth, they were like two trains going in opposite directions on the same track, headed for disaster. Liysa believed what she wanted to believe, shaping events and remarks to fit her own scenarios. Chris read her letters and was entranced, almost convinced that this might be the woman who would be willing to accept his lifestyle—that they could love each other but not be joined at the hip.

Chris's capitulation to settling down took several weeks, the marriage license notwithstanding. He really didn't want to marry Liysa, but he didn't want to leave her either. And she was expert at pushing his guilt buttons. She upped the pressure with very long, ultimately persuasive letters, often jotting down afterthoughts in the margins. It was obvious that she had reread the missives and edited them in spots where she realized her words sounded too blunt, but there were still jarring sections.

"First of all," Liysa once wrote to Chris, "I want you to *want* to marry me—at least as much as you did a few weeks ago." She acknowledged that marriage would never be as important to Chris as it was to her, but she begged him to look at her with love and to propose to her. She reminded him that he'd once told her he would never agree to marrying her without some pushing.

Liysa said she couldn't understand what had happened to change his mind. She mentioned other women who had been part of Chris's life earlier whom she now believed he'd used to "have fun" with for little while. When things got too serious, she felt he'd simply walked away.

Now, she asked Chris again for a commitment. "I want to know that you see potential. *Real* potential." (Later, she scribbled in *"I see us growing very old together,"* at the end of the paragraph.)

Liysa drove a hard bargain. Her letter continued, giving Chris many choices, but they all involved their living together and heading toward permanency. She was sure they were meant to be together, and she was worried now that somehow she had "blown it." If he saw a chance for them, she was willing to go back to their original two month trial plan to see if they could live together without arguing. She was sure she could prove herself to him. And, if she couldn't, she told Chris she was willing to end their affair.

"Also," she continued, "if at any time it strikes you during that two month period that, 'Hey! It could work,' feel free to ask. (Let's work out a prenup in the meantime.)"

Liysa felt their common goal should be marriage, and they should work toward that. She would, however, settle for Chris's loving her *and* giving her the free flight passes and other benefits from Hawaiian Airlines.

But, mostly, Liysa promised Chris an idyllic life if only he would marry her. She would prove that to him during their serious trial period of living together. And then they would have a wedding and a wonderful party to celebrate. Oddly, Liysa seemed oblivious to the odd juxtaposition of her flat demands as she kept reminding him of her monetary and special privilege requests in the very midst of her persuasive pleas for eternal love. "If you treat me well," she wrote, "I will be happy. I'm going to want you to get me as good of [sic] ticket prices as you can."

If Chris no longer loved her, Liysa said she needed to know that, so she could give up hope, he could move out, and she could set about "mending my shredded heart."

As she finished her long letter, Liysa warned Chris never, ever, to lie to her. She could not abide that. "I love you," she wrote. "I feel certain that *I'm* the one (for you), but I need to have your love, respect, consideration, honesty and fidelity."

For some reason, Chris put that letter into his safe-deposit box where it would stay for five years. Strangely, it was the *only* thing in the box, except for an honorary certificate presented to him by Hawaiian Airlines.

Liysa had written very similar letters to Kevin, the boyfriend of her youth and the man she attempted to seduce a decade later, but Chris didn't know that. When she wrote to him, Chris gave credence to her promised picture of their marriage: "I want to have a cottage on the Oregon coast," she wrote, "or up by a river with a fireplace and a piano where you can play and I can write or you can read and we can go for long walks in storms and just love each other. I have *seen* this vision.

"Or, if I consider the ranch, it is *only* with you as my partner. . . . And we are so comfortable and compatible—despite your 'Bull Elk' behavior. I know that we can engineer a life together.

"You give me hope by saying you view your parents' relationship as an ultimate role. I know in my heart that your life will be wonderful if you let me in. I know that there is a bond that is almost a mandate between us. I feel your resistance is almost humorous, considering the inevitability, the alchemy, the certainty I feel."

Her letter was romantic, but Liysa had more prosaic ways to turn the screws on Chris. He was now living in the eagle's nest in her backyard and she told him that he would have to move out if he didn't agree to marry her.

When Chris told Dave Story about her ultimatum, Dave looked at him in amazement. "That would be too bad," he said, "but you don't get married over a *rental!*"

It was, of course, far more than that to Chris. Liysa's persuasive rhetoric had begun to convince him that they *could* have a good marriage. He missed her when he was away on long flights, and he was glad to come home to her. She assured him that his life wouldn't really change that much if they got married. He confided to Arne Arnesen that Liysa seemed to be fine with his job; he could fly as much as he wanted, and she would take care of their home, keep it clean, and, of course, look after any children they might have.

So Chris and Liysa stayed together with the understanding that at some point they would get married. They worked out a simple prenuptial agreement. Basically, it was "what's yours is yours, and what's mine is mine." Each of them would retain the financial interests that they had going into the marriage. There would be no division of property if they divorced—except for any property that might be jointly titled. Neither would seek alimony.

However, if they should ever divorce, Liysa wanted full custody of any future children and Papako, and Chris would pay reasonable child support. Each of them agreed to buy a million-dollar life insurance policy with the yet unborn child or children as beneficiaries. It seemed a very benign prenup. But Chris would come to bitterly regret that he had ever even considered signing such an agreement. He had no inkling how much fathers can love their children.

CHAPTER THIRTEEN

IT WAS ALMOST SPRING in 1996 when Liysa and Nick were divorced and Chris still had the marriage license. He and Liysa were virtually living together in her house on Lanipo and getting along, even though Chris wasn't really comfortable with its total absence of order. He hoped that Liysa would begin to care more about the house.

"You keep your house so neat!" Chris once remarked to Dave. "Our house was only moderately neat," Dave recalled, "but Liysa's house was a 'minefield' of clutter, where you had to figure out a path just to get inside. There was *stuff* everywhere, and I know it bothered Chris."

Furniture didn't mean that much to either Liysa or Chris, although he would have been happier with some semblance of order. But he accepted the situation and could always retreat to his eagle's nest in the backyard, which he kept clean.

The main house had a tiny apartment in the lowest level, so small that everyone referred to it as "the camper" because it wasn't much bigger than a "cab-over" camper on a pickup truck. Randy Ore, Chris and Joe's old roommate, rented it. One day soon, he would own a million-dollar, three-acre estate on Maui, but Randy was going through a lean time. Northwest played hardball in salary negotiations with its pilots, and the former Hawaiian Airlines pilots who had hired on last were sacrificed. Randy ended up living with Chris and Liysa from September 1995 to August 1996. Chris, as always, invited friends to stay with him in Hawaii or Oregon when they needed a place.

Randy and Liysa became friends and commiserated with each other. She wanted to marry Chris, and Randy wanted to get back to flying. Eventually, he was rehired by Northwest and based in Honolulu.

Despite the bewilderment of many of his friends, there was no question now that Chris and Liysa were a couple. They socialized with Chris's circle of friends on both sides of the Pacific, who found, as Randy Ore, the Storys, and the Arnesens had, that Liysa could be a lot of fun. She and Chris certainly had a number of shared interests, hopefully more than enough to neutralize the areas where they were so different.

Liysa was extremely jealous of the women who had been in Chris's life, and she watched him warily whenever he was around any attractive woman. But Arne Arnesen began to see that it was something more than that. "She wanted to keep Chris away from *everyone* else. She didn't even like it when he spent time with us or his other friends."

For a time, Chris didn't find that worrisome. He wasn't interested in any other women, and he thought Liysa would stop being so territorial when she began to feel more secure.

Liysa flew to Oregon, where she visited Chris's parents, Dick and Jeanne Northon, bringing them a special bottle of wine. They invited her to stay for dinner. She said she had reservations to go to the Inn of the Seventh Mountain, but they all got along so well that she canceled her room and stayed with them.

"Chris was flying," Jeanne recalled, "and Liysa was so friendly. We all sat up late talking, and we liked her even more than the first time we met. I felt the chance was good that I was going to have a wonderful daughter-in-law."

* * *

ON MARCH 14, 1996, Dave Story played a pivotal role in Chris's life, a role that he would regret until the end of his days. "It was a Thursday," he said later, "and Chris called and tried to be casual. I remember that he wasn't feeling very well and he had a cold. Then he mentioned he and Liysa were thinking about getting married. I said, 'How about this weekend?' "

His wife, Debbie, was listening on the extension and she understood. She said, "Tonight—he means *tonight!*"

"I had to go to soccer practice for my daughter that night," Dave said, "and Chris said that was fine—they'd get married on the beach after practice."

Randy Ore remembered that day because what happened was so unexpected. "Chris called me and said, 'Come over later—I'm going to marry Liysa.' "

Randy thought Chris was kidding and said, "Can't you do it tomorrow?"

But Chris was serious. "Don't tell Joe or Drew," he said.

Randy wasn't sure why Chris wanted to keep his surprise

wedding secret from such close friends. A long time later, he realized that Chris was afraid they might try to talk him out of marrying Liysa.

And indeed they would have. Although Joe and Maggie Wilson had moved back to Hawaii and now lived only a mile away on North Kalaheo Road, they didn't learn about Chris and Liysa's impulsive gesture until it was over. One of their first Hawaiian roommates—Drew Fischer—was also in Kailua that night, vacationing. Randy kept his promise to Chris that he wouldn't let either of them know about the ceremony.

There wasn't time to do that, anyway. Once Chris finally proposed to Liysa, she said breathlessly they should get married right away before either of them changed their minds.

"Chris grabbed Randy Ore from the camper and called Dave Story, and they walked down the hill to the beach with Liysa and Chris and did it," Joe Wilson recalled. "I really wasn't miffed at being left out; I just thought that Chris was out of his mind—that he wasn't proud of what he was doing. . . ."

Dave Story, who would perform the ceremony, barely had time to put on a white shirt. Liysa wore a purple sleeveless blouse, a wrap skirt, and a lei made of white flowers. Chris was in a short-sleeved shirt and chino pants with a blue lei. Randy Ore and four-year-old Papako were the only witnesses as Chris and Liysa got married. The newlyweds and Papako all looked happy and triumphant in the snapshots that were their only wedding pictures. Liysa had been single for exactly twenty-six days.

CHAPTER FOURTEEN

BACK IN BEND, Jeanne and Dick Northon had been elated to hear of Chris's marriage. "We liked her so much when we met her," Jeanne said, "and she couldn't do enough for us. We were happy to have her in our family."

The elder Northons gave a party in Bend for Chris and Liysa to welcome her into the family and the community. Most of the time, Liysa and Chris lived in Hawaii, although Chris still had his house in Bend.

Chris met Wayland DeWitt and told Joe Wilson that he really liked his new father-in-law. Wayland had worked in Alabama for a while after his divorce from Liysa's mother, but his career as a college president seemed to be over. He was living in a beach cabin on the Oregon coast. Liysa's mother had remarried and was Sharon Fisher now, and she was living in Texas.

Liysa and Chris settled into her house on Lanipo Street, and they seemed to be happy. Their initial problems were predictable. Chris had never been a father, and Papako was a child who had always received a lot of attention from his mother.

Randy Ore remembered that Chris didn't quite know how to approach his new stepson. Sometimes he gave Papako an order to do something and expected instant obedience. Papako dawdled or ran to Liysa, and Chris would sometimes become impatient with him. He wasn't mean, Randy hastened to point out, "but he wasn't used to talking to kids—and he had to learn that they weren't just smaller adults."

Liysa was very proud of her skill as a surf photographer and looked to Chris for praise—but he wasn't particularly interested in endless discussions of her career. Maybe that was because the surf pictures were part of her marriage to Nick, and they were still in business together. Chris preferred to concentrate on the new life he and Liysa were building. He was, as he always had been, a man not given to lavish praise and empty compliments. He loved her and he had married her, and, for Chris, that was proof enough of his allegiance. But Liysa needed a *lot* of attention and affirmation and that may have been a problem.

Despite her promises to Chris that she wanted only to be a

wife who ran his life smoothly—as his mother had done for his father—Liysa still had so many career goals of her own. Even so, their sex life was perfect. According to Liysa, it was the most important part of their marriage. Their intimate life was as passionate as it had been during their courtship. Liysa rhapsodized about Chris's sexual equipment and technique to her closest girlfriends, to *his* friends, and even to his mother. Apparently, Chris was the first man since Ray who had brought her to orgasm so easily and frequently, and their reunions after his flights were great.

Even before Chris and Liysa were married, however, Arne and Carrie Arnesen had worried because Liysa's premarital adulation of Chris as a sex partner had gradually metamorphosed into a litany of his faults. She still talked—somewhat crudely—about how she relished Chris's lovemaking and how essential that was, but such praise was nearly buried under her grievances against him. Carrie finally came to a point where she had asked, "Then why do you want to *marry* him if there are so many things about him you hate?"

"Because of all the free flights I'll get," Liysa had said with a smile. At the time, Carrie thought she was kidding.

Among the people who were pessimistic about Liysa's third marriage was her second husband, Nick. He felt that Liysa had married Chris on the rebound and their union was doomed to failure. Although he and Chris were about the same age, he wondered about the depth of Chris's commitment to Liysa. "He'd really had no long-term relationships," he commented.

Nick saw Chris a couple times a month when he was picking up Papako for their time together or when he dropped him off. "Chris treated me fine," he allowed, "but I never felt any genuine feeling at the gut level."

Nick viewed Chris as merely being civil to him and that his broad smile was only a surface thing. That wasn't unusual, certainly; both men had been married to Liysa within the space of a month. Nick had cared about her, and he still did. Even though he was moving on with his life, it was to be expected that he wouldn't become tight with Chris.

Liysa and Chris had married in haste when she begged him to seize the moment. Their ceremony on a moonlit beach couldn't have been more romantic—or more hurried. It was the day-to-day living that was proving difficult. Chris was still the silent Swede who hated discussions that burgeoned swiftly into arguments. He had been with many women in his life and he had never liked to argue. Indeed, he preferred to walk away rather than stay and fight. Every woman he'd ever been close to could affirm that.

Liysa and Chris approached life from different angles. She was a dreamer; he was a realist. The things that had worked in their courtship still worked. They both liked watching old movies and swimming out to the Mokolua Islands. Both of them loved to surf and they shared a deep affection for Papako. In the beginning, Liysa seemed to enjoy going to parties with Chris's friends. He was very close to Debbie and Dave Story, and at first, Liysa joined him in visiting the Storys and in having them over. They had dinner with other pilots and their wives, and when they were in Bend, they saw John and Eva Gill and Arne and Carrie Arnesen.

But all too soon their expectations about marriage only highlighted some of their profound differences. Liysa had never had the slightest interest in housework, and legalizing their relationship didn't change that. This would become a huge bone of contention with Chris. He tried to accept unmade beds, dishes in the sink, unidentifiable food hardened on plates left sitting on the tables, counters, and floors, and rooms strewn with paper and clothing. Their home usually looked as if it had just been vandalized. For Chris, it was akin to living in a pigsty and he was embarrassed to have anyone see how bad it was.

At first, he tried to clean when he was home from a flight.

Then, he hired a cleaning lady to come in one day a week to do a thorough job, hoping that Liysa might keep things in order the rest of the time. But she didn't. It just didn't matter to her. No one could say she was not a doting and attentive mother, but she had too many interests and projects to waste time doing repetitive chores.

Moreover, she wanted to have another child and reminded Chris of his promise to try. Joe and Maggie Wilson had welcomed their first child, Graydon, in Honolulu in August 1996, and Chris could see how thrilled Joe was. Although neither of them knew it at the time, Liysa had already conceived another child with Chris. When she found that she *was* pregnant, she was pleased—and so was he.

Liysa began to renew old acquaintances and to make new friends of her own. Kit* and Cal Minton*—who was also a pilot—lived in the Bluestone area of Honolulu, where Joe and Maggie Wilson also lived, and Liysa became good friends with Kit. She also got back in touch with Ellen Duveaux, her friend from her teenage days working summer jobs on Walla Walla farms, and the ten-year high school reunion had reminded Liysa how much Marni Kelly meant to her. Marni was an attorney now and married to Ben Clark,* an M.D. with a practice in Walla Walla.

When Liysa found out she was pregnant, she bonded once again with women in her childbirth education classes. She was usually the center of attention among a dozen or more young women who met at a swimming pool near the Lanipo house to do gentle water exercises. Her new friends, like those who had known her when she was pregnant with Papako, adored her. It would be no exaggeration to say she was the most popular woman at the pool.

Most women would have envied Liysa's life. She was married to a handsome pilot, the man she had pursued so avidly. She was pregnant, something else she'd longed for. She already had

Papako, her beloved first child. If she *had* had cancer, she was healthy now and her pregnancy wasn't threatened. She and Chris lived in the paradise that was Kailua, in a house that was growing steadily in value. She had time to swim, stroll on one of the loveliest beaches in the world, or simply sit and watch Papako play and think about the coming baby. She had more close friends than she could count on two hands, and she had all the time in the world to pursue her ambition to be a successful author. Occasionally she could even take photography assignments.

Liysa's journals were filled with lovely scenes and descriptions of what an exquisite child Papako was, the glowing brilliance of a Hawaiian sunset, or some other wonder of nature. She rarely wrote about Chris. Now that they were married, he vanished from her writings—except for an occasional mention of his impatience with her. She spoke of how contented she was when Chris was gone on a flight and she and Papako could be alone with each other.

As she grew heavy with pregnancy, Liysa had even less inclination to clean house, but Chris understood that. He was looking forward to becoming a father.

BJORN* NORTHON was born on May 20, 1997, delivered by cesarean section. He was a miniature of his dad, a little blond Swede. Chris was shaken by how much he loved this little boy from the very beginning of his life. He, who had never really sought fatherhood, found more joy in Bjorn than he had ever imagined.

Excitedly, Chris called all of his friends, leaving messages on the answering machines of fellow pilots who were on flights. His old friend Dan Jones saved the tape with Chris's call—he had never heard him sound so happy.

Chris wanted to name his baby boy Hugo after his grandfather, but Liysa objected. They settled on the name Bjorn because it was Scandinavian, and it was also the name of one of Chris's best friend's sons.

Pictures of Chris, Liysa, Papako, and Bjorn in Liysa's hospital room show a wonderfully elated family. Chris called his parents in Bend, and Jeanne Northon caught the first plane to Hawaii. Sharon Fisher wasn't coming, and Jeanne assumed that Liysa would need some help—especially after a surgical birth.

She was stunned to find that she was not welcome, at least not by her new daughter-in-law. Liysa had been so nice to her and Dick when they'd met in Hawaii and again in Bend—before Liysa and Chris were married. She had seemed pleased at the reception the Northons threw for them in Bend. But this was a different Liysa.

"I realized my coming there was a mistake," Jeanne said a long time later. "Liysa didn't want me there. I stayed a week, but I only fixed meals and helped with laundry. Then I went down to the beach so I wouldn't be in the way. Chris was mortified when Liysa didn't care to have me around, but it was too obvious for either of us to pretend."

This was the first cloud in the relationship between Liysa and Chris's parents. It could well have been the usual postpartum blues that many new mothers get. Jeanne didn't take offense, although she was hurt. She could understand that Liysa needed her own "space," especially as she was adjusting to a new baby. Jeanne was sure she and her daughter-in-law would be fine together when Chris and Liysa began spending more time in Chris's house in Bend.

CHAPTER FIFTEEN

BEFORE BJORN WAS BORN, Chris and Liysa had swum side by side to the Mokolua Islands. It was one of their favorite things to share. Now they took turns while one stayed onshore to watch the baby. That was fine with Chris; he loved his son tremendously. He loved Papako, too, but Bjorn was flesh of his flesh. Even so, as time passed, their marriage wasn't working the way he had hoped, or apparently the way Liysa had planned.

Chris *had* let Liysa into his life, but there was no sign of the wonderful things she'd predicted would happen. She grew more angry at him because he wasn't responding the way she wanted. He was aloof and sometimes shut off from her as he mulled over a problem. He was a man who had always craved a certain amount of solitude, and he still did. He'd told her he was a "big dumb Swede," and she knew before she married Chris that he needed time alone and would leave a room or the house if she pushed him too hard. Now she really resented that. She accused him of reacting "like a nihilistic Jew from Cornell." That was how she had referred to her first husband when that marriage began to turn sour. When she learned that Chris's first love, Anna, was Jewish, Liysa accused him, albeit somewhat obliquely, of being an "honorary Jew," saying that made her feel "shaken and enraged."

Randy Ore, living on the lower floor of Liysa's house in the camper, occasionally heard them argue. Usually, it was Liysa's voice he heard. "She would yell at him that he wasn't helping her enough with the kids, and that it made her angry the way he'd walk away—like a bachelor—to go skiing or surfing."

Liysa's temper *was* mercurial, although not with her sons— only with Chris. She viewed his career as unimportant and stultifying, She expected him to baby-sit when she had a photographic assignment and complained to her friends that she couldn't count on him to be there.

Chris loved both boys. On one occasion in Oregon, he saved Papako from drowning near Tumalo Falls when he slipped off a log and was trapped underwater. And he adored Bjorn. But he wasn't a very efficient baby-sitter. "Oh, he could change a diaper and give a bottle," Joe Wilson said with a smile. "But the thing about Chris was that if they were off on a hike or on the beach, you couldn't count on him to remember to *bring* extra diapers or bottles."

And when the family hiked together, Liysa complained that Chris strode ahead and left her and the boys in his wake. Pictures of a smiling Chris with Bjorn happily tucked into his backpack warred with that accusation.

NICK MATTSON became one of Liysa's sounding boards—but reluctantly. They had to be part of each other's lives to a certain extent because they shared a child they both loved. Liysa confided to Nick that Chris had struck her in the winter of 1996 when she was in the early stages of her pregnancy with Bjorn.

"I don't want to hear the details of your new marriage, Liysa," Nick had said gently. "I think we should keep to the topic of Papako and what is best for him."

She had smiled wistfully and agreed. But Liysa had any number of friends who lent willing ears to her complaints about Chris. She had been obsessed with marrying him and now she continued to bad-mouth him to others when their marriage was less than a year old. Her most attentive listeners were the women friends she met at the pool, other expectant mothers or members of La Leche, a group that supported nursing mothers. She dropped subtle hints that Chris was physically abusing her. They felt sorry for her, although she tried to downplay the extent of her husband's abuse. The more she made up excuses for

Chris, the more they believed that she was suffering in a quietly brave way.

When Nick wouldn't discuss Chris's faults with her, Liysa turned to Randy Ore. "She was always wanting me to say or do things that would make Chris do what she wanted," Randy said. "She wanted to use me to manipulate Chris. The only way I can describe it was that she was like a junior high school girl, plotting and playing little games. She didn't act like a grown woman with marriage problems."

When Liysa wasn't griping about Chris, she was pleasant enough company. She was usually placid when Chris's friends were around, but she could be frosty, too, if she didn't feel like having company. "She would just walk in, say 'Hi,' and disappear," Randy said.

Randy Ore believed he would have heard any serious arguments because he lived right downstairs from the Northons, and he certainly would have heard any physical fights. But he never did. He thought Chris and Liysa were getting along quite well.

But one day in February 1997, Liysa came to the pool in Kailua with bruiselike spots on her neck. When the women in her group questioned her, she looked down and told them that they were an adverse reaction to prescription medication. Bruises had never been unusual for Liysa. She lived such an athletic life that she often had abrasions and cuts where a surfboard had clipped her. One woman at the pool recalled the spots looked like "boogie board" bruises, which were common among surfers.

Things were not going well at the Northons' house on Lanipo Street. On December 5, 1997, when Bjorn was about six months old, Liysa called the Honolulu Police Department. Officer Oliver Domingo took her report. Liysa told him that she and her husband had had an argument, and he had left before the police responded.

The Honolulu Police Department records indicated that

this was the third time she called the police to the Lanipo Street house. A year earlier, Liysa reported that someone had broken into her car and taken her credit card, $65, and a check that Chris had left her. On another occasion, she said someone had stolen her scuba bathing suit.

This time, Domingo was confused about what she wanted. She seemed upset and was quite vocal about her altercation with her husband. But Domingo couldn't see that she was physically hurt in any way.

The follow-up report read, "Argument between Liysa and Christopher Northon. Per Liysa. No abuse was present during the argument. Liysa did not complain of any pain. Christopher had already left the scene prior to my arrival."

Liysa told the officer that she'd been mistreated by her husband before, but Domingo found no record of that. Her complaint was filed in case she called again, and no disposition was made.

* * *

LIYSA WAS OFTEN JEALOUS of Chris. He had told her about "Maka" Makanani, whom he had loved so many years before he met her. But Liysa was intensely curious about *all* the women he'd known in the past, more curious than Chris was about *her* romantic past.

Liysa and Chris had been married for almost two years when he learned that Maka had succumbed to brain cancer on February 5, 1998. Although he was heartbroken that Maka had died when she was only in her mid-forties, Chris didn't go to her funeral services.

"He was too shy to go," Joe Wilson said. "He didn't want people who knew both him and Maka to stare at him to see how he was taking her death. They were both married by that time, but he had cared for Maka a great deal. People didn't realize how bashful Chris really was. He even snuck away to the bathroom at my wedding reception. He was afraid he'd have to get up and make a toast in front of everyone."

Although Chris didn't go, Liysa attended Maka's funeral in Honolulu. She had never known Maka, but she was very curious about this woman Chris had once loved.

*   *   *

AFTER BJORN'S BIRTH, Chris and Liysa started living half the time in Chris's Bend house. Now that he had a family, Chris made plans for a number of expensive improvements. He wanted decks built all around and decided to tear down walls to make the house roomier. Eventually, it would have a cathedral ceiling, too. He designed a special table for his "family." For Papako—and for Bjorn as he grew older—Chris set up a trampoline in the backyard and tents for backyard camping. There was a hot tub with a piped-in stereo system. To make housekeeping easier, he bought an expensive European-made washer and dryer, and drew up plans to build a storage shed behind the house.

The only things Liysa wanted were blinds for the house so no one could see in. She didn't think there was any reason for them to buy a bedroom set, and they slept on mattresses on the floor, with a little jury-rigged pad for Bjorn.

All too soon, however, the Bend house was in much worse disarray than the Kailua house. Chris had learned to pick his battles, and he accepted that Liysa would never care about housekeeping. He lived with it, embarrassed still when his friends or family came over.

Wherever he lived, Chris had always maintained a kind of "open house" policy for any of his friends who came to town, but Liysa discouraged that. Once, Gina Goodrich and the husband she'd reconciled with traveled to Bend, and Chris invited them to spend the night.

"We actually went there to stay with Chris and Liysa on a weekend," Gina recalled. "It was kind of odd. Liysa wasn't there when we arrived, and I just figured she was out of town. After we went to bed, she came home, but when we got up in the morning, she was already gone. I think that she wanted to avoid us—because we never really saw her, even though I know she spent the night there."

Chris remained close to John Gill, and Liysa and Eva Gill got along, although Eva's gentle mien was so different from Liysa's sometimes frenetic personality. Both were exceptionally devoted mothers and that common ground brought them together.

Liysa quickly made other women friends in Bend, many of whom she met when she sought out people to assist with Papako's homeschooling or for solo piano lessons. Dee Branch* lived across the street from Chris and Liysa, and she invited the couple to dinner when they first moved into Chris's house as a family. It was a good evening.

Later, Liysa asked Dee if she would homeschool Papako, but Dee declined. Soon Liysa enrolled him in a private school in Bend. Dee recalled that Liysa was happy and sunny until Bjorn was about six months old. "She and the boys were outside all the time," Dee said. "And then that slowed. I just thought she was homesick for Hawaii."

Liysa began to homeschool Papako herself, trying to follow the principles of the Waldorf School philosophy. Bjorn was still too young for any formal education, but Liysa doted on both her boys. If there was a skill they could learn, an art they could master, or a spot on the earth that she thought they should see, she made it happen, especially for Papako. He was old enough to work with Ellen Duveaux and learn about the art of glass and to begin piano lessons. He loved nature as much as Liysa did, and he was a brilliant little boy. If ever a child was exposed to all

the wonders the world had to offer, it was Papako. Liysa
planned to give him *everything*.

When Bjorn was still a baby and then a toddler, he was
never happier than bouncing along in his father's backpack.
Bjorn was the image of Chris, with the same blond hair and
apple red cheeks. Although he hated to admit it even to himself,
Chris began to enjoy his life more when Liysa was gone on one
of her frequent journeys. Papako would often stay with his father in Hawaii, while Chris looked after Bjorn. He and Bjorn
visited Jeanne and Dick Northon a lot during those times.
Sometimes Chris had both boys with him.

Jeanne and Dick had looked forward to spending more
time with their grandsons and with Liysa and Chris now that
they were all living for months in the same town. But that
wasn't to be; Liysa had been gracious to them *before* she and
Chris were married. And then, quite suddenly, there had been
her postpartum coldness after the birth of Bjorn. But Jeanne put
that down to jumbled hormones. Far more disturbing to the
Northons, however, was now that Liysa lived in Bend at least
half of the year, she seemed determined to avoid them.

Jeanne was puzzled when the warm relationship she had
with Liysa vanished. "She didn't have time for us any longer. We
never saw her, and we were never invited to their house. Chris
came to see us—but Liysa didn't."

When Dick went over to Chris and Liysa's house to see his
grandsons while Chris was flying, Papako came to the door and
said, "She's not here."

"I knew that Liysa was hiding in the back of the house,"
Dick said later. "I'd seen her looking out the window."

There had been no argument, no disagreement, nothing,
and the Northons were baffled. And then they could only accept
what seemed to be the truth: Liysa didn't care to be around
them. It was a tremendous disappointment—but they knew that

in-law relationships were often difficult. They'd seen friends in the same situation. They hoped that Liysa might like them better if they pulled back and let her initiate contact with them. But she didn't. Chris came over alone, bringing Papako and Bjorn. Nobody talked about why Liysa wasn't with them.

Liysa and her third mother-in-law *were* very different from each other. Liysa was career-oriented and independent. Jeanne was a complete homemaker who loved to cook and sew, things Liysa cared nothing about. Although Jeanne was athletic, too, and enjoyed hiking, boating, and skiing, she appeared delicate and was very pretty in a blond, blue-eyed old-fashioned way. Liysa was tan and her features were almost stark compared to Jeanne's.

Jeanne tried, always, to keep the peace and be optimistic, even if she had to play Pollyanna sometimes. Liysa thrived on argument and confrontation. Her favorite epithet for Chris's mother was "Jeanne's the queen of denial."

They were not a good mix. Every time Jeanne tried harder to bring Liysa into the family, Liysa shut herself off more, digging her heels in. She definitely didn't want the Northons to get the idea they could drop in anytime they felt like it.

"When I talked to Liysa the first time," Sally, Chris's sister, said, "we were in the hot tub and it was like talking to a robot. She was acting; she just wasn't connecting the way a real person would . . . she was only concerned about how she looked in her bathing suit."

Once, to convince Chris to marry her, Liysa had written that she wanted to have a marriage just like his parents'. That was what he, too, had always wanted and that statement impressed him. Now there seemed to be no truth behind it. Jeanne was a wife of the fifties, when most women deferred to their husbands' career needs and most men made the major decisions. Liysa had no intention of deferring to Chris. Ever. At her center, she was a most self-reliant woman whose ambition knew no bounds. And her very autonomy was one of the things that had drawn Chris to her. He didn't want a "little woman" at home any more than she wanted to be one.

It was clear that Liysa most certainly did not want a marriage like her in-laws had. Too late, she realized that she really didn't want to be married to Chris at all. She had allowed herself to elevate him to the rarefied status that Ray and Kevin and Makimo had occupied in her mind—the only three men she felt she had ever really loved.

And then she had added Chris to that list. Physically, they were still perfect together, but it destroyed her confidence when she perceived him as emotionally cold and disinterested. She could not bend him to her will. It was necessary for her to be with a man who found her perfect. Chris expected too much from her and he wouldn't always do what she wanted. Worse, he wasn't interested enough in *her* achievements.

What Liysa wanted and *needed* was absolutely perfect love, a love that asked nothing of her and would accept her, warts and all. Feeling betrayed, she began to see Chris as two—or even three—people. She thought of him as a kind of multiple personality who was sometimes sweet, sometimes cruel and aloof, and sometimes only boring and standoffish.

They had been married such a short time. Bjorn was only a baby, and Chris loved him fiercely. But Liysa now saw her third marriage as a major impediment to her happiness and fulfillment. But she didn't have another man in her life and wasn't yet ready to leave Chris.

CHAPTER SIXTEEN

LIYSA WROTE CONSTANTLY—journals, screenplays, a novel, even children's stories that she made up to tell Papako.

One of her screenplays was a historical story about the wife of a ship captain—almost a romance tale—but more often her journals and her exploration into movie scenarios began to revolve around complicated plots where the main character was always a caring—but desperate—woman who was fighting to escape a husband who was unbelievably cruel to her. Sometimes the woman was dying of a terrible disease. In other screenplays, the lead character believed her husband was going to kill her. One version had a faithless husband who had given the main character AIDS, and she knew she would surely die.

Liysa wrote extremely well. Had she been able to channel her thoughts and finish one solid proposal, she might have been offered a book contract or given the go-ahead on a movie treatment. And yet there was a sense of dread in every one of her plots, a terrible kind of thought process that might have chilled anyone who read what she had written. It was too real, and too focused on a single theme.

No one saw Liysa's journals or screenplays for a long time. She had always been secretive about her journals, and she wasn't ready to show her scripts until she found someone who would be in a position to help her. She needed a mentor or someone with strong contacts in Hollywood.

Although Liysa was determined now to be a writer, she still wanted more real estate, especially huge ranches. She still wanted to oversee the recovery and renewal of all those who would come there. Liysa had her two beautiful and brilliant little boys, and now she would pursue her career as a much sought-after author. That might very well reward her financially enough so she could realize both of her dreams.

All things being equal, it might have come to pass—at least the writing part. Chris was no more enthusiastic than Nick Mattson had been about buying countless properties or about becoming a rancher. Both men had interests other than riding the range and milking cows. Chris's dream was to make captain with Hawaiian Airlines and his chances were looking better and better. That mattered more to him than running a New Age spa—a lot more.

* * *

WHEN BJORN WAS ABOUT a year old, Liysa broke down in hysterical tears while she was taking a shower with her pool group in Kailua. She blurted to her friends that Chris was beating her. She sobbed that she had been hit and kicked, and she said Chris had pulled her hair out by the roots.

And it wasn't the first time.

As she stood naked with water sluicing over her, her friends gathered around. She did have a "good-sized bruise" on her back, and it appeared that a patch of hair was missing from the back of her head.

The women of the pool group were horrified that their sweet and caring friend who was a wonderful mother was suffering so badly. They urged Liysa to leave Chris, but she shook her head. She couldn't do that. Her tears, mixed with the shower water, coursed down her face as she said she was afraid of him. She sobbed that there was no place she could go to hide from him. She'd called a women's shelter and they had told her that she could stay there only forty-eight hours. *Then* where could she go?

"Chris will find me," she whispered. "He'll hunt me down. He's a pilot—he can go anywhere in the world. No hiding place is safe from him."

One of the women called her pastor. Another called a domestic violence hot line. Both resources explained that there was nothing they could do unless Liysa herself asked for help. The DV shelter did say, however, that there was no forty-eight-hour time line. Women could stay as long as they needed to.

Liysa's dilemma with Chris quickly became an urgent topic

of discussion among her friends at the pool, her friends in Bend, Ellen Duveaux (now living on a large wheat farm), and Walla Walla attorney Marni Clark. She didn't get such avid attention from her male acquaintances, however. Nick Mattson didn't want to listen to her endless complaints about Chris, nor did Randy Ore. Chris had always been a good friend to Randy. When he moved out of the Lanipo Street house, it was only across the street; he rented the same apartment that Chris had lived in when he first met Liysa. In either location, Randy recalled that he never heard any sound of domestic violence out of the couple.

One time, when she was in Bend, Liysa surprised Jeanne Northon by coming to visit when Chris was away. Although she occasionally showed up at family sports outings, Liysa never visited Jeanne by herself. On this day, though, she did. She had come to complain about Chris and his rage.

"Liysa told me Chris had tried to strangle her," Jeanne said, still shocked, "and she told me she had marks on her neck. I looked but I couldn't see anything. Her neck looked perfectly fine to me."

The thought of Chris hitting or hurting a woman was preposterous to Jeanne. Chris had never hurt anyone in his life, and certainly not a woman. She looked at Liysa with confusion. "I don't see anything," Jeanne said.

Liysa left, annoyed that her mother-in-law could be so blind.

* * *

IN ADDITION TO HIS REGULAR flight schedule, which kept Chris away from home about fourteen days a month, he was a training pilot, a coach, a member of the investigative "Crash Team" at Hawaiian Airlines, and an alcohol counselor for the airline.

The latter two were volunteer jobs. He was by no means a tee-totaler, but neither he nor any of his friends drank when they were scheduled to fly. He smoked marijuana occasionally and so did Liysa. It was far more common for young and middle-aged people to use pot in Hawaii than it was on the mainland. But of course the pilots didn't smoke within a specified time period before a flight. They faced fines and dismissal if they did, and drug and alcohol testing at Hawaiian Airlines was random and precise.

When he *did* drink enough martinis or wine to alter his mood, everyone acquainted with Chris knew that his reaction was to grow only more mellow. Alcohol didn't make him angry, and marijuana is famous for its calming effect on almost anybody. Even so, Liysa began to tell her friends that Chris was a "high-functioning alcoholic" who would probably be diagnosed with multiple personality disorder if he ever went to a psychologist or psychiatrist. She whispered that she was literally living in fear, afraid of what he might do next.

Chris had no knowledge of what Liysa was telling her friends. He knew the marriage wasn't good, and he agonized about that, but he didn't talk about it to anyone. He was a very private and stoic man.

Virtually the only thing Chris asked of Liysa was her understanding that he still needed to go surfboarding or bike riding for an hour or so to get rid of the "kinks" after sitting in one position in the cockpit for eight or ten hours. She couldn't see the point of that, complaining that he was selfish and inconsiderate. *She* needed a break from child care and expected him to come home as soon as he landed.

In a way, maybe Chris was selfish. A few of his former girl-friends had complained that he was too much a solitary man. That was his major flaw. He had been inflexible on occasion when they pushed him too far, refusing to put aside activities that meant a lot to him. He had lived under his own time plan for so long that it was hard for him to adhere to Liysa's. Although he never said anything negative about her to his friends or his family, he had begun to hate always doing *what* she said *when* she said it should be done.

His friend John Gill wondered how Chris's marriage could possibly last. He viewed Liysa as a "control freak." Chris was usually so easygoing, and now John watched him as he gradually bent to Liysa's expectations. The two men often took their boys on hiking or fishing trips, and if John stopped at Chris and Liysa's house in Bend after an outing, he noticed that when Liysa came home, she never said "hello" anymore.

"She would just ignore me. And if she had an issue with Chris, she'd call him on it as if I didn't exist," John said. "Chris wouldn't say anything. He'd stay positive. Chris was never negative."

John did note that any physical aggression in the Northons' marriage came from Liysa. Chris could be oblivious to what Liysa wanted and that made her furious. She would clench her teeth and punch him in the arm. That was like a butterfly trying to batter a steer.

During one ski trip to Oregon's Vista Butte that the Gills took with Chris and Liysa, John watched Chris put on his skis and climb up a bank. Liysa was having trouble getting up the bank and Chris didn't notice—so John reached down and pulled her up. The fact that Chris hadn't looked back to see how she was doing made her very angry.

"That was Chris being Chris," John said. "Oblivious sometimes—but it wasn't deliberate."

When Liysa lost her temper in front of other people, Chris was embarrassed. John had never seen him get mad in their decades as friends. Now Chris would quietly tell Liysa that they would talk about it later, but he wasn't angry; he was humiliated.

Arne Arnesen hadn't seen Chris angry either. When they were at games or in taverns and people started to fight, Chris always suggested that they leave. "Chris hated to fight," Arne said. "He hated to be around arguments."

MORE AND MORE NOW, Liysa tried to avoid her husband. If he was in Bend, she stayed in her house in Kailua. She used her free airline tickets to escape from him. Sometimes Chris and the boys were on one side of the Pacific and Liysa was on the other, although she usually had Papako and Bjorn with her. She preferred to fly at night. Either she was constantly searching for something she never seemed to find, or she was truly terrified of the man she had longed to marry only a few years before.

When he and Liysa *did* travel together, Chris always let her sit in the first-class section, while he rode in coach with the little boys. Children were not allowed in first class. But now their journeys together had become infrequent, and that became moot.

None of Liysa's friends could predict when she would show up for a visit. When she was feeling happy, she simply appeared, a youthful "Auntie Mame" character who arrived in an ebullient whirl. She was a scintillating—if sometimes exasperating—friend. Other people's plans didn't deter her. But if she was depressed, she filled them in on Chris's latest "cruelty." Viewed through Liysa's eyes, he did, indeed, come across as a monster.

*   *   *

IN 1998, LIYSA'S FIRST HUSBAND, Kurt Moran, was startled to receive a phone call from her. He hadn't seen her in years. Like Tim Sands, Kurt had soon come to realize that Liysa often revised the truth to suit herself. While they were living apart, she told him that she often suffered "blackouts," but he suspected that might have been her way of explaining away the other men she'd been intimate with during their marriage.

Liysa was warm and friendly when she called him. She announced that she was single again and went on to tell him that she owned many rental properties in Hawaii, and she had considerable real estate investments in Oregon.

Kurt wasn't interested in renewing their relationship. He had heard that she'd married a Hawaiian Airlines pilot named Chris. Now he surmised that the marriage must have been very short. He didn't know that Liysa was still very much married to Chris.

CHAPTER SEVENTEEN

CHRIS DIDN'T MENTION IT to his friends, but he had prevailed upon Liysa to go to counseling with him. She agreed, but Chris turned out to be the one who spent the most time with the clinical psychologist. He wanted to save his marriage if he possibly could, and although it went against his own preference for privacy, he was willing to try. He told his friend Arne, "I think this can make me a better father."

As the new year dawned in 1998, he and Liysa had begun counseling in Honolulu with Dr. Linda Carr.

Later, Chris confided a little in Arne about the first few sessions. When Dr. Carr asked Liysa and Chris what they hoped to accomplish in therapy, Liysa sat up straighter and said, "Okay," and began to talk. Chris said she spent the entire fifty-five minutes detailing his inadequacies, his annoying habits, and, in her opinion, his rage.

It was the same in their next session. Although they had been married for a little under two years, Liysa had a long list of traits and behaviors she wanted Chris to change. But when she continued her derogatory monologue in their third session, Dr. Carr interrupted her. "Wait a minute, Liysa," she said softly. "What about *Chris's* issues?"

When Chris finally got a chance to talk about his concerns, Liysa reacted with impatience and annoyance. And that was the end of their joint sessions. She refused to attend any more counseling with Chris.

Ethically, counselors cannot talk about what goes on in the privacy of their offices—unless, of course, their patients give them permission. There would come a time when Chris told Dr. Carr that she could discuss his therapy with others.

"I AM A LICENSED PSYCHOLOGIST practicing in Honolulu, Hawaii," a March 2, 1999, report by Dr. Carr began. "I have seen Mr. Northon for psychotherapy since January 1998. To date, he has had twelve individual sessions with me in the first half of 1998 and the remaining five since December. Additionally, there have been several sessions that included his wife, Liysa.

"Mr. Northon originally sought therapy in an attempt to deal with the conflicts in his marriage. He discussed problems with his wife, including frequent arguing and almost constant criticism of him by her. Mrs. Northon appears to blame her husband for everything, and has even stated that she believes he has caused cancer in her and in a previous girlfriend of his. In his therapy, he has expressed a desire to remain committed to his marriage, partly because of his wish to keep the family together for his young son, in spite of the conflict between husband and wife.

"He has been open about his anger, which, though slow to build, can be quite harsh once sparked. Mr. Northon is aware of

his stature and [of] how intimidating just looming over someone and raising his voice can be and is not averse to using this to
his advantage in an argument. *However, when angry, he is likely
to say hurtful words and not to become physically abusive."*

DR. CARR WORKED WITH CHRIS to try strategies "to monitor
his anger so that escalating arguments wouldn't do permanent
damage to the relationship . . . as might happen when someone
is so angry that they say something they later wish they could
take back."

His therapist suggested that Chris ask Liysa for some time
alone when he could see their bickering was heading in a dangerous direction. Chris told Dr. Carr he was already trying to do
that. That was why he had left the house on Lanipo Street in December before Liysa called the police.

"Overall, Mr. Northon has been a cooperative and honest
client," the evaluation read. "He has kept all the scheduled appointments or canceled in a timely manner with a good reason.
He paints a realistic picture of himself and has never attempted
to make himself look like a victim or a saint. If anything, he is
likely to agree to have *all* responsibility heaped on him, even
though, in fact, all of a couple's problems can rarely be blamed
on only one of the parties. . . ."

Dr. Carr advised Chris to avoid violent arguments by walking away from them and pondering the best way to respond.
Once, after Liysa had reacted by leaping on his back and clinging there, scratching his face, Chris told a friend, "I'm a big guy
and I can shrug her off, and leave the house. . . ."

That made Liysa furious. She was strong for a woman, but
she knew she couldn't hurt him much; he was so much bigger
than she was.

And that only made her madder.

* * *

LIYSA WAS TRAVELING more than ever in 1999. Her friends in Hawaii and in Bend believed that she was a woman on the run because she was afraid. However, she vehemently cried that she could never truly escape Chris, no matter where she went.

On February 2, 1999, both Chris and Liysa happened to be in Bend at the same time. They joined Arne and Carrie Arnesen in the lounge at Broken Top in Bend. Broken Top is a very exclusive country club with a wonderful ambiance, and it should have been a pleasant evening.

It was snowing and the ice was thick on the roads and sidewalks that evening as the two couples drank martinis in the cozy bar. Chris didn't have to fly for several days, so he was comfortable having two or three drinks. So was Liysa. But alcohol didn't make her feel relaxed or sentimental. Instead, it seemed to make her angry, and she began to say things that were clearly designed to cut Chris down, stinging complaints that hit like little arrows.

"These were things that made you turn your head and widen your eyes," Arne recalled. "Carrie and I were thinking, 'How can you do this to someone you're married to—someone you're supposed to love?' But every time Liysa realized she'd made a direct hit, she smiled."

Chris didn't fight back. He sat there uncomfortably as she kept pounding on him verbally.

"It was 'Chris doesn't care about this—and Chris doesn't care about that . . . ' and on and on," Arne said, shaking his head. "Liysa clearly meant to hurt him as much as she could."

The evening ended much earlier than they had planned; no one was having any fun.

Chris told Arne the next day what had happened after the couples said good night. He had confronted Liysa about her behavior toward him as they drove home. "We were really yelling at each other," Chris admitted. He stopped the car beside the road and got out, determined to get away from Liysa's harangue. He'd decided that it would be easier to walk home in the cold. But she wouldn't let him leave. She followed him with the car, yelling out the window, continuing the argument.

Then she stopped the car and walked over to him. Chris described how he had put his arms out in front of him to hold her away, pushing her toward a snowbank. Liysa grabbed his arm, and when Chris tried to shake her off, he accidentally hit her with his elbow and she lost her footing on the icy street. She fell heavily on her knees, cutting them on the gravel left by road crews.

"I wasn't trying to hit her," Chris said gloomily. "I was trying to get away from her."

Finally, they both got back in the car, but they were still arguing. Liysa was very drunk, and Chris had had too much to drink, too. "And then," he told Arne, "she just wound up and gave me a roundhouse punch between my eyes."

With blood streaming out of his nose, Chris pulled the car over again and asked Liysa to drive him to the hospital. Instead, she drove about two miles outside of Bend and eventually agreed to return home. They were both hurt. Chris's nose was swelling up and Liysa soon had purpling bruises on her knees.

Four days later, Liysa went to the Immediate Care Center, a walk-in medical clinic in Bend, where she was seen by Dr. Jamie McAllister. Dr. McAllister, who had never treated Liysa before, studied the small woman in her examining room. She seemed very upset. To the doctor, Liysa appeared terrified, and she listened as her patient told her about her life with a man who beat her when he lost his temper, which happened frequently. Liysa said softly that she was afraid for her life and for her children's lives.

Liysa had a slight infection in her knee wounds, which Dr.

McAllister treated. And then she told Liysa that she had to call the Bend police and report instances of domestic violence. It was the law.

Liysa begged her not to, citing her fear of reprisal from Chris. He would be so angry if the police were brought into it. She pleaded with the doctor not to write anything in her file about her injuries or what had caused them. Finally, Dr. McAllister agreed not to write down their conversation.

But the doctor *did* call the police and reported the incident. By the mid-nineties, the plight of women caught in violent marriages was no longer something to be hidden in the shadows. There was help—shelters, counseling, and even prison for husbands or lovers who seemed to view women as possessions to hurt and humiliate. Liysa was obviously a most intelligent woman and she said she was aware of her options. But she seemed so frightened, too afraid to reach out for help.

Bend Police Department patrol officers Kalin Ayhan and Lisa Susac-Nelson responded to Dr. McAllister's call and talked to Liysa at the clinic.

"Northon was very nervous and frightened," Ayhan's report began. "She stated she did not want to press charges against her husband but wanted to document her injuries. She stated the only reason she went to the doctor was due to the abrasions on her knee getting infected. She showed me a large bruise on her left thigh and healing abrasions on her left knee.

"She stated after they dropped their friends off after dinner, Christopher became angry with her for embarrassing him during dinner. He started the argument, stopped the vehicle on the roadway, and got out. She stated Christopher came around to the passenger side of the vehicle and threw her on the ground, causing the listed injuries."

Liysa admitted that she had hit her husband, giving him a bloody nose, and she said they had both had a lot to drink.

"She advised me that Christopher had an anger and drinking problem, and has assaulted her in the past—four abusive incidents since they have been married."

Liysa seemed so afraid of her husband that she didn't want to file a report.

The Bend officers drove to the Northons' house to talk to Chris, but he wasn't there.

Liysa went over to Arne and Carrie's house, looking worried. "It seemed genuine," Arne said. "She said, 'Oh boy. Chris is going to be mad. This is going to be costly.' She said she hadn't known about the law that said one party in a domestic violence complaint had to be arrested."

When Chris heard that the police were looking for him, he walked into their offices. He was advised of his Miranda rights, gave his statement about the argument and the resulting injuries to both of them, and was transported to the Deschutes County Jail.

His swollen and crooked nose seemed to be a more serious injury than Liysa's bruised knees. Chris was horribly embarrassed, and he bailed out of jail quickly. Arne went to pick him up and get his car out of the impound lot. Chris was in pain from his injured nose. Neither man said much; there really wasn't anything to say.

Chris had had his first and only arrest for domestic violence. His nose healed up, a little crooked, but his belief in the chance that his marriage would somehow make it through the fire was severely damaged. The thought of losing Bjorn made his heart ache, but he knew it might well happen. He had agreed to give Liysa custodial rights long before Bjorn was even conceived. Now he wondered if there was any way around that. He just hadn't known how much a father could love his children.

Chris hired Seana McMann Ash, a Bend attorney, to defend his interests. Ash learned of the marriage counseling that Liysa and Chris had had for a short time. Chris was the one who kept going. Ash's defense strategy proved to be unnecessary; the case never went to court. Liysa recanted her accusations against Chris, and when the trial date arrived, she failed to show up. She'd flown off to Hawaii to keep from testifying. The case was dropped. Later, a "destruction order" was received by the Bend police, asking that the photos taken of Liysa's bruised knees and Chris's battered nose be destroyed.

They were, and Chris began the process of having the incident expunged from police records.

THAT SPRING OF 1999, Chris and his dad went hiking in their beloved mountains in the Three Sisters Wilderness area. Chris, who had always tried to hide his problems from Dick Northon, sat with him as they gazed out at the magnificent view from their perch. Neither said anything, but there was a heaviness of unspoken words between them.

"Dad," Chris finally said, "I don't know if I can stand it anymore. I wanted to make it work with Liysa—for Bjorn—but I don't know if I can. . . ."

Dick nodded, waiting for Chris to say more—but he didn't. They sat together in the sweetness of the mountain air, where every problem in life could usually be left far below in the valleys. It was difficult for Dick to give advice; he hated to see Bjorn lose his father's presence just as Dick had lost his father more than fifty years before. But he also knew that Chris was miserable.

Later, still avoiding the subject that hovered over them, they took photographs of each other. In one, Chris had regained his wide, familiar smile as he knelt on a massive stone outcropping beside a mountain lake.

* * *

WITH CLUMSY BAND-AIDS still holding Chris and Liysa's wretched marriage together, they now spent even less time together than before. If Chris was due back from a trip, Liysa would fly away before he landed. He didn't mind avoiding more arguments, but Chris missed the little boys.

In mid-1999, Liysa returned once more to Walla Walla, this time for her *twentieth* high school reunion. She came alone, although most of her fellow graduates' husbands were with them. It was an important anniversary; the eighteen-year-olds of 1979 were now close to forty. Men were balding and a lot of the one-time high school girls were matronly. But not Liysa. She looked like a million bucks.

"Liysa was very different than she was at our tenth," one woman said. "This time, she wasn't partying, but she had a glazed look about her eyes. Either she didn't remember a lot of us, or she pretended not to recognize us. It was strange."

A twenty-year reunion mini-yearbook featured "then" and "now" photographs of those attending. Most of the graduates of two decades earlier had had happy but prosaic lives. They listed their spouses, children, and jobs in a line or two. Some had suffered tragedies and some had lived exceptional lives. Randall Edwards, who once took Liysa to the senior prom, stood a good chance of being elected state treasurer of Oregon.

Both Liysa's photos showed a pretty young woman, but her high school shot was softer than the 1999 view. The latter was obviously the work of a professional photographer. Her hair was very long and silky straight, and she held Bjorn in her lap with her arm around Papako. Even her address was exotic and foreign-sounding. Who among them had even been to Kailua, Oahu—much less *lived* there?

Liysa's short biography blew her peers' stories off the page.

"During the last ten years," she wrote, "I have fought a battle with cancer; sold a screenplay; had two unique children; been in the world championships at Pipeline [bodyboarding];

traveled the world filming the movie *Endless Summer II;* done stunts for *Baywatch; been* in a couple of commercials; "modeled" for and shot for Patagonia; *filmed* a couple of commercials; cemented wonderful friendships; gotten divorced; built a deck on my house; maintained my photography career despite homeschooling; learned to backcountry ski; designed several houses; started living part time in Bend. Experimented with life so that I'm almost ready to settle down a bit."

Those who had gone to dental assistants' school or whose husbands were chain grocery store managers could hardly compete. Liysa's life sounded like the kind that most graduates long to flaunt when they go back to their old schools—something to serve as payback for the emotional hits that wound all teenagers.

There were, however, several things that Liysa *didn't* include. One was any mention of Chris beyond the obligatory first name following "Spouse:". The fact that he was about to be a captain for a major airline wasn't anything she cared to brag about. She was proud of her sons—not her husband.

In reality, Liysa was far from being "almost ready to settle down a bit." She told her very close women friends that she was living in abject terror, trapped in a marriage with a maniacal, drug-addicted alcoholic, but she still had big dreams. From what she confessed in the poolside ventings, it sounded as if Chris were beating her almost daily—even though she'd told the Bend police that by her reckoning there were just four incidents in her marriage. If there were, indeed, four incidents, that was too many, but her stories varied ever so slightly. She told her sympathetic friends that she had no hope of even attempting to escape from him, and yet she often traveled, leaving Papako and Bjorn with Chris.

With Nick, Liysa had gotten a taste of moviemaking and the glamour of associating with people from Hollywood. And that only made her hungrier to be a really famous and respected screenwriter. Achieving her goals wouldn't mean neglecting Papako and Bjorn; she would still homeschool them and be there for them whenever they needed her. She was a wonderful mother. She still intended to have her ranches where she would minister to the emotionally broken souls who came to her. She would continue to be a surf photographer.

The only person who was an impediment to her life plans was Chris. As she continued to describe him to her friends, the big blond pilot with the hearty laugh wasn't at all what he seemed to be on the surface. According to Liysa, she woke and slept in cold fear for her very survival. Her voice trembled when she talked about her dread of him.

One of Liysa's friends in Hawaii was an elementary-school teacher named Hillary Radovich who had known her for eight or nine years. She had liked Liysa from the beginning because she was "fun, had an interesting and colorful life, and was a very devoted mother." Hillary was shocked to hear that Chris wasn't the person she'd assumed he was. She had found him to be a nice man, although "almost *too* charming," and now that she thought about it, he seemed "controlling" with Liysa.

Liysa sobbed when she told Hillary what Chris was really like. She confided that he had threatened to burn down their house with his family inside. Of course, Hillary realized, that kind of intimidation would frighten Liysa more than anything because her boys meant the whole world to her. What an awful threat for him to make.

Liysa also told her that Chris used illegal drugs, even when he was flying. She said he could get away with it because he had some kind of position with Hawaiian Airlines that involved drug testing and knew how to avoid being detected.

"I never doubted the truth of what Liysa told me," Hillary recalled.

In the summer of 1999, Hillary ran into Liysa walking in

their Kailua neighborhood. She was wearing sunglasses, but she lifted them and showed Hillary the blackened eye beneath. "See what Chris did to me?" she asked.

There were other danger signs: scratch marks on Liysa's neck, and the time that Liysa said her husband had ripped off her bathing suit in a fit of temper. But Liysa had begged Hillary not to say anything to Chris for fear he would kill her. She said she was more afraid than ever since she had been the cause of Chris's arrest in Bend.

All of Liysa's friends lived with the growing apprehension that the man who seemed so nice on the outside was a powder keg who might explode at any moment and murder her. They begged her to leave him, but she just shook her head sadly and hopelessly. "He's made it his mission to hunt me down and murder me if I ever try to leave him," she said.

Members of the pool group thought now that they *had* seen injuries that looked as though she was a victim of violence. One woman remembered that her lips were sometimes swollen and discolored. She wondered if Liysa had been struck in the mouth. "We talked about our families and our personal lives," she said. "We had no secrets from one another."

By 1999, the main topic of discussion among Liysa's friends was how they could get her to admit the truth. They decided that she was just being brave, especially when she wore a rash guard T-shirt to the pool, and a broad-brimmed hat and sunglasses—or when she waited to shower until they were finished. Perhaps they had no secrets from one another, but they were sure that Liysa was keeping things from them.

Even if Liysa wouldn't talk about what her husband was doing to her, her poolside friends were formulating a plan. They carefully researched ways that she could save herself from Chris. They offered her keys to their houses where she could hide, and they warned her never to have arguments in the kitchen—because of the potential weapons there. They told her that she must always have money and a backpack full of essentials in case she and her children had to flee their home.

Liysa finally broke down again and admitted that when Chris was drinking, he got "that look." Her main concern, she said, was saving her little boys from the man she had married. She said she had taught Papako to grab Bjorn when a fight started. He was to take his baby brother into another room and lock the door, and not come out no matter what.

The women nodded as one. They were in total accord that Liysa was a great mother, a sincere, caring woman caught in a trap. They knew her in any situation—past or present—only by what she chose to tell them. And they had all begun to look at Chris with very jaundiced eyes. He might be handsome and have a big smile, but they were sure it was all a facade. They were convinced that he was unbelievably cruel to Liysa and that she was walking a tightrope between his moods. They worried about her. They even called her when she was in Bend, just to be sure she was still alive. When she said that Chris had told a pilot friend—Dan Jones—that he wanted to kill his entire family and eat them, they shrunk back in horror.

My God, what kind of a monster was he?

CHAPTER EIGHTEEN

AFTER WORKING SO HARD to convince Chris to marry her, Liysa was totally disenchanted with her third husband. Quite apart from the chilling stories she told her girlfriends, her life certainly hadn't moved forward as she thought it would. She owned the house in Kailua and the property would probably sell for $750,000, but the house itself wasn't anything special. She couldn't set up her Chrysalis program there. It would go against the zoning codes. Chris wasn't any more eager than Nick to buy her the huge ranch in Oregon. He had fixed up the house in Bend—but that was *his* house, and she felt depressed when she went there. She pulled the blinds shut and stayed inside.

She didn't feel like cleaning house; she didn't like Chris's parents or his sisters or his friends. In her view, Chris was having fun flying so much of the time. Liysa loved being with Papako and Bjorn and finding activities where they—especially Papako—could learn new skills, but she hated being in Bend. There she was often depressed, *really* depressed. She didn't talk to the neighbors and she didn't wash her hair or even comb it. Maybe it was the cold and the snow; Liysa liked to ski but she was basically happier in Hawaii with the sun and the ocean.

The few neighbors she'd been friendly with noticed that she had changed. Days would go by when she never left her house. It was almost as if *she* had two personalities, something she accused Chris of having. When she did come out to buy groceries or take the boys someplace, her eyes were dull and her hair greasy. She kept her eyes downcast so she wouldn't have to talk to anyone.

Don Strain, the man Chris had hired to remodel the house, also did handyman and repair jobs. Chris called him on several occasions to fix holes in the walls. Someone had either punched or kicked the plasterboard or paneling so violently that it was almost as if a wrecking crew had crashed through. When Don looked at Chris questioningly, he grinned and said, "Somebody around here has a temper."

The odd thing was that the holes were small. Don glanced at Chris's very large feet and hands and couldn't figure out why the holes weren't bigger. He tried to fit his own fist into the holes, but they were too small for him, too.

"If I was to guess," he said later, "I'd say that it was his wife who was doing all that damage. It looked like somebody with small feet had been in a helluva temper and just whaled away at the walls. . . ."

Liysa still read real estate ads and kept a file with clippings about ranches and acreage for sale. Chris's reluctance on the subject was just maddening to her. "How are we going to take care of a herd of cattle when we're in Hawaii half the time?" he asked her. "When I'm flying, who's going to ride the range?"

"We will *hire* people," she answered, disgusted at how dumb Chris could be. "*Other people will do that work.*"

"Who's going to write the check for $2,000,000 to buy this ranch?" he asked her.

She thought his tone was sarcastic and demeaning. And she didn't have a good answer. It was the same old thing. Chris had no vision at all. If he wouldn't buy her what she needed, she would find another way to get it.

* * *

THE MAUI WRITERS CONFERENCE is held every year just before Labor Day at the Grand Wailea Resort or the Wailea Marriott Outrigger. It is probably the most desirable conference for would-be bestselling authors and playwrights in America, because it combines plush and exotic surroundings with a chance to learn from the top writers in their genres. Conference-goers not only attend classes, they actually have the opportunity to mingle with authors, editors, producers, screenwriters, and literary agents at glittering cocktail parties and a sumptuous banquet.

In any given year, the roster of instructors at the Maui conference reads like the *New York Times* bestseller list. John Saul, Elizabeth George, Terry Brooks, Sue Grafton, Frank McCourt, Dave Barry, Richard Paul Evans, Mitch Albom, Robin Cook, Ridley Pearson, Carrie Fisher, and Ron Howard have all taught at the Maui Writers Conference. So has this author.

In 1999, Liysa Northon signed up for the conference. She had written novel outlines and screenplays and felt it was time to find an outlet for her writing talent. She was already far more accomplished than most of those going to Maui.

Real writers know that they must write what they live, what they know about. All of Liysa's books and screenplay treatments still had a central figure—a very strong and courageous woman who had a circle of close women friends, male children, and a cruel and dangerous husband. Sometimes Liysa actually used the real names of her sons, her husband, and her friends; sometimes she changed the names. The theme running through various versions seldom changed. The woman was dying and she wanted to leave money behind for her children and her friends. Her goals were altruistic and she was very brave as she faced cancer or some other inevitably terminal disease.

If the *strong woman* had to die, she would have enough insurance so that her friends, who were victims of poverty or domestic violence, would have the means to escape their lives. The *cruel husband* would not win, and the heroine would destroy him completely to save her sons.

An important facet in Liysa's strengths as a writer was her grasp of Hawaii—the customs, the vernacular, the sea that she loved, the flora and fauna there. She was especially adept at visual effects, as if she had only to shut her eyes and see her script on the big screen. She was also terrific with dialogue, which, of course, is the entire substance of a screenplay. Liysa was very good at writing, just as she had been with almost everything she had put her hand to.

There were elements in one of her screenplays that were reminiscent of an old movie, a black-and-white film noir classic starring Barbara Stanwyck and Fred MacMurray: *Double Indemnity.* Stanwyck played a greedy and bored housewife who wanted out of her stifling marriage to an older husband, and also to be paid *twice* the face amount of his life insurance poli-

cies by his dying a violent death. MacMurray played a somewhat artless insurance salesman, too easily seduced into a
deadly plan.

But Barbara Stanwyck's character had no admirable vir-
tues. When she tricked her husband into taking out double indemnity insurance and then arranged his murder, it was only to
enrich herself. When Liysa's heroine met with an insurance
agent, it was to be sure there was money for those she loved
after she died.

And after her despicable husband died.

And so, in August 1999, Liysa caught a flight to Maui.
Chris had arranged to be at home in Kailua to care for Papako
and Bjorn for several days while she attended the writers conference. It seemed odd that she would entrust her beloved boys
to Chris after he had allegedly threatened to kill and eat the
whole family, but she apparently saw no contradiction in that.

There were hundreds of other attendees at the Grand
Wailea and the Wailea Outrigger, but Liysa was a standout. She
was talented, charming, very attractive, and self-possessed.
There were several producers and screenwriters at the workshop she attended, all of them with vast experience and successful careers. Liysa appeared to be far more savvy and familiar
with the writing process than the other workshop attendees. It
wasn't always easy to predict which would-be writers were truly
dedicated enough to carry on despite rejection after rejection
and which would fall by the wayside. But, of them all, Liysa
Northon seemed to be a winner. She sat with rapt attention as
they talked about the art of moviemaking.

CRAIG ELLIOT* was about Liysa's age, but he was already a
Hollywood success. Several of his screenplays had been both
artistic and popular successes, and he had been nominated for
screenwriting awards. As for many others, teaching at the Maui

Writers Conference was a kind of payback for his own great good luck.

Craig was Chris's opposite in most ways. He wasn't nearly as tall as the towering pilot, and he was muscular where Chris was lanky. Craig was a dynamite tennis player where Chris liked his sports free-form. Craig was as dark as Chris was fair. Soft-spoken, Craig had very sensitive eyes and was most responsive to Liysa's remarks in his workshop. He was impressed with her writing, and he found her attractive in a "nontraditional" way. But Craig Elliot wasn't a likely candidate to become Liysa's next husband. He was already married, he had a family, and he lived on the mainland.

Conference students could sign up for a ten-minute one-on-one meeting with instructors and agents. Liysa chose Craig Elliot and pitched her idea for her screenplay about the dying woman who wanted to change the lives of three friends by leaving them the money from her insurance policy.

Elliot was impressed with Liysa's creativity and her writing ability. He was encouraging about her screenplay, so enthusiastic about it that he agreed to help her shape it up and find a production company that would take a look at it. He couldn't do that in the few days they had left at the Maui conference, but he promised he would work with her later, as he had future workshops to teach in the Northwest.

One of the problems with the script was that the insurance policy part had to be believable, and to do that, there had to be an insurance agent character who was well drawn and authentic. That wasn't hard for Liysa. She had one in the family—or almost in the family. Chris's sister Mary had been married to Phil Hetz, a successful agent who knew everything about insurance. Even though he and Mary were divorced, he was still close to the Northons and to Chris. He was a good guy and Liysa knew that he liked her.

She assured Craig that Phil would be glad to help them with

the ins and outs of insurance policies and how they worked. If there were red flags that alerted underwriters who evaluated claims, Phil would know what they were.

Whatever happened on Maui between Liysa and Craig Elliot, it was very subtle and no one connected to the conference noted anything more than Craig's interest in a very exceptional protégé. He went back home, and Liysa went home to Kailua and then to Bend, knowing that they would be in touch.

The Northons' marriage suddenly smoothed out amazingly. Chris was elated that Liysa seemed more serene than she had been for months. She spent more time at her computer than ever, but that was fine with him. When Liysa was happy, everyone in their house was happy.

He thought that maybe their marriage was going to make it after all.

CHAPTER NINETEEN

AS THE DAWNING of the millennium approached, Liysa's life became much more exciting than it had been in a long time. She, too, had reasons to feel optimistic again. After a meeting in October 1999, Craig Elliot told Liysa he believed in her screenplay—so much so that he agreed to write it with her and both of their names would be credited as the screenwriters! It was a virtual "open sesame" to Hollywood. Doors would finally swing wide for her. She wouldn't have to depend on any man for money to finance her dreams. Craig and Liysa agreed that she would finish a rough draft of her screenplay while he was busy on other projects. Then they would hone it to perfection together.

They had a meeting with Phil Hetz in the somewhat unlikely atmosphere of a Japanese restaurant, where Liysa and

Craig asked him about how insurance companies handled their payouts of death benefits. Phil told them that underwriters knew almost every trick in the book, and that their screenplay would have to be written very cleverly to be believable.

The main character's terminal illness would have to be something very difficult to diagnose, he said, because any insurance company would be suspicious of an apparently healthy young woman dying suddenly. Liysa asked about the possibility of the woman's committing suicide and leaving money for her friends, but Phil shook his head, explaining that most companies didn't pay in the case of suicide. If they did, there was always a time stipulation between the issuance of the policy and the death of the insured.

"You can't have the woman buy a policy and then die in a month or two. They'd find evidence of suicide on autopsy," he said. "Suicide isn't easy to hide from a competent pathologist." Someone trying to collect on a double indemnity policy would be under even closer observation.

Liysa and Craig got together several times, and he pointed out to her that there were a number of avenues they could explore in their screenplay. The insurance agent character could be crooked—as in Fred MacMurray's role in *Double Indemnity*. Or he could be written as an heroic guy who *knew* he was writing a bad policy, but who wanted to save the heroine when he learned she was being physically abused. She suggested that John Travolta would be a natural for the tough but tender agent. Of course, if Travolta played the part, he couldn't die in the last scene. John Travolta was too big a star to die in the end.

It was heady stuff for Liysa to think that *her* screenplay might be a vehicle for a major star such as *John Travolta*.

They decided on a title: *Lesser Evil*. Phil Hetz realized that Liysa was almost paranoid about letting anyone read the script. She was afraid someone would steal her ideas. Only grudgingly had she told Phil about her plot outline, and she told him just *one* of her ideas. But the central theme of all her plots bore a definite similarity to Liysa's marriage, or, rather, to the way she portrayed her marriage to outsiders. Craig sensed early on that Liysa was very unhappy, and she hinted frequently about Chris's cruelty.

Craig was more concerned about her safety than he was about somebody stealing their ideas. He knew there wasn't a plotline in the world that was new; it was all a matter of timing.

He believed that he and Liysa had a fairly good chance of selling their screenplay, but he wasn't as wildly enthusiastic as she was. Craig had been around the film industry long enough to know how many near misses there were. A lot of perfectly good screenplays languished in dusty filing cabinets because they didn't happen to be the right script at the right time. Still, he believed in their collaboration enough that he was willing to invest some of his capital, and his name and reputation, if they continued to work so well together, and if the project looked like it was going somewhere.

At the very least, Craig figured that Liysa wouldn't lose. She would have some exposure in marketing her screenplays in the future, and she wouldn't be considered "a flake." He knew that scripts had to come in either through an agent or with an introduction by someone who was well known in Hollywood. Production companies were panicky about being sued by unknowns who claimed that movie ideas had been stolen from them. "Over the transom" submissions didn't have a chance anymore, especially after Art Buchwald's successful suit against the producers of *Coming to America,* starring Eddie Murphy, a film remarkably similar to a treatment Buchwald had written.

Craig would be Liysa's mentor and her verification that she was a professional. And, if everything worked out well, Liysa would sell her first screenplay and be on her way with a reputation of her own to count on. She did, indeed, have ability and panache as a fledgling screenwriter, but only the very naive would believe that an extremely successful Hollywood writer would take time away from his own projects to help her to the degree that Craig was willing to do—without having something to gain. Like so many men before him, Craig Elliot had been seduced by Liysa's charms. Whether it was a *physical* seduction, no one but the two of them knew—but he was enchanted with her.

Liysa enjoyed that. A man with his connections who moved in A-list circles in Hollywood had chosen her and that was great for her ego. She shared her feelings about this new chapter in her life with her friend Marni Clark by email. Marni wasn't naive. She was a working lawyer and she had seen all manner of human failings, but she believed in Liysa, her old friend for so many years. Marni had worried about Liysa when she heard her recount stories of the domestic violence that she lived with. She thought that the incidents of Chris's violence might be true, and she could understand why Liysa was hoping to leave Chris and start a future with Craig.

If that was Liysa's plan, Chris wasn't aware of it. He once met Craig Elliot in Oregon and viewed him simply as someone who was helping Liysa with her writing ambitions. Unlike Liysa, Chris wasn't jealous. Besides, Craig didn't seem her type; he didn't resemble the other men Chris knew she'd been with, as either boyfriends or husbands. Like Chris, all of her men had been very tall and broad-shouldered. Craig was short and slightly balding, an intellectual, where Liysa had always seemed to prefer athletic types.

But Liysa was calm and happy, apparently because she was going to succeed at something that mattered so much to her. Chris was willing to rearrange his flight schedules so he could take care of Bjorn while she met with Craig. Sometimes, Liysa took Papako with her and sometimes she left him with Chris or with Nick. She had breast-fed Papako until he was five and she planned to do the same with Bjorn, so she couldn't be gone for very long.

Liysa was totally optimistic. Chris hadn't seen her in such a good mood for years, and that made him optimistic, too. In November and December 1999, she asked him to get her reservations to fly to Los Angeles. She said that Craig had set up appointments with producers and agents there.

And, indeed, he had. Not only was he fascinated with Liysa, Craig wanted to help her. He had gently questioned Liysa when she dropped the first few startling hints that Chris was abusing her. He had to draw the details out of her, but when he did, he found her story shockingly similar to that of a friend of his who had suffered at the hands of her husband.

Craig had talked to Chris on the phone many times, and he seemed to be a friendly guy. But he noticed that Liysa was a different person when Chris was around. "She seemed terrified of him," Craig said later. "Scared of him." Liysa seemed "normal" when Chris was away, but she grew apprehensive when he was headed back to Bend. Liysa told Craig that she felt she was "walking on eggshells" around Chris, always trying not to make him mad.

Liysa confided in Craig, although she always seemed to be holding back. But she finally told him that Chris had beaten her so badly in Hawaii that she had to be hospitalized. The police had come and, she told him, she had to be taken away by ambulance.

That wasn't remotely true. She had never been in the hospital because Chris had injured her. The only time the Honolulu police came to their home in Kailua was the time they filled out a report that indicated she wasn't injured at all. Liysa told Craig that they had handed that report over to Chris because he had some kind of *in* with them. In truth, it was simply filed away in dusty police records.

"Chris was ordered to take anger management classes after that," she told Craig. That wasn't true either. Liysa didn't say that Chris had voluntarily gone to therapy to try to heal their marriage.

Craig felt sorry for Liysa, and he had strong feelings for her, too. She struck him as a woman who was "being tormented and beaten by her husband . . . [and was] financially trapped."

"I had no reason to disbelieve her." Elliot said.

Clearly, Liysa was exaggerating her situation. But when she spoke to Craig about Chris, he found her evaluation of him to be almost benign, given what she said he had done to her. She was forgiving and understanding when she explained to Craig that "alcoholics have blackouts," and she realized that Chris didn't remember blacking her eye or punching the Sheetrock beside her head and leaving holes in the wall. She told Craig that Chris was so attractive and fun when he was good. "He could convince a nun to turn tricks," she said, laughing.

But when Chris was drunk, Liysa described him as "psycho." She said she was very concerned because Chris was going dove hunting with John Gill and she didn't want a gun in her house. If she found one, she said, she would throw it out, but she had tried to reason with Chris about having a gun—citing a tragedy where one of her friends' children had accidentally shot and killed the mother.

"I omitted the part about being afraid that either he would use it on me in a rage, or that I would be tempted to use it on him," she told Craig later.

Liysa wondered aloud if electroshock therapy might work on Chris, and then she apologized to Craig for venting to him, even though she thought her feelings might help them develop the female character in their screenplay:

". . . How it seems easier [for her] to try to work with him from the inside, where she has a sense of being able to predict some of his movements and be able to persuade him of some things, because as long as she is *there,* she can use the threat of leaving as the only incentive she has to get him to behave most of the time. If she leaves, she has absolutely no bargaining chip, and he has every reason to destroy her."

AWAY FROM CHRIS, savoring her time in Los Angeles, Liysa was riding high. She usually stayed at the Airport Hilton because she could get pilots' room rates. Chris's job held a lot of perks for her.

Craig took her to visit friends of his and they all liked her. Most people who met Liysa were charmed. It had been that way most of her adult life. She and Craig also "took meetings" with some of the top production companies in Hollywood. She sat in beautifully appointed offices and talked to men and women whose names she had seen in the credits of popular movies. Liysa did a great job when she pitched the premise behind *Lesser Evil.* And Craig was there beside her, emphasizing why he thought the movie had great potential.

Liysa enjoyed her time in Hollywood, but she didn't feel any real physical attraction to Craig. Even so, she thought life with him would be a lot more stimulating and productive than it was with Chris. Of course, Craig didn't know that she felt nothing physical for him. She was half playful and half serious when she emailed him, telling him that they were very good together. She urged him to leave his wife and family, teasing him lightly because he was "too chicken" to do it. She had a feeling that they "would be in each other's lives in a positive way."

She began to write long letters to Craig, letters clearly modeled after those she'd sent to Chris and to her old high school boyfriend Kevin. Liysa's letters were quite possibly the most skilled writing she did; she could turn strong men into romantic fools with her dreams and her promises—always seeming to know what it would take to win each of them over to her side.

"When I'm in an altruistic mood," she wrote to Craig, "that is what I want. To be good for you—as long as I can be part of your life in some way. When I'm feeling selfish, I just want to be with you. . . ."

At the same time, she continued to tell Craig about Chris's "alcoholic rages," repeating how afraid she was. On one of her trips to Hollywood, Craig picked Liysa up at her hotel and noticed she was wearing a lot of makeup, something she didn't normally do. He looked closely at her and thought she had "a fat lip." She bowed her head and said softly that Chris had hit her again.

Liysa told Craig that she often passed David Kelley and Michelle Pfeiffer on the beach near her Kailua home. Their Hawaii home was a short distance away from the Lanipo Street house. Now, she said, Chris was so jealous, he actually thought she was having an affair with David Kelley. That was another exaggeration. She had barely said "hi" to Kelley and Pfeiffer. And Chris had never accused her of having an affair with anyone.

There were a number of things that Liysa didn't tell Craig. Although she had often told her friends that her mother had abused her and broken her bones when she was a child, she never mentioned it to Craig. Liysa also told friends in Bend that a producer or an agent—they weren't sure which—had hit on her during an interview, or, in one version, in a motel. She didn't tell Craig about that either.

Craig had been planning to get a vasectomy, but in the month or so that he was totally captivated by Liysa, he put that on hold. Liysa wanted more children, and she beseeched him to leave his wife and family to be with her. In case she did want to have his child, Craig decided not to go ahead with the surgery.

He was bewitched.

Liysa emailed Marni Clark, giving her Craig's phone number, explaining that he was so worried about her that he wanted Marni to be able to contact him "in case Chris kills me or something, he will know. He is really a hoot and I am enjoying the attention, the positive strokes, and the fun of imagining what it would be like to be a partner in one form or another with someone who believes in me, cares about me, and at least *says* he considers me a treasure."

Liysa wrote that she was getting so much love and attention from Craig that she wanted nothing more from Chris, and that Craig was so anxious for her to leave Chris. He, in fact, had moved into his office during the week to begin the transition from his family in preparation for a divorce.

But Liysa told Marni that she still wasn't ready to leave her marriage. She was just "too damn afraid" Chris might strangle her.

"Liysa hit me like a thunderbolt," Craig Elliot recalled of that time in 1999, "but that was in Maui and I came to earth with a thud. Liysa wanted a foxhole to hide in—she didn't really want me."

They had talked about having a sexual relationship, but Craig said he'd held back. He loved his wife and realized that he was on the verge of losing his family. The magic of being with Liysa wore off quickly, although they continued to have a business relationship.

And he still felt pity and concern for her, trapped as she was in a marriage with a man she described as cruel and crazy. She had talent, and she had brought him a good story. A long time later, Craig told Oregon detectives that he'd hoped to aid her in escaping her abusive marriage. He had used his professional contacts to try to help her make some money with her screenplays. Liysa had almost given up, he felt. She was fatalistic, sure that Chris was going to kill her because she had no money to leave. Craig told the detectives that he'd realized she didn't want a relationship with him, but she desperately wanted her movie to work out so she could regain some financial stability.

It was ironic in a way. Liysa had spent more than a year

telling people how dangerous her husband was. And yet, she didn't leave Chris. She confided to some of her very closest friends that sex with him was too good to give up. She also extolled his sex appeal in her writings and, of course, to Chris's friends. Odd, because sometimes she also shuddered when she said that he raped her and humiliated her during sex.

Chris's friends knew he was unhappy and they had seen for themselves how Liysa goaded and belittled him. She told anyone who would listen about her negative opinions of Chris. Dozens of people now believed that he was liable to snap at any time and wipe out Liysa and the boys.

It was as if her life were a screenplay, and she was creating some scenario that established Chris absolutely as a menace.

CHAPTER TWENTY

THE SCREENPLAY that Liysa and Craig collaborated on was a model of professionalism. And it was a compelling story. While it was being read by several big studios, the two of them made some outlines for other possible movies. Liysa saw herself on the same level as Craig, and began to offer him suggestions about what she perceived to be flaws in *his* work and how he could improve it. It didn't strike her that she might be overstepping boundaries. She hadn't sold anything but a thin travel book about a Hawaiian beach; *his* name was well known in Hollywood. He counted top stars among his friends, and Liysa's only acquaintance with fame—before she met Craig—was her work with Nick Mattson on the *Endless Summer* films.

She was sure that was only temporary; once the screenplay sold, her career would take off and she would be well known, too. But just as she was soaring with optimism, Craig had to tell her some crushing news. She sat, stunned, as he assured her that there was nothing wrong with their screenplay. However, he had just learned that Columbia Pictures had bought a script so similar that theirs was dead in the water.

Liysa was inconsolable. She had been so close to fame and to money. Even though Craig told her that they had other screenplays to work on, she had lost her belief in him. The first months of 2000 left her with a bitter taste of ashes in her mouth. He could promise all he wanted, but Craig hadn't been able to pull it off for her. She wasn't impressed when he said they could continue to work together; the next screenplay, or the one after, might be picked up by a production company. Her whole life had been ruled by her need for instant gratification, and she had wanted this movie deal tremendously. Now Liysa didn't think she needed Craig any longer. She knew how to write a screenplay herself, and she felt she'd learned the rules of the game.

Liysa and Marni Clark corresponded often by email, and Liysa wrote that she had grown weary of Craig. "It is getting increasingly irritating to be around him," she said. She had come right out and told him that she wanted nothing but a working relationship with him. But Craig had countered with "What if I said I wasn't going to do this screenplay with you?"

Liysa emailed Marni, "I said, 'I'd just go pitch it by myself.' It was nice to finally be appreciated, but I am now quite over anything. We do work well together though."

Marni wrote back, wondering how Craig could have become so infatuated with Liysa since he must have seen there was no reciprocation. She hoped that he wouldn't continue to fawn over Liysa or it might make it difficult for them to maintain even a friendship.

LIYSA WAS AGAIN on an upward swing, so confident in her own brilliance as a writer that she no longer needed Craig Elliot's help. It didn't matter to her that he had been ready to leave his wife for her; he was expendable.

Fortunately, Craig hadn't thrown away his life to be with her. In fact, he had come to his senses even before their movie project foundered. He loved his wife—not this wild, impetuous woman in Oregon—and he was able to rescue his marriage. "You don't know how glad I am now that there wasn't a sexual interlude," he confessed months later.

Offers from Hollywood didn't materialize as rapidly as Liysa expected, although she was sanguine in her belief that they soon would. She spent the first months of 2000 hunched over her computer, spewing out ideas, notes, partial screenplays, chapters of a novel, an outline for a book on weight control for children. She was soaring again, and part of what she wrote was fiction while other parts came from her own life. That is true for many writers, but most of them can differentiate one from the other.

* * *

PERHAPS AS A LAST-DITCH effort to work on their marriage, Chris invited Liysa to come along with him on a Hawaiian Airlines flight where he had a three-day layover in Tahiti. She and Bjorn joined him on the trip, and they stayed at the Park Royal Beachcomber, a very nice hotel and favorite among Hawaiian Air employees.

They arrived in Tahiti on March 1, 2000, but the trip was anything but a second honeymoon. The other pilot on Chris's flight was Captain Leroy Perry, who was surprised to see that Chris often came down to the swimming pool alone, while Liysa and the little boy went off somewhere else on their own. Perry could tell that Chris was angry with his wife. He complained that Liysa would also take off by herself without warning, leaving him to look after Bjorn. Two flight attendants had remarked to Perry that Chris was "short and mean" to Liysa, and had told her to shut up. "She cowered like a wounded puppy around Chris," Perry said.

On the other hand, John Crabbe, the flight engineer on that trip, had observed that Chris and Liysa seemed to get along fine. "Chris told me his son really liked the water, and that Liysa was gone on a photography shoot." Perry thought the Northons had an argument on the bus back to the airport, while Crabbe shook his head in disbelief. "Maybe I missed something because I was sitting near the front of the bus," he said, "but I didn't see any trouble between them."

They probably had argued. Things were so tenuous between Chris and Liysa that they weren't used to being with each other, and neither of them sought togetherness any longer. Liysa had grudgingly agreed to go to Tahiti, but once there, she didn't want to be around Chris. Tahiti might have been a paradise but Liysa saw it, at least on this trip, as a cage.

If Chris and Liysa were both disappointed in the way their marriage had turned out, Chris was so grateful to be Bjorn's father. He considered Papako a special bonus, and he loved his time with both boys. The love between Chris and Bjorn was mutual. As Bjorn grew, he clearly adored his father. At three, he sprinkled his conversations proudly with "mydad *did* this" or "mydad *flies* airplanes!" When Bjorn looked at Chris, his face was a study in awe.

It was fortunate that Chris and the boys bonded so well. Chris spent much of his free time looking after both his son and his stepson. Liysa was peripatetic, never content to stay in one place for long. As usual, Chris gave her her head. He realized that she needed an inordinate amount of freedom to do whatever she wanted to do. By the early months of 2000, he preferred to be on the opposite side of the ocean from her; she felt the same way.

Liysa had it figured out like a timetable. When Chris was about to land, she was ready to fly in the other direction. And she no longer spent any time with Chris's friends. She cut herself off from Carrie and Arne Arnesen. She *quit* everyone. Chris would make excuses. "She needs her space," he said quietly. "She's writing."

And Chris wasn't all that eager to visit Liysa's friend Ellen Duveaux or her family. He knew Ellen disapproved of him. Many members of Liysa's family also found her husband to be distant and aloof. If he made an appearance at a family picnic or accompanied Liysa to a friend's house, more often than not he soon left or walked off by himself. There seemed to be no point in either of them trying to nourish the marriage. It was almost moribund. And yet each of them wanted to be with the little boys—Papako and Bjorn. If they divorced, Liysa believed she had the legal right to custody of both of them, and Chris could not bear the thought of being separated from Bjorn.

The house in Bend that Chris had so recently remodeled was a "pigsty," the descriptive word that all of Chris's friends, family, and neighbors used: dirty dishes in the sink, food rotting in the refrigerator, floors covered with a layer of junk and clutter. Liysa was gone much of the time now, but Chris left a key with his father. And he'd hired his sister Mary to come and clean the house. That only made Liysa more annoyed. She cared nothing about Chris's house, but she didn't want his family poking their noses in it. Her things were there and she resented the invasion of her privacy.

Liysa spent all her time writing. Except for her little boys, she shut out the world and stayed in the back room of the Bend house typing furiously. And then a writer's worst nightmare came true. John Gill was visiting with Chris on Sunday, June 4, 2000, when Liysa rushed out of the back room, crying. "Someone has stolen my computers," she sobbed. "All my work from the last year is *gone. . . .*"

She said she hadn't made backup disks or printed out any hard copies, which was almost unthinkable for a professional writer. But Liysa had trusted that her writing was safe in her computers' memory. And now it was lost, every page, every sentence of it. Liysa seemed inconsolable.

Chris called the Bend police right away and filed a burglary and theft report. The responding officers noted that two computers, a 35-mm camera, and a watch were missing. It was the 4,179th crime reported to the Bend Police Department that year.

"We were gone for most of the weekend," Chris explained. "Someone must have come in when we weren't here."

While Liysa sat, white-faced with shock, the patrol officers checked the house. They discovered some small pry marks on the exterior door to the garage and figured that was the only possible point of entry into the house.

Neither Chris nor Liysa knew the serial numbers for the missing computers, but Chris called the Gateway help line and got them. The Gateway Solo 2000 desktop model's identifying number was #0004155980, and the Gateway Solo 2000 laptop's serial number was #0015336775. The numbers were important; they could be entered into law enforcement computer systems, and if they turned up, the stolen computers could be identified.

The chance that Liysa's writings could be recovered if her computers were found was anybody's guess. Almost every writer saves each day's work on a backup disk to avoid just such a catastrophe. But because she had apparently failed to do that or to print her work out as a hard copy, she was the only one who knew how much she had lost.

She had had bad luck with thieves before. Once, she reported that a bag of her most expensive cameras had disappeared at the Honolulu airport, and then there had been the thefts from her car and shed in Kailua.

Their homeowners' insurance policy paid off on the loss, and Liysa got another laptop computer—a MacIntosh—to keep up her voluminous email correspondence, but Chris felt sorry for her because she had lost her movie treatments, screenplays, and journals. He had no idea just how much work she might have had in the stolen computers.

Liysa appeared to be devastated and accused Chris of failing to show any compassion for her. Later, she wrote to a male friend, asking him to be sure to remember the computer theft incident, exactly as she related it to him. And then she added in an odd nonsequitur that she had once caught Chris looking at pornography on her computer. When she confronted him, she said he'd been so furious that he'd kicked her in the stomach.

Sharon Leighty, Chris's onetime live-in girlfriend from the mid-eighties, had moved back to Bend in December 1999. She called Chris's home twice to see how he was doing. She knew he was married, and her calls were only friendly. But Liysa hung up on her the first time, and the second time she wouldn't let Sharon talk to Chris. Sharon sensed that Liysa was jealous of her relationship with Chris from fifteen years before, which she found ridiculous. That was all in the past. Chris himself answered her third call and told her he hadn't gotten her messages.

"What's going on, Chris?" Sharon asked him.

He paused and then said, "I'm dealing with it."

He sounded so different, somehow flat. But he didn't explain *what* he was dealing with.

* * *

THE SUMMER OF 2000 was long and troubled for Liysa and Chris—and for their family and friends. Chris no longer spoke to his father about how desperate he was in the marriage. He didn't really speak about it to anyone.

Liysa still talked to many people about her dissatisfaction with Chris. Actually, it was far more than that; she complained to almost anyone who would listen about his brutality and her fear. Chris's friends were sick to death of hearing it.

None of their neighbors heard any sound of fighting from their house in Bend, but, of course, that didn't prove there wasn't something going on behind closed doors. Maybe they didn't fight because they were so seldom together.

In the spring of 2000, Liysa had adopted a white Great Pyrenees puppy after she researched the breed and found it would be a "one-person dog." Chris loved animals and he liked the puppy, but he was annoyed when KoKo chewed up one of his most expensive work shoes. He shouted at the puppy and chased it around the yard waving his arms. Liysa told Papako's piano teacher that Bjorn had heard Chris threaten to kill the dog. And according to her, it was *Chris* who put his fists and feet through the walls of their house.

He wasn't perfect, and it *was* Chris who had the recklessness to have a drink once at his parents' home and then ride his bike home with Bjorn on his back. Anything that put Bjorn or Papako in danger made Liysa livid.

Her confidences varied, depending on whom she talked to. She didn't denigrate Chris to everyone. Dan Jones, another of Chris's closest pilot friends, took his girlfriend Mindi Fox to Hawaii for a vacation, and they stayed in Chris's "Berchtesgaden" retreat behind Liysa's house in Kailua. Chris was either flying or in Bend, but Liysa was there.

Mindi found Liysa great. "She was nice and energetic, and I never would have guessed that anything was wrong. . . . I really liked her."

The two women got along very well, and Liysa didn't badmouth Chris. She made only humorous remarks like, "Husbands will drive you nuts," and laugh.

Mindi had met Chris a couple of times. "He was really cool, warm, and a sweet person," she said. "He had a total love for life. I just loved him. . . ."

Oddly, Liysa had claimed it was Dan Jones who had warned her that Chris wanted to kill his whole family and eat them. Later, neither Dan nor Mindi recalled that threat. "That . . . ," Mindi said slowly, "is *way* out there." Which indeed it was. Dan just shook his head, mystified. Such a threat wasn't something that anyone could forget, but it was also a thought that was totally alien to anything Dan had ever seen in one of his closest friends.

Liysa's brother, Tor DeWitt, had been away from Walla Walla for sixteen years before he returned in 1998 to open a chiropractic office. Actually, the whole DeWitt family had scattered: Tor; then Wayland to Texas and the Oregon coast; Sharon, living with her second husband in Texas; and Liysa on her worldwide travels that ended in Hawaii and Bend.

Although he himself was in the midst of a divorce marked by bitterness and custody issues, Tor DeWitt was enraged when Marni Clark told him that Chris Northon had assaulted his sister. It was June 2000, and the two met at a baseball game in Walla Walla. Marni had assumed that Tor already knew about Liysa's troubles with Chris. But he didn't, and he was so angry that he called the Northons' homes in both Bend and Hawaii, leaving a message for Chris to call him.

In a panic, Liysa called her brother from Bend and begged him not to confront Chris about hitting her. "He'll take it out on me," she sobbed.

But Tor was still mad. He called Hawaiian Airlines headquarters in Honolulu to demand that Chris be grounded, but he gave up, frustrated, when he couldn't get through to anybody in authority.

Tor didn't know Chris. He had met him only twice—for a

total of less than fifteen minutes. They saw each other briefly in midsummer of 2000 at the Chief Joseph Days celebration in Joseph, where Tor was working in the medical tent treating injuries.

Tor didn't know Chris, but he knew he didn't like him. He often said that he had heard a lot about Chris's bad behavior, even though those reports came from "a friend of a friend of a friend," or from his sister Liysa.

Indeed, none of Liysa's extended family knew Chris well, although she told them about how cruel he was to her. He accompanied her on a visit to Joseph once, the only time her aunt Bobbi Chitwood ever met him. Liysa's step-grandfather refused to shake hands with Chris, remarking that he wouldn't acknowledge a man who beat his granddaughter. Liysa reacted with horror, whispering that he "would just make things worse."

Not surprisingly, Chris strode off. "I think maybe he'd been drinking," Bobbi recalled later.

In August, Liysa stopped by Tor's house in Walla Walla to clean it, perhaps an irony in itself. But Tor was divorced by then and raising his children alone, and he said Liysa wanted to help him out. Tor would recall that, on that visit, Liysa had a round bruise on the front of her neck and a few more bruises on the sides of her neck. When he asked her what had caused them, she said, "I don't know."

Remembering that visit later, Tor said he'd told his sister, "If you were a juvenile patient, you would not leave my office. I would be required to call the police. I think you got those bruises from domestic abuse. . . ."

But Liysa wasn't a juvenile; she was thirty-eight and married to her third husband. If Chris had, indeed, caused those bruises, she wasn't going to talk about it—not to her brother. But she discussed it endlessly with any number of acquaintances, always warning them that they must never, ever, repeat what she'd told them to Chris for fear he would become enraged.

THAT SUMMER OF 2000, Liysa had tremendous emotional support from the friends of her girlhood, Marni Clark and Ellen Duveaux, and, most of all, from her father Wayland DeWitt. He apparently believed everything Liysa told him and his heart was heavy with worry. Heretofore, Wayland had met his third son-in-law only sporadically and most of their visits had been pleasant. They had always gotten along.

Wayland had been completely consumed by his career when Liysa was a child. Perhaps he was trying to make up for those lost years. Liysa confided to her father that Chris acted normally when other people were around, but when they were alone, he went into unpredictable rages, triggered by alcohol. She said that marijuana and cocaine made Chris "mellow." Wayland had always liked Chris, and the feeling was mutual—but not now. Wayland told Liysa she could count on him to protect her. If what she was telling him was true, she was in trouble.

As for Chris's friends, Liysa's descriptions of them made them sound like the epitome of depravity and evil. According to her, Dave Story, the minister/pilot who had performed her marriage ceremony on the beach, was really a drug dealer. So, she said, was his wife, Debbie. Liysa whispered that Debbie even used the Storys' *child* to deliver the drugs while she waited in the car.

Wayland, who had a Ph.D. degree in social work, often spoke of the professional counseling he had done in the Washington State Prison at Walla Walla. It's probable that his visits inside prison walls were on a volunteer basis. He considered himself, however, quite expert on aberrations of the human personality.

Now Liysa's father pulled out his copy of the *Diagnostic and Statistical Manual of Mental Disorders* (the psychiatrists' bible) and began to diagnose Chris's personality disorders. He encouraged Liysa to call him every week and describe Chris's current behavior. After each of her calls, Wayland refined his diagnosis.

He concluded that Chris was very, very dangerous. It didn't matter that he himself had never seen Chris "change" after he had a drink or two, or that he had never observed Chris physically abuse Liysa. Wayland had spent a few weeks each April with Liysa and Chris in Hawaii, and Liysa visited him on the Oregon coast three or four times a year, often accompanied by Chris. Wayland had found Chris "sociable," but now he listened to Liysa's weekly reports and began to try to find a way to save his daughter from the "drunken monster" she had married.

AS ALWAYS, Chris didn't talk about his problems, but most of his friends noticed that he seemed quieter than usual and his grin wasn't as wide as it normally was. But aside from the few things he'd mentioned to Arne Arnesen and to Dave Story, no one knew what was bothering him.

"Chris was always looking for *solutions* to problems," Dave remembered. "He didn't give up on his marriage because he always figured there would be a way to fix it."

RANDY ORE ASKED LIYSA to photograph him when he was windsurfing, and on one of her trips to Kailua, she arranged to do that. She had evidently learned to keep a stiff upper lip, and now, with Chris's friends, she pretended that things were all right in her marriage. "She took the pictures of me in August

2000," Randy recalled. "I asked her how things were going with Chris, and she just said, 'Fine,' and changed the subject."

Chris was even more close-mouthed. Sharon Leighty, whose phone calls to Chris had been refused by Liysa, ran into him in the Bend post office in late summer of 2000. It might have been the week that Liysa was in Hawaii. Chris and Sharon hadn't seen each other in more than fifteen years. Chris had Bjorn with him and it was clear to Sharon that the little boy was the joy of his father's life. Bjorn was the spitting image of Chris.

Chris looked strained, and Sharon thought he might open up to her about his life but he didn't. He said nothing even faintly derogatory about Liysa and assured Sharon that things were going well for him. She didn't quite believe him, but she knew that was like Chris; he had always figured out a way to deal with his problems on his own and never blamed anyone else for whatever predicament he was in.

It seemed another lifetime when they were in their twenties and Sharon had gone to Europe and Chris to New Zealand. He had lived to fly and he'd gotten that wish. They were only comfortable old friends now. Even so, Sharon was vaguely troubled as he walked away, carrying the curly-headed blond boy.

CHAPTER TWENTY-ONE

THE SUMMER OF 2000 was drawing to a close. There were no hits on the police network about Liysa's stolen computers. They appeared to be lost forever, along with her screenplays, journals, and correspondence—the most bitter loss a writer can suffer. It was a very despondent time for her. Her work was gone and her excitement about Hollywood had waned. When Liysa wrote now, it was mostly emails: desultory notes to Craig Elliot, intimate discussions with Marni Clark or Kit Minton, friendly dispatches to Ellen Duveaux, and the regular confidences she sent to her father, which only alarmed him further.

The marriage seemed to be irretrievably broken. Chris came home to an empty—and filthy—house, while Liysa, using her Hawaiian Airlines privileges, was winging her way somewhere else, anyplace she could go to be away from him. She wondered to her friends how long it would take him to catch on to why she arranged to be away when he was coming home.

If he faced the truth, Chris was just as glad to have her gone. When they spoke, they argued. Their goals in life seemed always to be at cross-purposes. The quiet moments together when he would play the piano and she would read—the idyllic times she had promised him in her premarriage letters—never happened.

LIYSA WAS OUTRAGED when Chris told her he was thinking of loaning his parents some money to help them buy a house in Joseph. Jeanne and Dick's home in Bend was very nice, but the one they wanted to buy in Joseph was a large rustic house right on the shore of Wallowa Lake. They could swing it financially themselves, but Chris loved his parents and knew how hard they had worked when he was a kid. He had the means to help them make a larger down payment, and his reasoning was that they could buy the property now, when they could enjoy it without worrying about money. Eventually, the house would come to him and Liysa.

Liysa was astounded. Chris wouldn't help *her* buy the ranch she wanted, but he *would* help his parents buy a house! As far as she was concerned, they had a perfectly good house in Bend and, furthermore, she didn't like the idea of Jeanne and Dick moving to Joseph. That was where *her* relatives lived, and she didn't relish the thought of her in-laws moving into her territory. She didn't like Chris's sisters, and she didn't like her in-laws period. She was very angry.

The Joseph lakefront property was a good investment, and Chris argued that his contribution to his parents' new house wasn't even in the same ballpark as the two million dollars that a cattle ranch would cost. The Joseph house would grow in value and, someday, it would belong to them. Chris wasn't anxious for that to happen—but it was the only argument that he thought would work with Liysa. It didn't. She continued to fume about buying the elder Northons a house, and the arguments grew heated. As always, Chris tried to defuse them by walking away.

Frustrated and angry with him, Liysa still wanted her ranches—*two* ranches—one in Hawaii and one in Bend. It didn't make sense to anyone but her, but she was more determined than ever to create two magnificent havens for her Chrysalis program. She pored over the real estate section in the Bend paper and picked up the free magazines real estate companies distributed in grocery stores. She tore out ads for the most interesting spreads and saved them in her cluttered house.

Chris remained pretty tight-lipped about his situation, although he did talk to Arne Arnesen a little in August 2000. In a rare candid moment of discussing his marital problems, he confided that he was thinking about separating from Liysa. He said he had told her if she couldn't control her temper or stop fighting with him, he was going to leave. He admitted to his old friend that he'd threatened it a couple of times before—but this time Arne could see he meant it.

Somewhat obliquely, Chris said, "Liysa's getting psycho— you have no idea how psycho she is. . . ." But, as always, Chris agonized over being cut off from Bjorn. He said he wouldn't stop Liysa from leaving if she wanted to go. That would be the easy choice. But if she left him for good, she would take Bjorn

away from him. He loved Papako, too, and a divorce would
mean that, for all intents and purposes, both little boys would
be out of his life. The man who hadn't been anxious to become
a father wondered now if he could bear losing his son.

Like her other husbands and lovers before him, Chris had
long since begun to doubt many of Liysa's stories. He didn't believe that she had ever been physically abused as a child. Very
few of the things she had promised him if only he would marry
her had come to pass. Even so, he kept up the repairs and addi-
tions to the Bend house, as if part of him still hoped Liysa might
change. He was very proud of the house, but she couldn't have
cared less. As usual, when she left the house, she simply walked
out the door, leaving food on the table to rot, dishes in the sink,
dirty laundry in the washer, and clothes on the floor.

"That was the mess Chris came home to," Arne said. "He'd
start cleaning up the minute he got home."

But then, quite suddenly, things did change. Chris began to
smile again and looked as if a terrible weight had been lifted
from his shoulders. In September, he told Arne that he was getting along a lot better with Liysa. He actually seemed optimistic.
"Liysa's calmed down," he said in the first week of October
2000, "and it's great!"

When Chris got back to Bend after a flight that week, he
discovered that Liysa had left on a trip to the Oregon coast to
see her father. When she returned to Bend a few days later, Chris
told Arne, she had suggested they take the boys and go on a
camping trip together in Wallowa County. To Chris, it seemed a
good omen that the marriage was getting better. Even so, he said
he wasn't too enthusiastic about going since the best of the season was past and it could suddenly turn bitterly cold at that ele-
vation. He also said he wanted to stay around home because
he'd just been flying for fifteen days.

But Liysa insisted. So the camping trip—from Friday, October 6, through Sunday, October 8—had been planned without

any consultation with Chris. Liysa had the spot picked out—Wallowa County. She suggested that they take only Bjorn camping with them, because the weekend would be a great chance for Papako to visit on the Duveauxs' farm. She had already called Ellen Duveaux and asked if she could bring him up to Dayton to learn more about glass artistry. That, of course, was fine with Ellen.

Liysa had it all figured out. She wanted to take two vehicles. She would drive from Bend to Dayton with both boys and spend Friday night at Ellen and Francois's house. It was a long trip from Bend to Dayton, more than three hundred miles. Then, on Saturday morning, she and Bjorn would drive south from the Walla Walla area to meet Chris at the Minam Store and drive together to the Lostine River campgrounds. He would drive from Bend, bringing their tent, camping gear, and supplies. Liysa would then drive back to Washington Monday morning to pick up Papako.

It meant a lot of driving for both Chris and Liysa for a cold two-day camping trip in an isolated forest. But Chris was willing to do it. That Saturday morning as he drove alone in his SUV with their camping supplies to meet up with Liysa and Bjorn, he believed that he and Liysa *were* getting along better. He hoped that this trip would be the beginning of a new, good chapter of his marriage.

CHAPTER TWENTY-TWO

IT WAS OCTOBER 9, only two days later, when Liysa ran up to Ellen Duveaux's door, bruised, soaking wet, and nearly hysterical. Ellen had questioned the wisdom of Liysa's camping trip with Chris, but, even so, she hadn't expected to see Liysa in such terrible shape. She was stunned to see her condition. It was so early on Monday morning, and suddenly the sunny day took on a somber and frightening tone. Liysa pleaded with Ellen to help her lift Bjorn from her SUV. She seemed frantic to get them all inside. She tried to help, but something was wrong with her arm or shoulder, it seemed, and Ellen brushed past her and picked Bjorn up.

"I need to hide my car, too," Liysa kept saying.

Liysa carried a backpack, which she dumped in a corner of Ellen's living room. Ellen barely glanced at it because she was too concerned about her friend. Liysa's teeth chattered as she blurted that Chris had beaten her up and tried to drown her. She didn't know how she'd managed to escape, but all she had been able to think of was getting to Ellen's house. Somehow, she'd been able to get Bjorn into her Explorer and head for Washington so she could be sure *both* her sons were safe.

Ellen took charge. She told Liysa to take off her sodden clothes and ran a hot bath for her and Bjorn. She found some dry clothes while she washed Liysa's. When Liysa finally got warm and calmed down a little, Ellen insisted that they call "Shelter from the Storm," a domestic violence center in La Grande. They advised Liysa to go to the Dayton General Hospital where she could be treated for her injuries. She had refused her brother's insistence that she go to a doctor, but Ellen was emphatic. Finally, Liysa agreed to seek medical help.

Liysa drove herself to the hospital, and while Ellen waited nervously at home taking care of her little boys, two nurses and a physician's assistant evaluated Liysa's condition. Initially, she appeared to have some bruising beneath one eye and faint scratches and abrasions on one knee.

Michelle Hooper, a registered nurse, had worked at the Dayton hospital for four years in the combined acute care and ER unit. When Liysa told her that she was a victim of a domestic dispute and needed to see a doctor, she struck Hooper as being very calm, and she didn't consider this an emergency. Still, she led Liysa into the ER area because she could have more privacy there.

While they waited for physician's assistant Andy Garcia, Hooper checked Liysa's vital signs and asked her what had happened. "She complained about her knee and her shoulder," Hooper recalled. "There were some small abrasions on her left knee and her left shoulder, and then the blackened eye. She complained that her back hurt, and I looked at it—but there were no visible signs of abrasions or scrapes there at that time."

The skin below Liysa's left eye *was* discolored, but the eye wasn't swollen and she was able to open it fully. She told Michelle Hooper that she and her husband, Chris, had been camping in Lostine—near Wallowa Lake—and that they had gotten into a fight sometime between eleven and two o'clock the night before.

"She said that she was sitting in a chair by the river," Hooper recalled, "and that he'd been drinking and taking pills. She said she asked him—or told him—that he needed to get help for his drinking. Then he got angry and threw her and the chair into the river."

Then Liysa graphically described how Chris had held her head under the water, choking her. Only her "baby's" coming out of their tent and crying had distracted her husband, allowing her to get away. She had gone up to the tent to check on the baby and stayed there, waiting for her husband either to fall asleep or pass out so she could escape.

She thought he was asleep when she tried to slip by him, she said, but he'd tackled her on some rocks, pinning her arms and choking her again. Liysa stressed that Chris had been drinking vodka. She said she had waited a while longer and then finally run by his sleeping bag and taken a shot at it.

Michelle Hooper asked Liysa why she had driven all the way from Wallowa County, Oregon, to Washington State to report what had happened. "I wasn't familiar with the area," she said. "I just wanted to get to where my other boy was staying in Dayton."

Liysa said that she would contact the local police after she was treated. She didn't know that the Columbia County Sheriff's Office had already been notified, and that Deputy Kevin Larkin was waiting outside the emergency treatment area.

LPN Patty Gallaher was working as a float nurse that morning, and she took over when Michelle Hooper's shift ended. PA Garcia had finished checking Liysa's condition. Deputy Larkin was questioning Liysa, and it was hospital policy to have another woman in the room when female patients were talking to males.

Michelle Hooper had whispered hurriedly to Patty Gallaher when the two passed in the hall. She said the patient was a "domestic—a shooting: she shot at her husband," so Gallaher was surprised to find Liysa so "collected and calm."

Andy Garcia felt the same way. Most of the domestic violence victims who came into the ER were frightened and crying. This woman clearly had her wits about her, although Garcia knew that people in shock can seem strangely calm.

Liysa explained to Deputy Larkin that she and her husband had two homes—one in Bend and one in Kailua, Hawaii. Chris was a pilot for Hawaiian Airlines, she said, and she was a freelance photographer who did a lot of surfing shots for outdoor magazines. Then she launched into assertions that her husband was a very bad alcoholic and substance abuser.

"What kind of drugs does he take?" Larkin asked.

"You name it."

"How does he get away with that being an airline pilot?"

Liysa said Chris hadn't been tested for five years. He tested

Vivacious, pretty, and popular, Lisa DeWitt, pictured here on the right as a cheerleader in her high school yearbook, grew up as a typical teen in Walla Walla, Washington, in the 1970s.

The DeWitt family home in Walla Walla. Lisa's father was president of the local community college and adored his daughter. But Lisa would later tell confidantes that her home life was very unhappy, and that her mother was a harsh disciplinarian.

A moment of triumph. Lisa, chosen as Homecoming Princess at Walla Walla High School, on the arm of her escort, Randall Edwards, who would later become the state treasurer of Oregon.

3

Dick and Jeanne Northon as newlyweds in 1951. Dick was a junior at Cal State, and Jeanne dropped out of college to support them until he graduated.

4

Jeanne and Dick's son, Chris, at age six. He loved the outdoors from the time he could walk.

6

The Northons realized a dream when they bought a ranch in Bend, Oregon, where Chris proudly posed on his own horse.

In junior high, Chris was a daredevil and a mischief maker—and taught himself to play piano.

7

After many false starts, Chris finally found his true calling and first love—flying. In Pago Pago, as a captain with South Pacific Airways, he clearly enjoyed his life of travel and adventure.

9

Chris with his sisters Mary *(left)* and Sally *(right)* at their ranch in Bend. They were a very close family.

Jeanne, Dick, Sally, Chris, and Mary at a Northon family reunion. "I used to think we lived a charmed life," Jeanne would later recall sadly.

Chris skiing with his parents near Bend. A confirmed bachelor, he said that if he ever wed, he would want a marriage just like theirs.

Liysa DeWitt, who was now Liysa Mattson, living with her second husband, Nick, and their young son, Papako, on Oahu, first met Chris when he was flying for Hawaiian Airlines. The physical attraction between them was immediate and intense.

13

Divorced from Nick, Liysa pursued Chris relentlessly until they were finally married impetuously on a moonlit beach. Dave Story *(center)*, Chris's close friend and fellow pilot, was also an ordained minister and performed the romantic ceremony.

14

Liysa kissed Chris joyfully after their wedding. She had made up her mind to marry him and have another child. It was only one of her many ambitions—and Liysa always got what she wanted.

Chris, Liysa, and Papako posed happily after the ceremony. When the elder Northons met Liysa, they were delighted to welcome her and her son into the family.

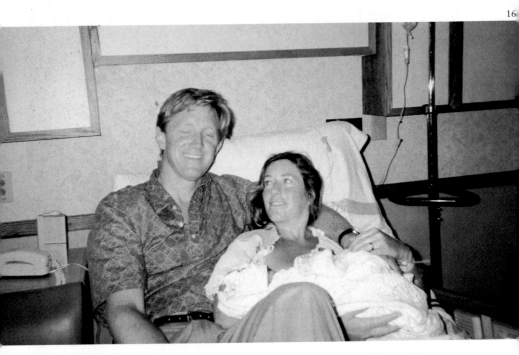

Liysa's wish was fulfilled when she and Chris had their son, Bjorn. Chris was thrilled to become a father.

Liysa holds Bjorn, her son with Chris Northon, at her in-laws' home in Bend, although she rarely spent time with Chris's family.

A picture-book young family in August 1997. *(Left to right)* Liysa, Papako, Bjorn, and Chris in his parents' pool in Bend. Chris was a pilot for Hawaiian Airlines and Liysa was a successful surf photographer who was also writing books and screenplays.

Liysa spent a lot of time with her boys on the beach. Here with Bjorn, she wanted him and Papako to appreciate all the joys of the changing seasons and nature at its most beautiful.

Chris hugged Bjorn for the camera. But beneath the smiling surface of their lives, deep trouble lay ahead.

19

Chris, a copilot in 2000, was about to become a captain when his marriage began to unravel. Here, he flies a DC-10 with Captain Dave Wolz and Don Gore. Liysa complained bitterly about his long absences from home.

21

Concealing his own unhappiness from family and friends, Chris nevertheless thought he could save his marriage. He put on a brave front on a hiking trip with his father, who took this remarkable photograph of Chris that would come back to haunt his parents.

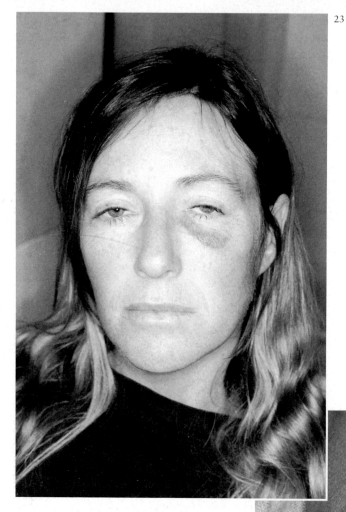

On October 9, 2000, Liysa arrived at a hospital emergency room with a bruised eye and abrasions on her knee. She had been camping with Chris and Bjorn in Wallowa County, Oregon, that weekend and told authorities that Chris had beaten and tried to drown her.

When authorities investigated the campsite expecting to find an abusive husband, they found instead a dead body encased in a sleeping bag.

Wallowa County District Attorney Dan Ousley *(far left)* would pursue the mystery of Chris's death with the same tenacity he had in running marathons. Friends and family, and women's support groups, were outraged when he charged Liysa with murder.

Oregon State Police Detective Pat Montgomery assisted in the probe into Chris's death. In three decades of law enforcement, he had never encountered a case that aroused such contradictory testimony and conflicting emotions.

The venerable Wallowa County Courthouse in the picturesque little town of Enterprise, Oregon, was the scene of a sensational murder trial in the summer of 2000.

Oregon State Assistant Attorney General Steve Briggs *(left)* assisted Dan Ousley in the prosecution's case against Liysa. Earlier, Dennis Dinsmore *(right),* an investigator for the A.G.'s office, had paired with Pat Montgomery to gather evidence crucial in her trial.

Liysa's high-powered attorneys, Wayne Mackeson *(left)* and Pat Birmingham, flank their client in the crowded courtroom. They considered using "The Battered Woman Syndrome" in her defense.

(Left to right) Birmingham, Mackeson, and private investigators Harold Nash and Robin Karnes worked for Liysa's acquittal. When shocking new evidence suddenly turned up during her trial, both prosecution and defense teams conferred heatedly to determine Liysa's fate.

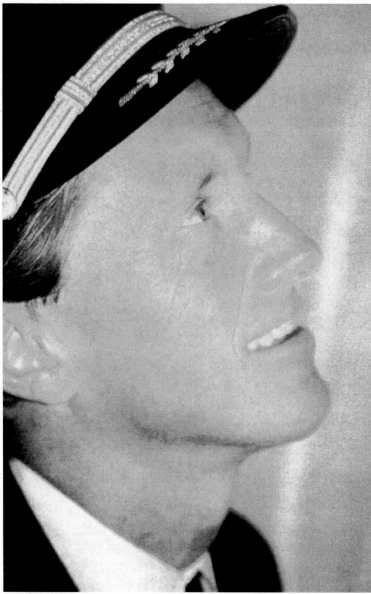

Chris Northon never got to be a captain with Hawaiian Airlines, but his son, Bjorn, has become a "son" to the Hawaiian Air family and Chris's fellow pilots. Chris's legacy makes his little boy proud.

himself, and if his tests came back "dirty," he would simply call in sick. She continued her monologue about how violent her husband was, often repeating the extent of his drug and alcohol use.

Patty Gallaher noticed that the woman with the black eye was being very vague with the deputy. "She would have different ways of saying it—and he would keep asking the questions to get the answers he was after."

Kevin Larkin was frustrated. "Even though I would specifically ask her questions about her fight with her husband," he noted, "she would continually drift off onto different, irrelevant subjects."

Still, when Larkin pressed Liysa to try to remember what had led up to the assault by her husband, she was able to do it in a methodical, coherent way, although it was a slightly different story than she had told before. After she took her older son to Ellen Duveaux's house, "She said she met her husband on the road [Saturday] near Wallowa Lake and they decided to go to the Maxwell Campgrounds."

Liysa told the deputy that earlier in the day, she had taken a hike by herself, leaving Bjorn with his father. It was when she returned that she'd found the tent moved down near the river. "Things were fine until suppertime," Liysa recalled. "But when Chris started drinking from a red cup, he became verbally abusive to Bjorn."

"Then she stated he had a hunting knife in his hand and started shaking it at the child, saying, 'If you don't behave, I'll come after you,' or something to that effect," Larkin said.

Liysa told Larkin she'd "slapped the knife out of his hand" and he'd apologized. But she said Chris was getting "edgy" and so she'd taken Bjorn with her for a twenty-minute drive.

Liysa had yet to mention anything about a shooting to Deputy Larkin, although she did say there had been a violent fight. In this recounting of the events of the night before, she said that Chris had tried to choke her twice, and dunked her head in the river—but she had relaxed and he let go.

"She said she took the baby, got in her car, and went for a twenty-minute drive," Patty Gallaher recalled. "Where I don't know—and then she came back."

Liysa had fixed dinner for them, and after they ate, she said she was sitting in her chair near the river with her sleeping bag draped over her shoulders. She had begun to lecture Chris about his drinking, pointing out where he would end up, and warning him that he would lose his children.

"With that," Gallaher said, "Liysa told us that he picked her and the chair up and threw her in the river and tried to choke her." Their baby was on the shoreline crying and both Chris and Liysa had apparently turned toward Bjorn. Liysa said she had picked him up and taken him to the tent.

"Why did you begin that discussion about drinking when you must have known it would provoke an argument?" Larkin asked.

Liysa brushed his question off and began to speak again of how frightened she was of her husband. Larkin took notes as she spoke.

Patty Gallaher remembered the whole conversation well. "[After dinner], she said, she put the baby down to sleep and she kept watching her husband through the tent. He was cleaning up the campsite, picking up garbage and taking it to his pickup. She noticed that he had moved his sleeping bag to the middle of the trail. When she tried to walk by him to get to her vehicle, he jumped out of the sleeping bag naked and choked her again and threw her down. Then she snuck out of the tent and went behind it, up the steep embankment."

Chris usually slept outside the tent, Liysa said, because the baby made noise and bothered him. She said he was lying across the trail from the beach to their vehicles because he wanted to stop her if she tried to leave with Bjorn.

During the interview in the ER, Kevin Larkin looked hard at Liysa's neck, but it wasn't red nor did it have scratches on it. Her Ford Explorer had been locked, but Liysa said she'd found a hidden key, opened the door, and retrieved a gun from her camera bag. She found the bullets, which she'd hidden in a separate place in the vehicle, and loaded the gun.

Liysa said that Chris had passed out on the beach, sprawled naked on the sand, when she came back. Despite her fear, she'd gone down to him and helped him into his sleeping bag. And then she said she had grabbed the baby and raced by the sleeping bag, shouting, "I'm taking the baby and leaving!"

Kevin Larkin kept asking her how *much* Chris was drinking, but she didn't seem to know. She said only that his condition went from "drunk" to "really drunk and smoking dope."

They had been talking for almost an hour, and it was near the end of their interview when Liysa finally told Larkin that she'd fired a shot at her husband in his sleeping bag. She had Bjorn under one arm, and her gun in her free hand. She'd shouted that she was taking the baby and leaving.

"How far away were you when you shot him?" Larkin asked.

"Six . . . maybe eight feet."

"Why did you shoot at him?" he asked. "Did he jump up at you?"

Liysa shook her head, explaining that Chris was a really light sleeper and she didn't want him to try to stop her from leaving.

"He didn't wake up as you got near him?" Larkin probed.

"It was too dark to tell—but I didn't see him move or anything."

Liysa said that Chris had made a funny grunting noise

when she fired the gun, an *umph*. But she was so frightened that she had kept running and then driven all the way to her friend's house in Dayton.

"Why did you stop to put your son in the car seat," Larkin asked, "if you were so afraid that your husband was coming after you to kill you?"

She looked up, startled. "I don't know why."

"Did you think you'd hit your husband when you shot?"

"Yeah, maybe."

"Where did you get the gun?"

Liysa explained that it was a small handgun her father had given her some time before so she could defend herself. It was out in the car now, in the hospital parking lot. She asked Kevin Larkin if he wanted it and he nodded. Then Larkin took Polaroid photographs of Liysa's injuries—two of her face and the others of the shoulder and her knee that she said had been injured as her husband tried to drown her.

When she was dressed, Larkin followed her out to the parking lot. She reached to the floor of the passenger seat of her Explorer and brought out a small plastic wastebasket. She held it out for him to check. He looked into it, and among other items, he found a handgun. It had been zipped into a large baggie. It was a Taurus Model 85 .38-caliber five-shot revolver.

"Is it unloaded?" Larkin asked.

She nodded.

As he had been trained to do, Larkin checked it anyway. Without removing the gun from the baggie, he pushed the cylinder and it slid to the side. He could see that there were *two* spent bullet casings inside, and three live rounds.

"I thought you only fired one round?"

"Oh," Liysa said, "one went off when I was loading it in the car."

"What did Chris do when that round went off?"

Liysa said nothing.

"You told me that he was a very light sleeper," Larkin said. "I find it hard to believe that he didn't hear a handgun being fired when he was only fifty or sixty yards away."

She had no answer for that.

Liysa pointed to a small fleece bag in the bottom of the wastebasket, and Larkin retrieved the three unfired rounds inside. So far, it looked like a "domestic," all right. Chances were that Liysa Northon's husband hadn't been hit and was sleeping off too much vodka down by the river a four hours' drive away.

Kevin Larkin wanted to get a taped statement from Liysa Northon. He directed her to go to the Duveauxs' house where her little boys were and wait for him to call her. She agreed to do that. She said she was going to call a friend of her brother's who was a police officer in Milton-Freewater, Oregon: Dick Bobbitt.

THAT WAS WHERE THE INVESTIGATION had begun. Kevin Larkin was a deputy in Columbia County, Washington, and it was his request to Wallowa County Sheriff Ron Jett that had sent Undersheriff Rich Stein to the Maxwell Campgrounds to check out the information.

Ironically, Jett had initially felt that Stein would be making an arrest. When Stein said he'd located the subject, Jett had been a little exhilarated that they had found the prime suspect in a domestic violence assault and that an arrest was imminent.

But, of course, it wasn't that way at all.

* * *

WHEN LARKIN CALLED the Duveauxs' phone, Ellen answered. The Columbia County deputy talked to her briefly. She said she'd been shocked at the sight of Liysa that morning. She had barely been able to speak and seemed to be suffering from hypothermia. Larkin asked Ellen if he could come to her house and take a taped statement from her as well as Liysa, and she said okay.

But when Larkin arrived a little while later, he found that Liysa wasn't there; she had left with her brother to see Dick Bobbitt. And now Ellen said she would prefer not to make any statement on tape. But she did tell the deputy that she had been encouraging Liysa to leave Chris for years. The camping trip hadn't been Liysa's idea at all, Ellen said. It was *Chris* who had insisted that they go camping because it was probably the last chance they would have before winter set in.

Ellen said she had heard all about Chris's abuse from Liysa and had no reason to doubt her. She assured Larkin that she herself had seen Chris intoxicated many times.

Ellen didn't mention that Liysa had left her backpack at her house. Perhaps she hadn't even noticed it yet; so much had happened since Liysa's arrival that morning. But when she *did* notice, she still didn't tell the detectives.

CHAPTER TWENTY-THREE

DR. TOR DEWITT and Umatilla County Sheriff's Deputy Dick Bobbitt were longtime friends. For twenty years, Bobbitt had known that Tor had a sister, Liysa, although he had met her only once. At 10:53 A.M. on Monday, October 9, Bobbitt was notified by a sheriff's dispatch officer that he had a message to call Tor DeWitt. When he reached him at his chiropractic office, his friend told him that Liysa was in the hospital in Dayton because she'd been assaulted by her husband. They had been camping down in Oregon on the Lostine River.

"She took a shot at him," Liysa's brother reported, "and then she left."

Tor asked Bobbitt for advice about what they should do. The Umatilla deputy said that as soon as he talked to Liysa, she should report the assault to the police jurisdiction where it happened: Wallowa County. "I gave Tor my office number and my cell phone number," Bobbitt said, "and told him that he or Liysa could contact me when she got out of the hospital, and he said she was already reporting the incident to the police in Dayton."

Bobbitt called Wallowa County Sheriff Ron Jett and told him about the conversation with Tor DeWitt. Jett said they were already checking the Northons' campsite because they'd had a call from Columbia County. No one had known at this point if Chris Northon was alive and well, alive but wounded—or dead. All Liysa had said was that she fired wildly, in the dark, as she was running past her sleeping husband.

Deputy Kevin Larkin had asked Liysa to remain at Ellen and Francois Duveaux's house until he could get more information from the Wallowa authorities, but she hadn't done that. After thinking about it, she evidently decided it would be prudent for her to go with her brother to talk with Dick Bobbitt, someone who had a connection to her family.

And so, at 1:15 that afternoon she called Bobbitt and said she didn't know what she should do. She repeated to the Umatilla County deputy her horrific story about how Chris had beaten her, tried to kill her, tried to drown her, and threatened to take her baby away. She emphasized that her husband drank a lot, smoked marijuana, and took some other kind of drug. "I don't know what it was," Liysa said, "because I never do drugs."

"Has your husband abused you in the past?" Bobbitt asked.

"Yes. A doctor filed a report about him once after he beat me and I had to go to the hospital."

Liysa sounded distraught and admitted that she had, indeed, fired a shot in her husband's direction, but only because she was afraid he was going to take her baby away from her.

Bobbitt told Liysa what he had told Tor DeWitt—she had to contact Sheriff Ron Jett in Wallowa County. He said she could come to his own office in Milton-Freewater, Oregon, to talk with him, and then she could call Jett from there.

Liysa had sounded so frightened and upset on the phone, it was hard for Bobbitt not to be touched by her plight. But before she arrived at his office, he received word from Jett that they had found a body on the beach next to the Lostine River. At this point, the Oregon State Police had been notified that help was needed to sort out the fatal shooting. And so Pat Montgomery had headed for Wallowa County while OSP detectives Jim Van Atta and Mike Wilson set out for the Umatilla County Sheriff's Office to talk with Liysa when she got there.

Bobbitt's first glimpse of Liysa Northon matched her voice on the phone. She was a thin little woman with a bruised eye, who held herself stiffly as if she was in pain. Two young boys clung to her anxiously. Liysa wore sweatpants and a sweatshirt. She had no makeup on and her long hair hung straight to her shoulders. Her brother, Tor, stood by with a look of deep concern. Their father, Wayland, was on his way, he said.

Liysa seemed very fragile to Dick Bobbitt, and his heart went out to her.

"Is Chris okay?" she asked softly.

"He's been located," Bobbitt said evasively. And then he asked Tor DeWitt to take the little boys out of the room while he spoke with their mother.

"The Oregon State Police want to talk with you," Bobbitt told Liysa. "They're on their way."

"Can I wait with my children until they get here?"
"Of course."

* * *

CHRIS NORTHON had been dead for only about a dozen hours, his body had been located, but already some of the most adept investigators in the state of Oregon were working the case. When a small Oregon county whose police department isn't used to handling unexplained death cases needs help, it can always ask for assistance from the State Police or the Oregon State Medical Examiner's Office.

For the moment, the Wallowa County detectives and the Oregon State Police would take a look at a case that wasn't even a day old yet to see if anything further needed to be done. On the surface, it sounded as if a family fight had escalated to sudden death. It was a familiar tragedy.

In earlier decades, police had pretty much thrown up their hands in frustration. The wrong people got married to each other, fought, made up despite police intervention, and while some eventually divorced, other misalliances ended in violent death. Too many wives who wanted their husbands arrested on a Saturday night refused to file charges on Monday morning and came and bailed them out of jail instead. Then again, too many beaten and bruised women kept quiet about what was happening to them. There was no place for them to go. How would they support their children?

Protecting battered women has become a major focus for law enforcement and the public over the last few decades. Young officers are trained to spot injured spouses, and to be gentle and supportive in dealing with them. In many jurisdictions, a domestic battle means that one party is *always* arrested and taken off to jail—even if the other cries and begs the police to let him or her stay at home.

Liysa Northon might very well prove to be a terrorized woman who'd been forced to a point where she had to shoot her own husband to protect their child. If that should be the end result of an intense probe, Liysa could gather up the shreds of her life and take Papako and Bjorn back to Hawaii, no longer afraid of Chris. However, if the circumstantial evidence and the physical evidence didn't match, disposition of this case might take much longer.

* * *

DICK BOBBITT BELIEVED Liysa's story. But already some of the people who had heard her describe the aimless shot that brought instant death to Chris Northon were feeling prickles of doubt.

Patty Gallaher and Michelle Hooper had comforted any number of abused wives and girlfriends in the little ER room at the Dayton General Hospital, but something about Liysa made the hairs on the back of their necks stand up. She was too calm, too evasive, and her wounds didn't seem that bad.

When they met Liysa in Bobbitt's office, Oregon State Police detectives Jim Van Atta and Mike Wilson were inclined to agree with the nurses. Although they took careful notes on the faint bruises and small cuts on her eye, back, shoulder, knees, and one hand, they, too, found her in remarkably good shape after the physical battles she described with a man who must have outweighed her by almost a hundred pounds.

Liysa maintained her flat affect when she learned that her husband was dead. She might have been in shock or perhaps she was a woman with remarkable self-control. She was, however, visibly upset when the State Police detectives advised her of her rights under the Miranda Act. She told them she understood them perfectly. And then she said she wanted to speak to an attorney before she answered any questions. The interview was terminated, although Liysa did allow Van Atta to document her injuries with photographs.

Mike Wilson stepped out of the interview room to tell Dick Bobbitt that Liysa was being placed under arrest on one count of murder.

It clearly wasn't what she had expected. She had told four law enforcement officers how she had barely escaped from her husband alive—and now *she* was going to jail. Stunned, Liysa made arrangements for Papako's and Bjorn's care. Her brother would take them for now. Van Atta and Wilson drove her to the Union County Jail in Pendleton. She fully expected that she would be out on bail shortly.

Dick Bobbitt asked Tor DeWitt to drive Liysa's vehicle to his office. It would be towed and impounded at the Oregon State Police office in Pendleton.

Liysa had impressed Bobbitt with her courage. Once, when the State Police investigators had left the office for a few minutes, she had lifted her chin bravely and said, "Dick, at least my kids are safe."

"And you're safe, too, Liysa," he answered, trying to comfort her. "You're safe and they're safe."

Wayland and Tor DeWitt were shaken as they watched Liysa being led away. Bjorn and Papako were bewildered and frightened, not sure of exactly what had happened that was tearing their mother from them. She had made herself such a presence in their lives that it was like losing the center of their universe. Papako had his dad—who was on a plane headed to Oregon. But Bjorn's beloved dad would never be there for him again. The essence of his father was gone. His body now lay motionless in the Bollman Funeral Home, awaiting a postmortem exam that might answer some of the many questions about his death.

* * *

TWENTY-FOUR HOURS BEFORE, Liysa had allegedly been cooking dinner at the campsite on the Lostine. And now she was in the Union County Jail, charged with murder.

Although she told any number of people that she was so relieved her children were safe at last, it was highly unlikely that Liysa expected this turn of events. She was not free to come and go as she wished—something that had always been essential to her well-being. And she was subjected to body searches and to the indignity of a search warrant conducted at the request of Detective Matt Cross of Wallowa County. She had no choice but to allow technician Danielle Moss of the Interpath Laboratory in Pendleton to withdraw her blood and collect her urine. Dick Bobbitt was the deputy who drove her to the lab and then back to jail, so at least she had a friend with her.

But because the lab samples were retrieved the morning after Liysa's arrest, it would be unlikely that an accurate reading could be taken on what she might have ingested or drunk two nights earlier.

Liysa hated being in jail and evinced great concern over her boys, but there was one thing she could be sure of: her friends would stand by her, and so would her father and brother. They all were convinced that Chris had put her through hell. She had told them over and over about his cruelty and his drunkenness.

And they believed her. Confiding in Dick Bobbitt, Tor DeWitt said that Chris had abused Liysa for a long time. He had tried in vain to get her to move in with him. Liysa had refused, saying—as she had to so many others—that Chris would kill her if she ever left him. And then she had told her brother the same thing she told Carrie Arnesen, "Chris would cut me up in little pieces and eat me."

* * *

SHERIFF RON JETT had driven up to Dayton to talk with the Washington witnesses. He was surprised to learn that Papako was still with Ellen Duveaux and not with his uncle, Tor. Jett faced the unsavory prospect of questioning a little boy about his mother and the violent death of his stepfather.

It was easier to talk to Patty Gallaher, whose wry frankness painted a different picture of the suspect than Deputy Dick Bobbitt saw. Women tend to judge their own sex a bit more harshly than men do—just as men can spot flaws in other men, men that females gush over. It's a theory proved true time after time.

Patty Gallaher was the nurse who had been present during Deputy Kevin Larkin's questioning of Liysa in the Dayton General Hospital's ER. She was a no-nonsense woman who described things the way she saw them. She told Ron Jett that it took so long to get the story out of Liysa because she continually brought up nit-picking details. "He [Deputy Larkin] kept wanting to get back to that issue [why the fight started], and she was so concerned about giving us every detail under the sun of how the event took place. Without her having a watch, she knew what time it was and how much time elapsed between each event. It was bizarre. I mean—the guy has a history, supposedly, of 'domestic' with her for three years. Right away, he threatens the child—the *baby*—she kept calling it 'the baby.' I don't even know if 'the baby' has a name. He threatened the baby with a hunting knife so she takes the baby, gets in the car, and knows she's gone for twenty minutes on a ride with the baby. And then comes back! *I* would have just kept on driving."

Patty Gallaher was puzzled that Liysa said she wasn't sure what her husband was drinking from the red cup the night before. "He went from 'maybe drunk' to 'oblivious drunk,' I don't know how quickly, but she said she never saw him take a drink.

"[She said] his sleeping bag was on the trail leading to her vehicle. When she tried to walk by, he jumped up stark-ass naked out of the sleeping bag, grabbed her around the throat, threw her on the ground, and tried to choke her until she relaxed again. And then he let her go. [Her Explorer was locked] but he didn't know she had a hidden key. So then she went back to the tent again where the baby's at. And she looks out and sees him sprawled, stark-ass naked, out on the beach. And this *really* doesn't make sense: she said she put him in his sleeping bag, and all this time she's telling us she can't subdue him in any other way because he's so big and violent. . . ."

Patty Gallaher continued to tell Ron Jett about how her antennae went up as she listened to Liysa. "It's light out at night usually in the mountains and you can see pretty well—except this is a canyon, you see, so everything's really, really dark. And I said, 'How do you know you hit the sleeping bag?' She knows she hit the sleeping bag because he made a moaning sound. She takes time to put the baby in the car seat and drive off. He was not following her. I said, 'Do you think it's a little odd that he hasn't showed up in Dayton yet?' And she didn't know. And then she wanted to know if she could go back home to Hawaii.

"She was not excited. She was not depressed. She got teary-eyed only when we brought up the fact that she's been in a domestic situation—because that's our job to be advocates and help people. So you offer all the services that you know are available, which we kept offering, and she's done all this and it's never worked. And she even had him in court one time, but she refused to show up to take care of the situation. And so she said she's been down that route. She was one of these type of patients, sitting there nodding her head at us but you know it was just not sinking in."

Patty Gallaher told Ron Jett what *she* would have done if she had been in Liysa Northon's place. "My thought would have been to grab the baby and walk as far as I could get. Because if this guy is this drunk and this stoned and passed out nude on the beach, I would think it would take him a while to come to. That's what I told her."

CHAPTER TWENTY-FOUR

THE DETECTIVES and the criminalists from the Oregon State Police and Wallowa County were back at the death site early Tuesday morning, October 10. When they were finally satisfied that every possible scintilla of physical evidence had been bagged and labeled, they loaded the containers into the back of Chris Northon's Chevy. It was then towed into Enterprise by a wrecker and left in the county impound lot until Matt Cross could get a search warrant to check out everything that was in it. They left the Shady Campground as pristine as it had been when Chris and Liysa arrived to spend the weekend there.

The site was cleared at 11:27 A.M.

* * *

DR. KHALIL HELOU, a pathologist, had come from La Grande to perform the postmortem exam of Chris Northon's body at the Bollman Funeral Home. As the medical examiner of Wallowa County, Dr. Lowell Euhus stood by. Pat Montgomery, Matt Cross, and Jeff Dovci observed as the sleeping bag was carefully tugged away from the body. Chris Northon had lain on his left side, frozen by rigor mortis into the position he'd been in when he died. Lividity, the dark purplish deposit of blood on the nethermost portion of a body when the heart no longer pumps, was present. Both of Chris's hands were tucked up under his neck and chin as if he'd been sleeping when he was shot.

He was completely naked, and his entire body had fine beach sand clinging to it. He had many bruises—on top of his right shoulder, on both knees, and on both shins. There was a deep, fresh scratch near his little toe on his left foot. Both of his eyes were black, but that was likely the aftermath of a bullet to his brain.

There were a number of vertical marks that looked like fingernail scratches on Chris's left chest above the nipple. They were several inches long. These wounds were puzzling. They *looked* like ordinary fingernail scratches, and yet, in some ways, they looked almost like burns. Those watching couldn't be sure just what had made those marks. Chris's hands weren't bruised and his fingernails were not broken, as might be expected after a violent fight.

The immediate cause of death was obvious. Dr. Helou found that the bullet had entered the head just in front of the right ear and coursed at a slight upward angle through the temporal lobes of the brain. The brain itself was pulverized and the bullet completely severed the brain stem, exiting just above the left ear. "Death would have been instantaneous," Helou said.

Montgomery nodded, his mind racing back to the statements Liysa Northon had made. In a homicide investigation, witnesses' statements always have to be weighed against the standard of physical evidence available. Chris Northon could no longer tell anyone what had happened; his "testimony" would be silent. And yet his body might very well harbor important physical evidence.

There wasn't any gunshot residue marking the victim's skin near the entrance wound, so Liysa would have to have been at least four feet away when she fired, too far for Chris to have reached out to grab her and keep her from leaving. But then Liysa herself had said she was between six and eight feet from Chris when she fired her gun.

Montgomery now pondered Liysa's recollection of the night of the tragedy. She said she had been running in the dark on the steeper of the two trails, holding three-year-old Bjorn under one arm, when she fired blindly toward where she thought Chris was. He had lain with his head almost touching one of the two logs that marked the boundaries of the grassy area—*not* across the trail to block it. The question was, where was Liysa when she fired?

If Chris was sleeping on his left side, facing *away* from the path, Liysa would have had to be almost directly over him, shooting *down* in the dark into his right temple area but the trajectory of the bullet was odd. If she had taken the sloping trail on the *other* side and Chris had been lying on his back, she would have shot him in the *left* side of his head.

No, that could not have happened. The entry wound was on the right side. Exit wounds do the most damage, and the left side of Chris's skull was shattered.

Jeff Dovci, from the Oregon State Police Crime Lab, had already come to a similar conclusion. "The most logical approach for a shooter or someone trying to shoot someone on the ground in the head would obviously be from the rear," he said.

Actually, the shooter firing from the rear and achieving the entrance angle that matched the wound would also have to have been standing above the victim. She might even have been *beside* him. The only angle that made any kind of sense was the "straight down" theory; the bullet had ended up two inches deep in the sand, carrying hair and feathers with it. What were the odds that Liysa could have been so deadly accurate in the total black of night? It almost looked as if she had stood directly above her husband and aimed down at his head. Something that could, arguably, have been accidental—depending on how dark it was. They had found the miner's light just above Chris.

As is so often true when relatively young people die in sudden violence, Chris Northon had been in excellent physical condition, save for two rather unusual findings. His heart and lungs were those of an athlete, with only minuscule fatty streaks. His liver was "unremarkable" and didn't appear to be that of an "alcoholic." All other organs, joints, and bones were normal.

However, Chris had been suffering from chronic inflammation (gastritis) of his stomach. In layman's terms: an ulcer. He also had chronic thyroiditis, inflammatory changes in his thyroid gland, known as Hashimoto's disease. The latter was unusual for a male, since it's more often found in middle-aged women or people with a family history of thyroid disorders.

Myriad things could have caused the two conditions—everything from emotional stress to environmental pollution to poison. The thyroiditis wasn't hard to explain; as it turned out, both Dick and Jeanne Northon had had slight thyroid abnormalities since they were in college, and Chris had obviously inherited that. The chronic gastritis was more problematic. Either the stress of his marriage had formed acid that was eroding the protective membrane of his stomach or he had ingested something corrosive.

Chris's stomach was empty. Liysa said she had cooked supper, but she hadn't noted the time—as she never wore a watch. She had also said that Chris was full of vodka, drugs, and she didn't know what else. She blamed his alleged attack on her on the medication and alcohol coursing through his veins.

Now blood samples were drawn from Chris's body so that they could be tested for the percentage of alcohol in his bloodstream and for drugs. Dr. Helou also took urine samples.

The samples collected for blood alcohol and urine analysis went to a State Police lab. The samples for drug testing were sent to a lab in Willow Grove, Pennsylvania. Laboratory results for drug concentrations in the blood are notoriously slow in coming back, as they stack up on waiting lists in labs all over America. It would probably be weeks before the results would be known.

* * *

THE FIRST FEW DAYS after Chris's death passed with agonizing slowness. It was still Tuesday, October 10, when Pat Montgomery placed a phone call to Dick and Jeanne Northon at their home in Bend. Talking with bereaved parents is one of the most disturbing tasks any police officer ever has to face. Montgomery knew that all too well; he had been on both sides and said softly to Jeanne that he could empathize with her pain. He, too, had lost a son to murder. He didn't give her any details, and she didn't ask, but both she and Dick realized that he was someone who could understand their agony.

Still in deep shock—they had known that Chris was dead for only sixteen hours—they tried now to tell Montgomery anything that might help him understand what had happened. They couldn't understand it themselves, but Dick Northon started with dates, cold facts. He said that Chris and Liysa had been married approximately five years ago—in Hawaii. "Chris never discusses . . . ah, *discussed* his personal life," he said haltingly, "but if there were any arguments or fights in the marriage, it wasn't one-sided."

Asked if Chris had ever been violent in the past, Dick instantly said, "*No!* Never."

It was unthinkable. Already, their phone had rung constantly with calls from Chris's friends, mostly in Bend—because others spread around the world didn't yet know he was dead. When they were told that Liysa was insisting she'd shot Chris in self-defense because he was physically attacking her, his friends were unanimous in their belief that that could not be.

Dick Northon asked Pat Montgomery about the gun. "To the best of our knowledge," he said in confusion, "Liysa and Chris never owned any guns. Neither of them."

"We're checking on the gun," Montgomery said noncommittally.

The Northons were very worried about Papako and Bjorn. They told Montgomery that Nick Mattson, Papako's father, would be in Oregon later that day, and that he might have temporary custody of both boys. They had been together since Bjorn was born—they were *brothers*—and they needed each other.

Nobody knew yet exactly what had happened. Not the Oregon State Police. Not the Wallowa County Sheriff's investigators or the Columbia County deputy, Kevin Larkin, who had taken Liysa's statements; not Deputy Dick Bobbitt in Umatilla County. Not the Wallowa County district attorney, Dan Ousley.

All they knew was that things didn't quite line up as they should have. Everything was just a little off center, slightly skewed. Dick Bobbitt tended to believe that Liysa had been the victim of savage abuse; Kevin Larkin found her demeanor bizarre. But if anyone had thought that a shooting in a remote county with a small sheriff's office would be handled quickly and forgotten, they were mistaken. There were a number of jurisdictions who were curious about it.

Jim Van Atta and Mike Wilson drove to Dayton on October 11 to contact Ellen Duveaux and Liysa's son Papako. Van Atta talked with Ellen, who remained adamant that Liysa, her friend since 1978, had suffered mightily at Chris Northon's hands. As far back as July 1996—only four months after her wedding on the beach to Chris—Liysa had come to Ellen's farm and said that Chris had choked her and hit her. He also had pummeled her on the inside of her thighs—in places that didn't show—she told Ellen.

"Liysa even went to Chris's parents once and showed them the marks, and they didn't believe her," Ellen said.

Liysa had once told Jeanne that Chris had tried to choke her, but Jeanne couldn't detect any bruises. Ellen obviously believed everything that Liysa told her.

Ellen recalled that it was Papako who had called her on Tuesday, October 3, to ask if he could come up on the weekend to work on stained glass. She had agreed and said that Chris had called her Friday about two in the afternoon to say that Liysa had left, but was running a little late.

Ellen said she had taken that phone call as an opportunity to talk to Chris about his marriage. She had asked him what his "love relationship" with Liysa was and if he loved her. There was a long pause on his end of the line, she said, and she had pushed further, saying, "If you don't love Liysa, why don't you let her go?"

Ellen said Chris had answered, "My parents have been married for fifty years. Once you're married, you stay married."

She had then tried to convince Chris to come to her house and they would all spend the weekend together and have a great time, instead of the Northons freezing in the mountains.

"I can take the cold—I'm Scandinavian," Ellen quoted Chris to the State Police detectives.

Van Atta and Wilson exchanged glances. Ellen Duveaux seemed to be a very intrusive—or a very naive—woman who had asked deeply personal questions about someone else's marriage.

Liysa, Papako, Bjorn—and their dog, the Great Pyrenees named KoKo—had arrived at the Duveaux farm on Friday, October 6, about 9:00 P.M., and stayed the night. Liysa and Bjorn had left to meet Chris on Saturday.

And then, of course, Liysa had showed up damp and disheveled on Monday morning.

WITH HIS MOTHER IN JAIL, Papako Mattson, who was only nine years old, gave a taped statement to Sheriff Ron Jett. He was still a little boy, but clearly intelligent. After a number of innocuous questions, Jett asked Papako if there were times when his stepfather and mother didn't get along.

"Lots of times," the child said, nodding.

"What did he do?"

"Well, I remember when he threw her out of the car—"

"Was it moving or stopped?"

"Moving."

Papako didn't remember where that happened. He repeated almost word for word what Liysa had said about Chris. "[He said] he was going to burn the house down and kill us all and burn the house down."

Just as his mother claimed, Papako said that Chris drank a lot. But he wasn't sure what "a lot" was. And his mother had told him that his stepfather took pills.

"Did you actually see him taking any pills?"

"No."

"But you've seen him when he was drunk?"

"Uh-hum."

Ellen and Francois Duveaux were present during Papako's questioning, and Ellen made comments or helped remind the little boy of people's names.

Papako said his mother had instructed him to take Bjorn into another room when she and Chris were arguing. "Basically, what I would do is keep my little brother out of it."

He said his mother had come to him where he was sleeping in Ellen's house on Monday morning. "Then she told me what happened."

"What did she say?" Jett asked.

"That she shot Chris."

"Did she say why?"

"Because he was trying to drown her. And he fell asleep by the river and he, and sh—, ah, when she was dragging him back up to the campground, he started hitting her and beating her."

"Okay. She was dragging him or he was dragging her?"

"She was dragging him 'cause he fell asleep on the river-bank."

"Did she say anything else about what happened down there?"

"Not really."

"Did you notice any cuts on her hands or anything?"

"Well, she had gravel stuck in her hands and her knees."

Papako said his mother had been "really, really depressed" when she told him that she had shot his stepfather.

It had not been an ideal setting for the questioning of a child. Ellen Duveaux hovered, her eyes darting from Papako to Jett. It would have been better if Pat Montgomery had done this interview; he had so many years of experience asking questions of child victims of sexual abuse.

Still, it was clear that the child believed his stepfather was angry and mean. Was Papako Mattson telling the truth about what he had seen or was he merely repeating what his mother had told him? That question would haunt the investigators for months. Papako and Liysa were far closer than most boys and their mothers. Would he have believed that the ocean was the sky if she told him it was?

Perhaps. Or maybe he was only a very confused little boy whose mother had vanished suddenly from his world and whose stepfather was dead just as suddenly.

But Papako had one parent who was there for him. Nick Mattson was on a plane to the mainland within hours of hearing that Chris Northon was dead. Nick and his second wife, Lora Lee,* had a new baby boy, but they wanted to get Papako home as soon as they could. Even though they had a very small house—designed for a couple and a tiny baby—there was no question that they would make room for Papako.

Bjorn was being bounced around among Liysa's friends and

relatives while she decided where she wanted him to live until she got out of jail. She was adamant about one thing; she would *not* let Chris's family care for the child who was as much their blood kin as her own family's.

_____ CHAPTER TWENTY-FIVE _____

CHRIS WOULD HAVE two memorial services, just as he had lived in two homes. The first service was held on October 17 in John and Eva Gill's Rock Springs Guest Ranch in Tumalo. Dave and Debbie Story had come from Hawaii, along with several other pilots who had flown with Chris. Four poster-sized pictures of Chris dominated the room: Chris in his uniform and hat, the actual hat now resting rakishly on the frame of the photograph; Chris on skis with Bjorn on his back; Chris and Bjorn laughing; and, finally, Chris half kneeling on a huge rock with a mountain lake behind him, smiling. Through some slant of light or reflection, perhaps some flaw in the film, there was a shining cross inside a halo above his head.

The men who had come from Hawaii wore leis of black leaves around their necks. The mourners gathered in a large room that Chris had always liked—knotty pine walls and a massive mica stone fireplace. Scale models of every plane he had ever piloted were displayed in the room.

Dave Story stood at the lectern with tears streaming down his face. He was accustomed to preaching, but the overwhelming emotion he felt at the loss of the man he considered his best friend made it difficult for him to speak. Time after time, he took off his reading glasses, as if he could see better through his tears, and then put them back on because it didn't help. Young and middle-aged men who stood up to remember Chris also cried unashamedly as they recalled what he had meant to them.

Arne Arnesen spoke of how things had always seemed to come easily to Chris. "The ability he really had was that he found a way to do the things we all have to do—but he always found time to *live* life. He taught me not to put off living. . . ."

Buck Zink, Chris's partner in crime in junior high pranks, sounded stunned as he said, "I thought Chris would be there forever."

Chris's abundant joy in the life he lived was part of every eulogy. "He instilled in me a great love and respect for life," an old friend said. "The last time we talked, we spoke of instilling this into our children."

Dave Story recalled the last time he saw Chris. "He had a layover in Honolulu eight or nine days before he was killed," he said. "Chris called me, and we sat out by our pool and drank a beer. I remember we talked a lot about pilots who had left Hawaiian Air. Some had retired, some were ill, and some had died. Chris said, 'You never know when it's gonna happen . . .'

"I keep thinking about that, and I wonder if somehow he knew."

Three hula dancers swayed to a song of farewell, and someone played "Für Elise," the first song Chris ever learned to play on the piano. Then a Hawaiian song, "The Beauty of the World with My Own Eyes," "Amazing Grace," and, finally, "Somewhere in Time," which had been Chris's favorite melody.

Chris's ashes had been divided. Half were scattered over the Oregon mountains where he and his father had hiked so often. Half were taken to Hawaii. In an old biplane, fellow pilot Warren Kitchell flew over Kailua and Lanakai and the Mokoluas with the ashes, but the weather turned so stormy and rainy that he thought he would have to go back. And then, suddenly, the sun burst through and a rainbow appeared. Down below, Dan

Jones and many of Chris's friends and fellow pilots were on surfboards. Kitchell released Chris's ashes and they drifted past the rainbow, melting into the ocean he had loved.

All of the Hawaiian Airlines pilots wrote letters to save for Bjorn to read when he was older.

And then, for Chris, it was over. For the detectives investigating his death, it was really just beginning.

* * *

THE INVESTIGATORS were about to receive some possible evidence that was almost more confusing than it was illuminating. Before he flew to Bend to lead Chris's memorial service, Dave Story had responded to a request from Chris's parents. They wanted the photos of Chris to use at his memorial service, and they were also concerned about the prenuptial agreement he and Liysa had signed. Given the circumstances, it seemed wise to retrieve Chris's personal papers.

The Storys routinely took care of the Northons' Kailua house when they were in Bend, just as the Northons watched their home when they were away. Chris and Liysa's front door in Hawaii might be locked, but the entrance from the porch was always open. The two couples were used to borrowing things back and forth and had easy access to each other's houses. While Dave and his wife, Debbie, were searching for the pictures, Debbie had come across a purple and black canvas bag on a shelf with Chris's belongings. Curious, she looked inside and found four or five spiral notebooks with handwriting that looked like Liysa's. Some of it appeared to be old letters to Chris and some of the entries seemed to be journals.

As she glanced at what Liysa had written, her heart contracted. She wondered if Chris had had any idea how much his wife had hated him. "Dave," she said slowly, "the police would be *very* interested in what's in here."

If the Oregon investigators had known that Liysa's writings existed, they couldn't have asked the Storys to look for them. Had Chris's friends' search been instigated by the detectives, anything they found would be thrown out of court. Evidence retrieved by detectives without a search warrant is barred. And so is evidence discovered at the *suggestion* of law enforcement personnel, which is deemed "fruit of the poisonous tree."

This "fruit" was not poisonous—not legally. Debbie had heard Liysa complain about how she'd been abused most of her life by family and friends. She'd even said that Chris left bruises on her. Debbie, who was both a real estate agent and a massage therapist, knew that was an exaggeration because she'd often given Liysa massages and knew that she was thin-skinned and bruised easily. Moreover, she had seen Liysa have temper tantrums and become so violent that Chris had to hold her arms to quiet her. With Liysa's tendency to bruise, even that left light violet marks.

Debbie hadn't had any idea what to do with the notebooks, so she'd thrown them into her luggage to take to Oregon for Chris's memorial services.

Dick Northon had served as the caretaker of Chris's house in Bend when he and Liysa were both away. He'd gone to the house the first time to find Chris's Rolodex for names and addresses of people to notify that he was dead. He'd taken his son's flight bag to see if the address list was there, but later returned it to the house.

Dick had long held two general powers of attorney to represent Chris if he should ever be unable to carry on his own affairs. He had never expected to need them, except for taking care of the Bend house. He was also listed on Chris's bank account.

Now, still in shock after Chris's sudden death, Dick moved to protect what he'd left behind. Liysa's own prenuptial agreement spelled it out: the house in Bend was Chris's; the house in

Kailua was hers. But Dick was unable to find a will or any papers that might indicate Chris's wishes for Bjorn if anything ever happened to him.

Dave and Debbie Story and Arne and Carrie Arnesen went back to the Seventeenth Street house to help box up Chris's property to store in the garage. The story had been in the papers; most people in Bend knew that Chris was dead and Liysa was in jail—an ideal setup for a burglary. Sadly, it was also an occasion for a confrontation. Wayland DeWitt had already written to the Northons, warning them not to sell Chris's grand piano or his rental properties because those should be saved for Bjorn. They hadn't even thought about selling anything of Chris's, but it disturbed the Northons when they realized Wayland was carrying out orders from Liysa. They were amazed at the timing of her thoughtless request and they hoped never again to deal with the woman who was—legally—Chris's widow.

Arne and Dave had packed more journals and paperwork, along with some of Chris's personal things, and Debbie and Carrie were cleaning the refrigerator, which was full of spoiled food, when a huge rental truck pulled up. It was Tor and a male friend, Tor's ex-wife, Jimmie Rhonda, and Liysa's newest friend, Mia Rose.* Tor stubbornly insisted he had a police detective's permission to take whatever items Liysa wanted from the house.

Dave Story called Dick Northon, who pulled his car in front of the moving truck, blocking it. It seemed like grave robbing for Liysa's brother and friends to swoop down to divide the possessions in Chris's home when the pain of his death was still achingly fresh. In his grief, Dick felt rage, too. It was an easier emotion to deal with than deep mourning. He swallowed his anger, however, and began to point out innocuous items that DeWitt's entourage could take. They ignored him and strode in, loading up the new washer and dryer first. Eventually, they packed almost everything of value. Liysa had told them that it all belonged to her now. In the end, they removed everything—save Chris's piano—hauling away photographs, books, mementos. DeWitt would recall that he saw a "bag of marijuana" in Chris's gray filing cabinet. Perhaps he did.

Tor DeWitt continued to insist that he had police permission to remove what he wanted from the house. That couldn't have been true; Pat Montgomery instructed Dick and the Arnesens *not* to take anything away because it might have evidentiary value. And they hadn't; they were putting things in the garage. In fact, Montgomery had told Dick he'd prefer they didn't even go *in* Chris's house.

Later, somewhat contritely, Dick met with Montgomery. "I told you not to go to that house," the State Police detective said. "It would be better if you and Arne had never been there."

Dick nodded grimly, but he turned over a box with an Olympus microcassette recorder in it that still contained a tape, and five spiral bound notebooks that Chris's friends had taken from the house. Now all of Liysa's journals from Kailua and her more recent writings from Bend were locked into evidence by the investigators.

The contents of those journals and letters would intrigue D.A. Dan Ousley, Pat Montgomery, and Matt Cross tremendously, although it was virtually impossible to wade through the thousands of pages. None of them had ever dealt with a murder suspect who memorialized virtually everything she did or thought in writing. They realized that they were *not* investigating a slam-dunk case of self-defense, however, and there were probably scores of people who would have to be interviewed.

So many things didn't add up. Montgomery was puzzled about why Liysa had driven so far before she asked for help. He'd seen the pay phone on the corner in the hamlet of Lostine, right where the river road crossed the main street. She could have called an ambulance or the sheriff from there. Apparently, she'd had Chris's cell phone, too. She could also have driven to Enterprise, the county seat, which was only ten miles south, and contacted the sheriff's office.

LIYSA'S FRIENDS on both sides of the ocean formed a solid wall. Those who lived in Oregon assured detectives that she had lived a life of quiet desperation, too afraid of Chris to leave him. If they had any information that might make Liysa look guilty of murder, they were not about to tell detectives anything that would harm their dear and enchanting friend. *No.* She couldn't be guilty. They were incredulous that anyone would even suspect Liysa of murder.

One of her old high school friends served on the board of directors at the Y.W.C.A. in Walla Walla, and the "Y"— traditionally a protector of frightened women—agreed to be listed as a supporter in flyers and posters printed to solicit money for Liysa's defense. She was in jail, yes, but she was a heroine, a fragile woman who had barely survived, one who had fought desperately to protect her children from harm.

Even before Chris's memorial services, women in Walla Walla, Bend, Joseph, and Hawaii had beaten the drum to gain support for Liysa. Some of her friends stood behind her by remaining silent, while others were vocal in her defense. In Wallowa County, the consensus of strangers was that Chris Northon must have been a tyrant who had terrorized his slender little wife. Very few of the county's residents had ever met Chris *or* Liysa, and none of them knew what had really happened on the Lostine River. But the rumors circulating seemed to assume the worst about Chris.

One flyer read:

LIYSA NEEDS OUR HELP

On Monday, October 9, 2000, Liysa shot her husband, Chris, after he had badly beaten her. Liysa is being held in the Union County Correctional Facility on a murder charge.

Some of you are aware of the years of abuse she had suffered from Chris.

Liysa needs our support through cards and letters.

All mail will be opened and inspected. Mail without a complete return address including your first name and full last name will be refused.

Donations to Liysa's defense should be sent to:

Liysa A. Northon Defense Fund
American West Bank
P.O. Box 1598
Walla Walla, WA 99362

Thank you for your support of Liysa and your stand against domestic violence.

This flyer was signed, "Sharon Fisher, Liysa's Mom, and Cathy/Dick Cook." And supporters were asked to spread the word about Liysa by email.

Although Liysa's wasn't a high-profile case and didn't make headlines around the state of Oregon, it certainly was the subject of gossip in Wallowa County, in Bend, and in Walla Walla.

_____ CHAPTER TWENTY-SIX _____

BOOKED ON A MURDER CHARGE, Liysa remained at the Union County Jail in La Grande, Oregon. There was a very small jail on the first floor of the Wallowa County Courthouse in Enterprise, but the county contracted with Union County to house its prisoners because long-term confinement wasn't really an option.

Liysa's first experience in court had been on October 11, when a telephonic bail hearing was set up with Circuit Court Judge Philip Mendiguren, who listened from his courtroom in La Grande. Liysa pleaded not guilty to murder charges, but Judge Mendiguren denied bail. Although she couldn't see them, she was heartened to hear that her family and volunteers from the Safe Harbor shelter for abused women were present in the courtroom to lend their support.

"She seemed to be very scared when she was first booked in," a female corrections officer in the Union County Jail recalled. "But most people are. *I* never seemed to see her the way she was portrayed as vulnerable and anxious. I thought she was a pretty 'together' person, even with her circumstances."

The corrections officer said that Liysa was slightly bruised when she came in and had a black eye and a few scratches. "I cannot say if the bruises were consistent with the attack she claimed happened," she said. "I am not an expert. I would have thought, however, that she would have had more injuries than she had."

Throughout her stay in the Union County Jail, Liysa stood out as being "very bright," and she seemed to love her children deeply. "She was one of the best female inmates that I have dealt with," the corrections officer recalled. "She never whined or complained about anything. She is the only female inmate I ever witnessed writing to her children every day. Large letters—sometimes ten to twenty pages."

But there were other aspects of Liysa's behavior that struck her guard as atypical. She had seen scores of women who had suffered from domestic violence come into jail and found they had fairly predictable patterns. "Even women in abusive situations will talk about the man they fell in love with initially, or even how they still loved them," she said. "But Liysa never spoke of *any* good times with Chris Northon. Personally, I don't think she had any love for him, but married him out of convenience. But that's just my opinion."

Perhaps the corrections officer's supposition was right, although Liysa's letters begging Chris to marry her warred with that. Still, it is certainly true that most women locked up without men tend to remember the sweetest side of the men they once loved. B movies linger over scenes of women in prison garb, sobbing when they hear lyrics from blues songs like "He Was My Man—but He Done Me Wrong." In the Union County Jail, Liysa spoke almost lovingly about Nick, her second husband, but she had only negative things to say about Chris.

* * *

CONTINUING THEIR INVESTIGATION into Liysa's case, Matt Cross and Pat Montgomery interviewed Nick Mattson on October 16. He said she had admitted to him that Chris became violent with her on their wedding night. In the years following, she had often complained that Chris was threatening her. Although Nick had found Chris to be "a nice guy" when they met, Liysa told him the opposite. Nick thought that maybe his son Papako was afraid of Chris. "I feel Liysa would have left him long ago," Nick offered, "but she didn't want to lose either of her children."

Possibly as conflicted as anyone about what the truth really was, Nick also called Jeanne and Dick Northon on October 16. He told Jeanne that Papako wanted to go to Chris's memorial services because he had loved him. But Liysa wouldn't allow it, and Papako didn't go.

IN JAIL, Liysa rapidly developed a new coterie of friends. Other female inmates were drawn to her and admired her. She listened to the stories of the younger women, many of whom had been through domestic abuse, some who were in jail because they'd been persuaded by boyfriends and lovers to participate in robberies or burglaries. They gravitated to her just like the women who had once shared pregnancy and delivery classes with her in Hawaii.

Many of the female corrections officers felt sorry for her, and one male officer went out of his way to be protective. Liysa's acceptance in jail was almost unanimous. As Randy Ore once said, "She made a wonderful first impression." Although it sounds odd, Liysa was one of the most popular inmates the Union County Jail had ever housed.

One of her fellow prisoners, a young woman who was in jail for assault, was booked in a day before Liysa, and she noticed that Liysa had written reminders on her hand. The words read, "Keep your mouth shut!" and "Don't talk."

"My lawyer told me that," Liysa said with a smile.

"But she talked to everyone anyway," the young woman said. "Liysa told me her husband was always checking on her if she didn't come home on time, and he accused her of having an affair. She said he held her head underwater and she had shot at him to get away.

"She was shocked to learn her husband was dead—but she didn't seem sorry," the young woman remembered. "She told me that one split second can change your life forever. . . ."

Another prisoner looked upon Liysa as a mother figure. She

and her boyfriend were awaiting trial for shooting at a law enforcement officer. She and Liysa shared a cell for three weeks. The girl was pregnant and Liysa was very solicitous of her.

"She told me what to eat and stuff that was good for me—and what was bad," the girl said.

Liysa also told her how she had suffered at the hands of her "ex-husband," and the way she had gone limp in the river when he choked her and allowed herself to just "float away." She spoke of fearing for her children for a long time. She said that once when Chris was feeding Bjorn, the baby bit him on the finger and Chris tried to kick him. "I covered the baby with my own body to protect him and *I* got kicked," Liysa said.

As for Chris's shooting, Liysa recalled now that she had been running backward when she fired at him, but she had no idea if she'd hit him.

Many of the wives of Chris's longtime friends wrote to her, more out of grim curiosity about how she could have shot him than out of friendship. But they were careful not to alienate her because they were very concerned about what would happen to Papako and Bjorn. It wasn't a question of there being no place for the boys to go while their mother was in jail; it was that so many people wanted to take care of them. Liysa still had her own group of Oregon friends, women who were involved with the private school Papako attended and others she'd known for decades.

Papako was okay for the moment with his father. It was Bjorn who needed someone. Liysa detested Dick and Jeanne Northon, and looked down her nose at his sisters, Mary and Sally, who had marital troubles of their own. She pondered over which of her friends should have him for what she assumed would be only a matter of weeks, or at the most, a few months. Eva and John Gill offered to take Bjorn, and so did Joe and Maggie Wilson. Dave and Debbie Story felt he would be happiest with them because Dave and Bjorn had bonded just as Dave and Chris had. The Gills were in Oregon, the Wilsons in Stockton, California, and the Storys in Kailua.

But Liysa didn't want any of Chris's friends to have Bjorn. Her high school friend Marni Clark was looking after him until Liysa selected a temporary home for him. She finally decided that the best choice among *her* friends would be Cal and Kit Minton, who also lived near Kailua. Kit Minton was one of her closest friends and, like Chris, Cal was an airline pilot.

If Bjorn went to the Mintons, he could see Papako, and Liysa trusted Kit implicitly to keep any secrets they might have shared. Kit was definitely on Liysa's side about the abuse. She readily agreed to look after Bjorn, even though she had young children of her own.

Liysa granted the Mintons a special durable power of attorney so they could make decisions about Bjorn, and Tor DeWitt flew with Bjorn to Oahu to deliver the little boy to them. Bjorn was too young to understand how much his world had changed. At first, it seemed normal to him to have his father away because Chris's job meant he was gone on trips to far-off places half the time. But he was used to having his mother around; she was still breast-feeding him. That was an argument she had used in asking to be released from jail. She always called him "the baby" or "baby Bjorn," as if she wanted to keep him an infant instead of a little boy on his way to being self-sufficient. He was three and a half and as highly intelligent as Papako. Now Liysa's hovering maternal style only made it more difficult for Bjorn. And Papako was going through a similar confusion.

John and Eva Gill flew to Hawaii and visited with Bjorn at the Mintons' house. Eva wrote to Liysa and assured her that Bjorn was doing as well as could be expected, and Liysa wrote back, thanking Eva profusely for being in touch. Eva and John wanted so much to have Bjorn with them; it would be something they could do for Chris. And so Eva strived to remain on good terms with Liysa, who, even behind bars, still controlled so many lives.

In her letters to Eva, to Maggie Wilson, and to Phil Hetz, her former brother-in-law, Liysa stressed that none of them had ever seen *both* of Chris's personalities. She pointed out to Eva that the Gills had seen only the "great side of Chris," when in fact he had had a "Jekyll/Hyde" personality. Liysa assured Eva, who was such a protective mother, that she would have done just as Liysa did—*anything* it took to save her children from a malignant force.

Eva and John didn't believe it, not for a moment. Liysa's letters painted Chris jet-black. He was capable of things the Gills could never have imagined. Besides unleashing his fury when they were alone in their homes, according to Liysa, he was a perverted personality whom she once found passed out drunk in front of their computer. Liysa said she'd been horrified when she hit the "go back" arrow to find "site after site of pornography—some homosexual, some kids. . . . It was shortly after that that our computers were 'mysteriously' stolen," Liysa wrote.

The computers stolen from the Bend house had never been recovered. Now Liysa was suggesting that Chris had gotten rid of them to hide his addiction to pornography—or even to hurt her in the worst way he could—by destroying all her work.

Liysa was distraught and impatient as she told Eva that she had "no idea" how the legal system worked and decried that it was not "logical."

WISELY, LIYSA "LAWYERED UP," retaining one of the top criminal defense attorneys in Oregon, Pat Birmingham, whose offices were in Portland. Birmingham resembled a tintype of an old-time attorney. He had prematurely white hair and a bounteous handlebar mustache. His eyes were like an eagle's—slightly hooded and piercing. He was a very, very good lawyer. Later, Birmingham would be joined by Wayne Mackeson, who had wavy brown hair and a wide friendly smile. The two lawyers were often called "Mutt and Jeff" by their peers—even though they were about the same height—because Birmingham did most of the courtroom questioning and Mackeson did the research.

To retain attorneys who were in so much demand, Liysa had no choice but to sell her house in Kailua. She had wanted *more* property, and now it galled her to realize that her most viable asset was her house with a view of the Mokolua Islands, this pied-à-terre that meant so much to her. But neither her father nor her brother had the means to pay a top-notch lawyer for the billing hours it would take to prepare for a murder trial, and then defend a client three hundred miles across the state from Portland. Pat Birmingham agreed to represent her for $200 an hour or a flat fee of $100,000—with the understanding that he would also need money for defense expenses, which would include transporting witnesses to the little town of Enterprise and hiring forensic experts. It was a lot of money, but compared to the defense of a truly high-profile murder defendant in most jurisdictions, it was a legal bargain.

The two Portland lawyers soon began conferring with Liysa as they researched her case. She had a telephone in her cell and was able to call Birmingham every day, and either he or Mackeson—or both—would eventually travel across the state for more than forty hours of in-person talks with her prior to her trial.

Liysa gave Birmingham essentially the same version of the night of October 9 that she had told to Deputy Dick Bobbitt and Deputy Sheriff Kevin Larkin. However, in this retelling, she wasn't holding Bjorn as she ran by the sleeping bag. She said Bjorn was sleeping in the tent because he had the sniffles and she'd given him some cold medication to help him sleep. As she raced past Chris, she recalled now that she held the sack with the bullets in one hand and extended her other arm as she fired. She'd meant only to hit the bag to "warn" Chris not to follow her.

"I didn't intend to *hit* Chris," she said. She'd shouted that she was leaving with the baby and gone to the tent to get Bjorn, who hadn't wakened at the sound of the shot. Her only thought was to get to Ellen Duveaux's house and to file assault charges against Chris for trying to drown and choke her.

Birmingham consulted with a dozen experts on the "battered woman syndrome," and read as many research papers on the problem that has become so pervasive in America. He found that few women had actually been acquitted with this defense, although some had their murder charges reduced to manslaughter.

Perhaps more enlightening reading was the thousand-plus pages Liysa herself had written: short stories, letters, manuscripts, and screenplays, provided to Birmingham through discovery by the State. There was a central, repetitive theme that troubled him. In the screenplay Liysa had discussed with Phil Hetz, the abusive husband was shot in the temple with a speargun that the main female character had hidden under a towel.

She had written of another woman, also abused by her husband, who fantasized about shooting him in the temple as he slept. Indeed, the character hated her husband so much that she visualized a bull's-eye on the side of his head whenever she looked at him. Yet another fictional spouse succumbed to a murderous wife who smashed his head in with a rock. And one female character had electrocuted her husband with a stun gun while he was in a Jacuzzi. Aware that the State also had copies of Liysa's almost stream-of-consciousness writing, Birmingham had to wonder if any of this would play well as part of a battered woman defense.

Mackeson and Birmingham asked Liysa if she had any life insurance policies on Chris and she said no. She told the same thing to the defense investigators. They were to discover later that there *was* a large policy on Chris. Liysa explained that away by saying that Bjorn was the sole beneficiary. However, Birmingham found that it was Liysa who was the primary beneficiary, and she was paying the premiums.

Liysa's defense demanded a great deal of research and multiple court appearances. Indeed, Birmingham would record 847 hours of preparation. He encouraged her to assist in her own case, although he often became frustrated because Liysa could not resist discussing the facts of her case and the legal theories that her lawyers developed by brainstorming, with the guards, her family, friends, nurses, and counselors, and even other inmates in the jail.

With Pat Birmingham beside her, Liysa first stood before Circuit Court Judge Philip A. Mendiguren in La Grande in November. She had never imagined that she might still be behind bars on Thanksgiving, with her sons thousands of miles away. But she was.

IN HER VOLUMINOUS CORRESPONDENCE from jail, Liysa even wrote to Craig Elliot, giving him helpful criticism on some of his screenplays, and sounding pleased that their relationship had transformed itself into a solid friendship that could survive even the murder charges against her. She told him that her children were the greatest "opus" of her life, and that she felt "artificial" without them.

Liysa's attorney had requested that she be able to leave the Union County Jail, and Dan Ousley argued against that. A section of Oregon statute 135.240 goes against the release of prisoners charged with murder, aggravated murder, and treason—if there is a strong presumption that the defendant is guilty. Ousley cited Columbia County Deputy Kevin Larkin's police report on his interview with Liysa.

Somewhat bizarrely, both the State and the defense offered the same police reports to support their arguments, but then the case would always be built upon a matter of inference. Liysa had shot Chris because she was a battered woman *or* she had shot him because she wanted to be free of him.

At the end of the short hearing, Judge Mendiguren denied bail for Liysa, saying that there was overwhelming evidence to support the charges of murder against her.

She spent Christmas in jail, too, but she was flooded with mail and holiday cards with photos of her friends and their happy children sitting on sleds or near Christmas trees. It was heartbreaking for her to be shut off from her sons, and so many people felt sorry for Liysa.

CHAPTER TWENTY-SEVEN

THE PHYSICAL EVIDENCE from the death scene was piling up. Most of it looked as if it had come from a well-organized family camping trip: ice chests, a camp stove, plastic totes, fishing gear, the tent, adults' and children's shoes, blankets. But then there was also the gun, the Taurus model 85, the bullet that Lieutenant Jeff Dovci had found in the sand beneath Chris's body, the spent casings, the unfired rounds. There was also the miner's light, meant to be worn on an elastic band around the head, found on the path where Liysa said she had run past Chris and fired in the dark.

How dark had it been? In the early hours of October 9, 2000, the moon was only four days away from being completely full. Even in the shadow of the mountain, it probably wasn't pitch-dark.

Strangely, the keys to Chris's SUV were missing. So was his cell phone. After the autopsy, the blue mummy bag had been hung up so the blood-soaked layers would dry, and Dovci had noted that the velocity of the slug had driven it through the down from the sleeping bag, then through the foam pad and the tarp beneath, ending two inches into the sandy beach.

After Chris's Chevrolet Suburban was processed, it had been released to Dick Northon. He didn't realize that the foam sleeping pad and tarp were still in it. When he did see the items there in the evidence bag, he didn't touch them, sickened by the dark, dried bloodstains. He returned them to the State Police. They *had* slipped outside the chain of evidence, but there was no way the two items could have been tampered with; each had a single hole that matched the holes in the sleeping bag.

* * *

THERE WAS NO QUESTION that Liysa had fired the single fatal shot at Chris. The real question was her motivation. If Chris's former girlfriends validated that he'd been physically rough on them, Liysa's claim of self-defense would probably hold up in court. Pat Montgomery hadn't known either Chris or Liysa. He had to learn as much as he could about both of them.

Chris's friends didn't believe that Liysa had shot him out of fear that she and Bjorn were in physical danger. They insisted that Chris adored Bjorn and believed that he had never hit a woman in his life. Certainly, they had watched as the Northons' marriage wound down, and seen Chris bounce between his concern over Liysa's bizarre behavior and his hope that they would somehow make it through after all. Now old conversations and incidents came back to them.

Pat Montgomery had talked to Rob Ezell in Bend three days after Chris's death. Rob had gone to high school with Chris in 1975 and had spent a lot of time with him since 1989, when Rob moved back to Bend. "I taught him how to fly-fish," Rob said. "Chris and Bjorn would come fishing with me, but Liysa never participated. They didn't do things together."

However, Rob said that he liked Liysa and had met her about a dozen times during her marriage to Chris. Chris often bragged about what a good mother she was, and a talented photographer who made money to help cover their bills. But Chris always seemed worried about staying away from home too long when he was out with his male friends. "I need to go home and make my wife happy," he would say.

"She was very jealous of Chris," Rob said, "and she didn't want him to spend time with his friends. If we called him, Liysa always said she would give him the message, but the next time we saw him, it turned out he never got our messages. It was like she didn't want him to spend time with anyone but her."

"Did you ever see marks or bruises on Liysa?" Montgomery asked, a question he would repeat at least fifty times to different people. "Did Chris have a temper?"

Rob shook his head. "Chris is real laid-back—he didn't get excited about anything. One time, he was driving and another car cut us off and was driving all over the road. I was upset, but Chris remained calm. He said it was no big deal."

"Did he drink heavily?"

"He was an average drinker—like after fishing all day—but it never made him lose control or turn mean."

"How about watching porno on the Internet?"

Rob looked bewildered. He'd never heard of such an accusation about Chris.

Rob said that Chris wanted to spend as much time as he could with Bjorn, and he seemed to have "nothing but love" for both Bjorn and Papako. "If we went to the park, it was Chris who was watching the kids and chasing after them if they got out of sight."

Asked to describe Liysa, Rob characterized her as being a

"very deep person with many different interests." He'd found her independent, a woman able to take care of herself. "She even went through some kind of S.E.A.L. training." He said the idea of "poor little Liysa" was wrong. That didn't describe her at all. She always seemed in complete charge of her life.

"Look," Rob told Pat Montgomery, "Chris was a really nice guy and I don't believe that he could do anything to provoke anyone to do what Liysa did. He had a zest for life, and he wouldn't get down when negative things were going on around him. If their relationship was bad, I can see him throwing up his arms and saying, 'Enough is enough—and *I am out of here!*' He'd probably say something like, 'You take the house in Hawaii, and I'll take the house in Bend,' but he wouldn't hurt anyone."

"When was the last time you saw him?"

Rob Ezell looked down. "I saw him on his birthday last month. He was having dinner with Liysa and the kids at Honker's Restaurant. I stopped by to wish him a happy birthday, and everything seemed to be fine. He was opening his presents and they both seemed happy. . . ."

Pat Montgomery interviewed a number of Chris's associates in October. He asked Dave Story, Arne Arnesen, and Joe Wilson to make a list of all of Chris's former girlfriends, and they'd known him so well that Montgomery was soon armed with a number of names. Joe Wilson recalled that Chris had never had "a woman in every port," even though he had been single for twenty-two years of his adult life, and he had always gotten along with women.

There was a long list of former girlfriends. Dave Jones remembered a woman named "Kat," who was a flight attendant for Delta. Joe said her name was Katherine Wellington and she was based in Los Angeles, but her father had lived in Konaloi. She was an African American woman, coolly beautiful. She and

Chris had dated in 1994 and 1995. There was Anna, of course, whom Joe said Chris always referred to as "the special girl whom he let get away."

There was also Kelly Coffey from Tennessee, with whom Chris had a three-year relationship between 1987 and 1990. Chris met Kelly when she was traveling through Australia, and she took him up on his invitation to call if she ever got to Hawaii. "They had a good relationship," Joe recalled. "A very nice relationship."

Kelly lived on Maui for several years, but then she moved back to Tennessee, became involved in politics, and she and Chris gradually stopped calling.

And, of course, there were Sabrina and Gay Bradshaw.

Chris had enjoyed a great time as a bachelor, but as far as Joe knew, none of the women he'd been with had a bad word to say about him. "Chris liked women," Joe said, "and they liked him."

Montgomery went to Portland to talk to Sabrina Tedford, the last woman Chris had dated before he met Liysa. Tears filled her eyes as she answered his questions. It was obvious she was brokenhearted that Chris was dead.

"We dated in 1989," she said, "but I'd known him for twenty-six years. We got together again six years ago."

"How did he treat you?" Montgomery asked.

"He was wonderful to me," Sabrina said. "He liked and respected women."

"What kind of a drinker was he?"

"Moderate. I only saw him drink too much on one occasion, and then it just seemed to make him happier. Chris didn't get upset or angry about things most people do."

"When did you see him last?" Montgomery asked.

"Two years ago in Bend. His wife was in Hawaii for two weeks, and he was taking care of his little boy—Bjorn."

"That was one of the hardest interviews I ever did," Montgomery recalled. "Sabrina really loved Chris, and she was broken up over his death."

Joe Wilson's wife, Maggie, called Pat Montgomery and asked if she could speak to him. She had come to La Grande to visit Liysa in jail, and to offer their help in caring for Bjorn until the case was resolved. "Liysa said she'd already made other arrangements for him."

Maggie was obviously troubled. Her husband, Joe, of course, had known Chris for many years when they shared rentals, and Maggie herself had known Chris and Liysa for about five and a half years. "Liysa and I talked while we were all still dating," she said. "Her relationship with Chris wasn't good—even before they were married. She told me that he was mean and always yelling. But she gave him an ultimatum that if he didn't marry her in six months, she was gone. He gave in."

Maggie said that Liysa had been "obsessed" with Chris's old girlfriends—with his life before her. "I tried to talk to her, but it seemed as though she was angry from the beginning. She'd swear me—or Joe—to secrecy and then she'd tell us about their fights—verbal fights. It was so hard because we'd promised not to talk to Chris about it. She wanted him to drop his whole lifestyle and stop doing most of the things he enjoyed, and he would sometimes say that he'd told her before they were married that there were things he liked to do, but she was trying to change him."

"Did you ever see marks and bruises on Liysa?" Montgomery asked.

"*No!*" Maggie said vehemently. "Life in Hawaii was so casual. We never wore makeup and we saw each other every day at their house or on the beach. She never had any bruises on her."

Initially, when Liysa had described Chris as a "raging alcoholic," Maggie and Joe Wilson had stared at her, surprised. "I'd seen him drink socially—but not like that," Maggie said. "I've never seen him drunk or showing any kind of mood swing. If he drank, he just got sleepy. Liysa described a Chris we didn't know and have never seen."

"Once she brought this to our attention, we did watch Chris *like hawks,* and we *still* didn't see what she was talking about. He never said a bad thing about her. And if *we* said anything about Liysa's behavior, he always said, 'She's having a hard time,' and left it at that."

But Maggie had noted that Liysa enjoyed saying things that upset Chris. "She pushed his buttons and that was what she liked—the *intense Chris.* She smiled when she was talking about that."

Maggie explained that Liysa was a woman of independent means who traveled all over the Pacific Islands taking photographs on important assignments. "She had the ability, knowledge, and experience to pick up and move on. She would think nothing of just getting on a plane and going somewhere else to live. If she wanted to get away from Chris, she could have just taken off to one of the islands and disappeared. And he would have let her go without any problems—but he would have looked for Bjorn. He and Bjorn were always together."

Once, when Chris was in Texas for training, Liysa and Papako had attended a wedding of friends in Hawaii. "She wore a long fancy dress—but no shoes—to the wedding," Maggie recalled. "She talked to me all night and was pounding down one hard drink after the next. The whole time, she was saying what an 'asshole' Chris was. The next day she called me and said that Chris had called her and everything was fine and I should forget about everything she said about him."

Maggie recalled how Liysa had tried to isolate Chris from his old friends and his parents. "When we first met her, she seemed very low-key, sweet, and nice. After we got to know her, we realized she was mixed up with a lot of other emotions. And she didn't want us in Chris's life."

"She would never say she loved him, and she didn't seem happy with him. The only thing she said was how great the sex was, and that she had never had sex with anyone as good."

"She didn't seem afraid?" Montgomery pressed, having heard about Liysa's obsession with sex before.

"No. I never saw her talk or act like she was afraid—only angry."

Montgomery was getting totally opposite evaluations of the kind of man Chris had been—from Liysa's statements and then from Chris's friends. But he knew that men tended to treat the women in their lives in predictable ways. All too often, abused women learn that the men they are with have demonstrated rage to their previous girlfriends or wives. But women in love rarely check references—especially not with ex-wives.

Oregon State Police investigator Rob Ringsage, who was stationed in Bend, helped interview Chris and Liysa's acquaintances. He talked to Don Strain, the handyman who had done several jobs for Chris. Don told Ringsage that he was surprised about the October camping trip. Chris had already made plans with Don to paint the newly finished storage shed on the weekend of October 7 and 8. "He had a week off and he wanted to get that done before winter."

Don Strain had learned otherwise. Liysa had come out on the deck while Chris was on a flight and informed him that her family would be camping that weekend. "You can go ahead and paint," she said, "as long as it's dry before I get back. I can't stand the smell of it—it makes me sick."

Don said that Chris was "dumbfounded" when he got home and learned his plans had been changed. "I told him I'd paint the shed by myself," the handyman said, "but I could see that Chris didn't know anything about going camping. He finally said, 'Well, if Liysa says we're going camping, then we probably are.' "

Ringsage also interviewed a woman who was vehement about how badly Liysa had suffered during her marriage to Chris. Mia Rose said she had met Liysa in 1999 through the private school where they both had children attending. Mia felt that Chris had never wanted to socialize with her and her ex-husband, Billy Shamir*. "He was very standoffish." But she found Liysa very warm and friendly.

Mia and Billy, who led a Bend religious organization that was well out of the mainstream, had remained good friends after their divorce. He assured Liysa that counseling was part of his calling, and he visited her in Hawaii in the waning days of summer, 2000. She spent hours telling him about her smothering marriage, how she had realized early on that Chris was repressing her talents, although she didn't mention that she had felt the same way about Nick Mattson. "When I needed to be out shooting photos, Chris wouldn't look after our children," she said. "So I had to cancel shoots. I thought of leaving him after Bjorn was born."

"Why didn't you?" Billy asked.

"He would have killed me. I just had to hide the marks and bruises and try to explain his verbal abuse to the kids. He strangled me once, you know. My father was so worried about me that he gave me a gun."

Less than a month before Chris's death, Liysa confided to Mia that she was living with violent domestic abuse. She bemoaned her mistake in not getting to know Chris better before she married him. She had found out too late that Chris had beaten and terrorized the women he'd dated. While Liysa told Mia all this in the Northons' home in Bend, she was crying, afraid that Chris might come home and suspect she had been talking about him.

"She told me he beat her once because he thought she'd told someone what he was doing to her," Mia said. But when she asked her if anyone had ever witnessed his abuse, Liysa said Chris was too smart for that. "She said he'd slapped her across the face recently and when she asked him why, he said, 'It's the way you looked at me.' "

Both Mia Rose and Billy Shamir were convinced that Liysa was desperately afraid, that Chris had, indeed, warned her that if she ever tried to leave, he would find her and kill her. He would drive off cliffs, set fire to their house, even kill them and eat them. Liysa said that she might have a chance if she had only Papako—but she knew that Chris wouldn't let her take Bjorn, and she was afraid to give him custody. "She said he was always threatening to kill the kids."

Liysa told Mia that she had asked an attorney what she should do and been told she had only two options: "Flee the country, or kill Chris in self-defense."

By September 2000, Liysa had convinced Mia Rose and Billy Shamir that she was married to a monster. She couldn't flee because all Chris would have to do was put her picture on the Internet and offer a $5,000 reward. "I wouldn't last ten minutes."

But when they offered to help her, Liysa begged them, as she exhorted all of her friends, to stay away. She didn't want Chris or the police to know she'd told anyone. It would just make her life worse. "I think the police are connected to Chris's family in some way," she whispered. "They never do anything to him. They wouldn't help me."

It was Mia who had given Liysa KoKo for protection, but even that had apparently brought on stress. Liysa told her that Chris had threatened to kill the dog, and that he kicked it when he walked by. That story was passed from one of her friends to another. And so were other confidences. Liysa said Chris was terribly jealous of her career as a surfing photographer and cinematographer, and that he was always trying to sabotage her work. He didn't like the way she dressed when she was working and he'd once torn her bathing suit off. As Mia had listened in rapt horror, Liysa pulled at her loosely fitting clothing and said, "Why do you think I dress like this?"

Liysa had tried so hard to keep her abject terror from her family, Mia explained, but she had finally told her father and brother. Apparently, Wayland DeWitt had compared Chris to prisoners he'd visited in the Walla Walla penitentiary and stated flatly that Chris was "as dangerous as anyone in the penitentiary is."

"Liysa said her family refers to Chris as 'Ted Bundy,' " Mia Rose told the Oregon State Police detective.

According to Liysa, Mia said, Chris had once assaulted a flight attendant while they were in the air. Another flight attendant had actually recognized Liysa's last name on one flight and told her, "Oh, honey—I pray for him every day . . . the devil has his soul."

Ringsage took notes on Mia's recitation of the dangerousness of Chris Northon, all of it derived from Liysa herself. When Mia had talked to her in jail, and Liysa told her how Chris had dragged her down to the river and held her head underwater; during the struggle, Liysa had gone into a "different state of mind" and somehow found the strength to free herself. Now, whenever she spoke to Mia on the phone, Liysa repeated her mantra: "At least my boys are safe."

Surprisingly, Mia, too, had known that Liysa had a gun, and that she took the gun on the camping trip to the Lostine River—a trip that Chris had insisted upon. Liysa said she'd had no choice but to go.

"Where did she keep the gun at home?" Ringsage asked.

"She said in the garage, where he wouldn't find it."

Mia said Liysa had given up on her own chances of survival and had bought a big insurance policy so that her sons would have an income they could count on.

More and more of Liysa's friends and family knew that she had a gun, but no one ever thought of letting the police know.

Every new interview seemed to make the case more complicated. Had Liysa shot her husband in a last desperate attempt to defend herself and three-year-old Bjorn? Or had she cold-bloodedly shot him because she hated him?

——— CHAPTER TWENTY-EIGHT ———

LIYSA REMAINED in the Union County Jail, writing stories for her sons, sending out massive correspondence—and receiving as much—visiting with her jailers, her fellow inmates, her father, and her brother. She seemed very gentle, almost a martyr for domestic violence. She, who had been accustomed to having complete freedom to come and go as she pleased, was no longer free, and her agitation about being locked up was serious enough that a jail doctor prescribed drugs—Paxil and Neurontin—to help quiet her anxiety. She worried constantly about Papako and Bjorn. She sometimes had panic attacks, and sympathetic corrections officers sat with her until she was calmer. She explained that she was "reliving" how Chris had stalked her as she hid in the tent with Bjorn. Her whole body shook and her teeth chattered.

Her days in jail dragged on and it became apparent that Liysa might not be released until her trial. Although she hated jail and called the fenced-off exercise yard "The Kennel," she continued to get along well with her jailers and the other prisoners. They found *her* "awesome."

* * *

ON NOVEMBER 7, 2000, five weeks after Chris Northon's death, the election to choose a sheriff of Wallowa County was held and a new regime began. Ron Jett had chosen not to run again, Rich Stein, the undersheriff who found Chris's body, lost his bid for sheriff to Fred Steen, and Matt Cross, the head county detective on the Northon case, resigned, regretting that he would not see the end of the investigation. His new wife worried too much when he was out on night patrol, and they decided to set up a small business together in Enterprise.

When the old guard changed, the investigation into Chris Northon's death slipped into the background for a while. It *was,* however, desperately important to Oregon State Police Detective Pat Montgomery and D.A. Dan Ousley. They both had a gut feeling that something wasn't right in Liysa Northon's statements about spousal abuse. It didn't matter how many women stood behind Liysa Northon, something was—in police parlance—"hinky."

Ousley agreed with Montgomery that they were a long way from being ready for trial. In fact, neither side was prepared to go to court. There were so many potential witnesses, and they were spread across thousands of miles, far away from the serene little town of Enterprise.

Dan Ousley had gone over to the sheriff's office and asked for the file on Chris Northon's death. He pored over it again and again, scrutinizing it for chinks in the facade of the sweet wife who'd been brutalized by the cruel husband. He found some tentative cracks, but he also realized that there was still a lot of legwork to be done. And there was no question that they needed help. Ousley put in a request to Oregon Attorney General, Hardy Myers, whose offices were in Salem, asking for assistance in the State's case against Liysa Northon.

Myers assigned Assistant Attorney General Steve Briggs to the case, and Briggs requested the help of Dennis Dinsmore, a criminal investigator in the attorney general's office.

Steve Briggs was barely thirty, but for court appearances, he wore near pince-nez glasses, which added years and authority to his mien. Briggs graduated from Dartmouth College and then from the University of Oregon Law School. He'd been an assistant district attorney in Washington County, Oregon, for three years before he moved to the Oregon Department of Justice as an assistant attorney general.

Briggs looked like a long-distance runner, but it was Dennis Dinsmore, two decades older, who *was* the runner, even though he didn't look like it. Briggs was a backpacker and a mountain climber, when he had the time. But with a new baby in their household, he and his wife, Marla, had little time for camping trips.

Briggs and Dinsmore, whose wife was named Marlene, worked well together in investigating and trying cases.

* * *

PAT MONTGOMERY CONTINUED to follow up every lead he could, but the crime site itself was gone. Snow covered the Shady Campground and clogged the road leading to the trailhead into the mountains. The place where Chris Northon had died was literally cut off by snowdrifts from midfall until spring. They probably couldn't even go to trial until the snowpack melted. If any jury wanted to view the crime scene, someone would have to persuade the Forest Service to open the road with a snowplow. Even then, it would be dangerous to try to get twelve jurors and several alternates up there.

But a trial did lie ahead. Dan Ousley was in his second term as the district attorney of Wallowa County, and he had chosen Enterprise because he liked the lifestyle there. He'd really never expected to be prosecuting a case so different from the usual felonies and misdemeanors that came across his desk. Thus far, he had prosecuted one homicide case—an uncomplicated one. His sisters, Kathleen Erskine, a federal judge, and Patty Ousley, a registered nurse who was the head of Emergency Medical Technicians' training for King County, both preferred the more fast-paced ambiance of Seattle.

Dan's wife, Lisa, had spent twenty years in Germany, and the mountains and lakes of Wallowa County were reminiscent of that country. The Ousleys lived in a big house only a short walk from the courthouse, and their lives revolved around music, running, and the law. Lisa was active in the Chautauqua Program, played the violin, and was just starting to learn western fiddling. Dan banged the Irish drum, and they both were participants in the musicales held in the bandstand on the courthouse lawn. Dan had been the volunteer cross-country coach at Enterprise High School for eight years, and he always ran in the 10K Lostine River Run.

The old courthouse in Enterprise, where there was a fire siren—but no bell—in the tower, hadn't changed much in a hundred years, and Dan Ousley's office was up the steep steps to the second floor of the building. The furniture was time-weathered oak, including a tall cabinet with dozens of narrow drawers that had held records from eighty years before anyone ever envisioned such a thing as a computer.

Tall windows looked down on the flower beds below. There were legal files on Ousley's desk, but there was also a fragment of a bright blue robin's egg and a miniature glass Volkswagen. A couple of shotguns—unloaded—leaned against the wall, evidence left over from a recent trial. The courtroom where Liysa Northon would be tried for murder was across the hall, an expansive room that looked like a soundstage for a Gary Cooper movie set in the 1890s.

Pat Montgomery's office in the Oregon State Police station

in La Grande was more modern, but with a population of 12,000, La Grande is a big city compared to Enterprise, and an hour's drive away if the weather is good. Still, far eastern Oregon is so different from the coast, just as eastern Washington is dissimilar to Seattle. The tempo is slower east of the mountains, the seasons more defined, and the air sweeter, redolent with the smell of alfalfa in spring and sunburned wheat at summer's end.

That doesn't necessarily mean that there are no violent crimes in the little towns beyond the passes. Human emotions don't change just by crossing towering mountains. A certain percentage of the population of any town or city is going to act out violently; it was just that there were far fewer people in Enterprise and La Grande.

Pat Montgomery had graduated from the Oregon College of Education over on the coast in Monmouth in 1972, and he worked as a counselor at the state penitentiary in Salem for eighteen months. He was good at that; he had a soft voice and was a sensitive, intuitive listener. He learned a lot about the psyches of criminals in that job, but what he really wanted as a young man was to be a state trooper who was "outside, pulling people in."

He joined the Oregon State Police in La Grande and worked on patrol for six or seven years. And then he moved up and became a criminal investigator. Over the next three decades, Montgomery worked every kind of criminal case there was. Ironically, he came full circle. His ability to listen and understand people was perhaps his strongest tool as a detective. He was the investigator in his territory who worked child abuse cases.

"Abusers love to talk," he said with a faint smile. "You can make a difference in a kid's life. You can't help all of them, but some of them you can."

Montgomery was really happy with his job. He was never

tempted to take a test for a higher rank because he liked the investigative part of it. Union and Wallowa counties were his areas, but often he would be called out to surrounding counties, too. He was most astute at deductive reasoning, looking at a case from every angle and never coming to a conclusion until he had weighed all the variables.

Montgomery's enthusiasm for his job was catching. His daughter joined the Oregon State Police as a trooper. Lisa Sater had been with the department for seven years.

Now Pat Montgomery and Dan Ousley would be the initial core of the probe into the shooting of Chris Northon.

But not for long. By early December 2000, another new partnership was formed, one that would prove to be a natural. Dennis Dinsmore and Pat Montgomery had both come up through the ranks of police work, but they faced a daunting job. They were prepared for it. Compared to a lot of detectives working in Oregon, they were "old cops" with sixty years of experience between them. Dinsmore, like Montgomery, had investigated dozens of homicide cases, some slam dunks and some that almost defied solution. They had both worked one-man cars where backup was too far away to count on, and each of them had been intrigued with investigative work. Their knowledge came from a baptism by fire working murder cases.

"What I didn't think of," Dinsmore said, "Pat thought of. We just worked together perfectly because we had all that experience behind us. We kind of thought as one person."

Dennis Dinsmore had been captivated by police work from the time he was twelve. He'd found a "big, giant book called *The G-Men*" in his junior high's library in Bandon, Oregon, and read it several times, but didn't really believe *he* could be a cop. After graduating as valedictorian of his class at Bandon High School and completing one year of college, he married young. Dinsmore was the first member of his family ever to *go* to college, but he didn't get to graduate. Instead, he went into the kind of work most people in his area did: a job in the sawmill in Eureka, California.

"Working in a sawmill wasn't that much fun," he recalled, "and I decided I was going to do what I'd always wanted to do. There was an opening in the sheriff's office in Humboldt County, and I hired on in 1971."

Like all California new hires, Dinsmore worked in the jail first, and then was assigned as a resident deputy in a substation smack in the middle of marijuana-growing country. "We worked alone. If you were on a paved road, you were an hour and a half from backup; if you were on a *back* road, you were on your own."

After several years with Humboldt County, Dinsmore returned to Oregon and worked his way up to detective in the Coos County Sheriff's Office. There, he had several run-ins with major fugitives who were passing through Oregon and handled an inordinately large number of homicides. One year, Coos County had fourteen murders, giving it the dubious distinction of having the highest homicide rate per capita in Oregon. Dinsmore got a lot of experience in ferreting out evidence and questioning witnesses to homicidal violence.

In 1994, he was hired by the Oregon State Attorney General's Office as an investigator. There were two units in the A.G.'s office—one to investigate organized crime, and the other to work "D.A. Assists." Dinsmore did both. There were usually fourteen investigators working at one time, most drawn from a pool of the top detectives in local agencies around Oregon.

Dinsmore kept a framed quotation from Ernest Hemingway on his office wall that indicated how much he loved his job:

There is no hunting like the hunting of man, and those who have hunted armed men long enough and liked it never care for anything else thereafter.

Now he and Pat Montgomery were, in essence, hunting an "armed woman," but it was much more difficult than the days when Dinsmore had been privy to the crime scene itself and able to observe evidence from the very beginning. As an A.G.'s investigator, he came in as a consultant and had to play catch-up weeks or months—sometimes years—after the crime had occurred.

CHAPTER TWENTY-NINE

LIYSA HAD NO CHOICE but to put her house on Lanipo Street on the market so that she could pay her attorneys and provide money for witness expenses. The house was worth well over $700,000, and she eventually sold it to Nick Mattson, at what she said was "$100,000 below its real value." Nick had bought this house once before, but he'd never lived in it because Liysa filed to divorce him almost before the ink on the real estate contract was dry. The Mattsons would finally move in on March 26, 2001.

When Liysa accepted that she was really going to trial for the murder of her husband, quite possibly something she had never visualized in any real sense, she stepped up her rhetoric to gain support. She had the best defense possible, but from the beginning, she had ignored Birmingham and Mackeson's requests that she not discuss her case with anyone but them. She continued to rely on her own intelligence and instincts to make the right choices, talking continually to anyone she wanted to, giving details about her relationship with Chris and the night he died to all who would listen. She wrote letters, too, either unaware or unconcerned that jailers could read all mail going out and coming in—with the exception of communication between a prisoner and her attorneys. Her "legal mail" to Birmingham consisted of 545 pages of letters, most of them written in her familiar small script on both sides of the page. She had strong opinions, concerns, and demands.

Liysa intended to testify in her own behalf—something that makes defense lawyers cringe. Birmingham and Mackeson assured her that the statements she had already given to deputies Dick Bobbitt and Kevin Larkin were more than adequate and it would be wiser not to take the witness stand, where she would be subject to cross-examination by the prosecution. But Liysa was not a malleable client. As she continued to butt heads with her attorneys, she was in danger of crippling their ability to defend her.

Her first trial date was set for March 5, 2001. By that time, there was a good chance that the snow in the Maxwell Campgrounds would melt and jurors could be taken to the crime scene on the Lostine River. And that would be important. Unless they saw the campsite with its two trails, narrow beach, and shallow, rushing river with their own eyes, it might be impossible for them to choose between the prosecutors' stance and the defense team's version of the night Chris died.

Liysa's lawyers asked for a delay. That was an expected first move, but it was more than that; until the house sale to Nick Mattson was closed, there were no funds to hire expert witnesses or to have lab tests done. Although she was eager to get the trial over with so she could be with her sons again, Liysa grudgingly agreed to resetting the date.

The job of a criminal defense attorney is, of course, to get the best possible result for his client. That is usually an acquittal, but in some cases, it can mean a life sentence rather than the death penalty. A defense attorney *does* need the truth from his client, however, even though he isn't going to tell anyone else.

Pat Birmingham and Wayne Mackeson advised Liysa that she must tell *them* the absolute truth, and made her aware that their investigators were working hard to validate her claims— not because they doubted her, but because they needed backup at the time of trial. She assured them that she was being honest with them.

To prepare for a homicide trial, the defense conducts its own investigation—one not so different from the State's. The last thing they want is a surprise rearing its ugly head in the midst of a trial. While a defense attorney hopes that his client is telling him the whole truth, few are so gullible that they believe without some confirmation.

Pat Birmingham and Wayne Mackeson relied on their own investigators, private detectives Harold Nash and Robin Karnes, who were most experienced in winnowing out the truth. They would either speak to or attempt to interview a hundred witnesses in eight states. The two defense attorneys also enlisted help from a firm with computer techniques that made locating witnesses and information far easier than it once was.

Oregon has a policy of reciprocal discovery: both the State and the defense technically have access to any information unearthed by the other side. But handing over hard-won information to the other team is never palatable. In most jurisdictions, only the State is required to show the defense team what cards the prosecutors are holding.

* * *

LIKE THE DEFENSE INVESTIGATORS, Pat Montgomery and Dennis Dinsmore needed the trial delay. They, too, planned to interview literally scores of people who had known either Chris or Liysa, or preferably *both*. If they talked to enough people, they might just shake out the truth. Montgomery had already begun the process, but there was much more work to be done.

Liysa's disciples remained steadfast. Mia Rose was still insistent that the Liysa she knew couldn't possibly have hurt her husband—not unless she was pushed to the wall trying to save

Bjorn. Ellen Duveaux, who had known Liysa for more than twenty years, was just as adamant that it was Liysa who'd been victimized by Chris, not the other way around.

On January 10, 2001, Pat Montgomery had sought out Phil Hetz, the insurance salesman who had once been married to Chris's sister Mary. He had a long history with both Liysa and Chris, but he wasn't actually a member of the family and might be able to give a less biased opinion on their marriage.

Phil, stunned at the news that Liysa had shot Chris, said he'd been close to both of them since before they were married. He and Chris shared a love of skiing and enjoyed being outdoors, but Phil had custody of his two sons by Mary, and he said he "couldn't keep up with a single guy."

"Liysa was very nice in the beginning," he recalled, "and she seemed to fit into the family." Because they were both "in-laws," Liysa tended to confide in Phil. She complained to him that Chris was physically abusive, although he personally had seen no evidence of that. "I told her if what she was telling me was true that she needed to leave Chris for the kids' sake, but she always said she wanted to save her marriage."

After the Bend incident when Liysa reported Chris to the police and he went briefly to jail, she had called Phil in a very emotional state. Again, he suggested that she leave—that this was the perfect time. "But she never did. Once she showed me a bruise on her arm, and I saw a red mark on her neck another time."

Phil Hetz recalled helping Liysa and Craig Elliot on their screenplay with his knowledge about insurance. "She was talking about being abused," he said, "but she was laughing. I thought it was weird that she would laugh it off."

During one of their "research meetings," Liysa had asked Phil if it would be possible to get insurance on someone without his knowledge. He shook his head. "Most companies wouldn't pay a beneficiary if the claim is based on illegal activity—and, besides, the companies require a physical exam before they'll issue a policy so the person would almost have to know."

Phil said he'd read part of Liysa's movie treatment and recalled that it was about a house on a beach in Santa Barbara, diving, and a strong female character who was "married to a womanizing asshole—whom she kills with a speargun."

Liysa had constantly berated Jeanne Northon to Phil, calling her a bad mother who had raised "a monster for a son," and ruined her children's lives. She had seemed intent on finding some skeleton in the Northons' closet that she could exploit. Phil allowed that the elder Northons had been, in his opinion, too easy on their three children, often letting them slip past house rules without the promised punishment, but nevertheless he found his former in-laws "great people."

Chris had stood by Phil when he and Mary got divorced, and soon Phil had made his peace with Jeanne and Dick, who had supported Mary. By 2000, the elder Northons often visited with him, and his two sons looked forward to vacationing at their grandparents' home.

Phil said that Chris had never complained about Liysa, although he would occasionally mention that there were some "difficulties" in his marriage. "He didn't bad-mouth her—ever—he'd just say she 'didn't understand.' "

"Did you buy her complaints about Chris hurting her?" Montgomery asked.

"Only once," he answered, "after the fight they had in Bend. The other times she talked about violence, it didn't seem real. She always told me to keep it confidential. I said I would if she would take care of herself—but she stayed with Chris, and she continued to complain about him."

Phil said he'd washed his hands of Liysa and stopped talking to her after she'd written him a letter from jail, in what he felt was an attempt to orchestrate what she wanted him to remember. She told him that she was slowly coming out of shock, and was concerned now about Phil's little boys. She didn't want them to remember Chris as totally bad, but they needed to understand that drugs and alcohol had turned him "evil."

"They need to know that Chris almost killed me and Bjorn and I did what I had to do to save our lives."

Liysa reminded Phil of their discussions about her fear of Chris as they sat in the Northons' hot tub. She urged him to recall her bruises. "*You* know the power of Dick and Jeanne's denial," she wrote. "Your loyalty may be divided and you have to just tell the truth."

Liysa stressed how worried she was about Phil and Mary's grade-school boys. She urged Phil to tell them that Chris had imbibed an entire fifth of vodka and used drugs, too. That had seemed inappropriate to Phil. But she continued, detailing the physical injuries from which she was healing, *as she explained she still couldn't get dressed without help.*

Phil told the detectives that Liysa had repeated the story of her near drowning and her assertion that Chris had done wicked things. "Chris was a [one-time] hippie who became responsible," he said sadly. "Chris was *always* responsible, especially to his work schedule and he didn't jeopardize that."

On January 17, Montgomery and Dinsmore went to Walla Walla to talk with the woman who probably knew Liysa better than anyone—her longtime friend Marni Clark. Over the last twenty-five years, Marni and Ellen Duveaux had been, perhaps, equally devoted to Liysa and concerned for her future.

Marni, the dark-eyed pixie who'd been a champion on the gymnastics team at Wa-Hi in 1979, was now an attorney, married to a physician. Liysa nicknamed Marni "Bear," and Papako and Bjorn called her "Aunt Bear." Now, as the investigators sat in Marni Clark's law offices, she was obviously troubled about her old friend. Dinsmore asked the questions while Montgomery sat nearby, listening to what could be the key to their investigation.

Marni made it clear that she wasn't representing Liysa in a professional sense, although she had assisted Liysa and the DeWitt family in locating and interviewing Pat Birmingham. She had also helped them get certain powers of attorney and discussed child custody issues. It was Marni whom Tor DeWitt had sought out when he needed somewhere to leave Bjorn and Papako that first night. Marni ended up caring for Bjorn for three weeks, and her own family was plunged into upheaval by Liysa's situation.

Although Marni was an attorney, she was now, in essence, only a very good friend trying to find the best way to help Liysa. She agreed to talk to the two detectives, but she warned them that if they wandered into matters that were confidential, she would have to invoke her right to refuse to answer.

Marni recalled that she had been a member of the wedding party in Liysa's first marriage and then had lost touch with her for about a decade. She and Liysa didn't see each other that often in the late nineties, but Chris and Liysa had occasionally stayed with her family and the Clarks had visited the Northons in Bend.

As for Chris, Marni liked him; she described him as "very vital and smart," a man whose life was quite "ordered." She thought that his many years as a pilot had probably caused him to be precise in his habits. Liysa, on the other hand, was an artist, an idealist, "a free spirit."

Marni had felt that she understood Liysa well, and it was obvious that she loved her somewhat flamboyant friend, whom she described as a wonderful storyteller who sometimes embellished for dramatic effect. She found the grown-up Liysa an eccentric, but also a woman who was "bright, creative, full of joy, loving, mirthful."

Marni admitted that she hadn't known whether to congratulate Liysa when she married Chris—or feel sorry for her. The two were so very different, and Liysa complained to her that

Chris wasn't able to be intimate—not in a sexual way, but in terms of opening up his life to her. Within a year of her third marriage, Liysa confided that Chris demeaned her with verbal and physical abuse. She seemed very afraid when she told Marni that she had contacted several shelters for women.

Montgomery and Dinsmore were becoming familiar with this scenario. They listened quietly as Marni Clark said she had never observed any abuse on Chris's part, but she recalled telling Liysa that she was afraid for her and feared that the violence might get worse. Once, when Bjorn was about a year old, Liysa had appeared at their door unannounced "very upset," after what she said was a fight with Chris. She showed Marni some marks on her neck, but they weren't bruises. They seemed to be "more pressure marks."

"Liysa was convinced that he would kill her," Marni told the investigators, "and she left. In my logical mind, I didn't believe Chris would kill Liysa, but I don't think she did a full disclosure either."

Marni had offered to serve as a mediator between Liysa and Chris, but Liysa panicked, begging her not to call him. "He will take it out on me," she pleaded.

Two weeks before he was killed, Marni had spoken to Chris on the phone for about an hour. They had discussed a number of things, but Chris was hesitant to talk about Liysa. He said they were doing "pretty good—better than it was." When Marni pressed, Chris said only, "Liysa and I are not perfect partners. I'm a little volatile."

As for the holes in the wall in the Bend house and the books Liysa said he tossed at her during arguments, Chris had only said quietly, "She did it, too, Marni."

Marni had found Chris to be somewhat self-involved and unable to see how unhappy Liysa was, while she could see that Liysa was growing more and more depressed over the years.

Her former effervescent personality had deflated to a shadow of what it had once been until Liysa apparently felt there was no way out of her hopeless life. "Their marriage was nontraditional," Marni explained. "They were only together two or three days a month because of Chris's schedule—not much commitment, although Chris was very committed to Bjorn."

As for Liysa's fear of Chris, it seemed real enough to Marni, but when she asked her old friend why she would stay in a sham of a marriage, Liysa always claimed that she had to stay or Chris would kill her. She didn't want Chris to have any visitation rights at all if they separated, and she had mused about leaving the country for ten years until Bjorn grew bigger and stronger.

Marni and her husband had been out of town at a wedding in Portland on the weekend of Chris's death. Actually, Marni had been gone for most of the prior week, attending a seminar in Spokane. Her practice dealt chiefly with being a guardian ad litem for the disabled and elderly. So it was Dr. Ben Clark who had answered the phone when Liysa called on Tuesday night, October 3, saying that she and Chris planned to go camping the coming weekend. Marni had tried to return Liysa's call but failed to reach her.

Back home on Monday afternoon, October 9, Ben Clark took Liysa's call again, only to hear her telling him in a tight but relatively calm voice that she was in jail for "accidentally" shooting her husband. When Marni grabbed the phone, she had difficulty understanding exactly what had happened. Liysa was saying that Chris had either tried to drown her or kill her—and that he was in the hospital.

"He's dead," Liysa announced flatly.

"*He's dead?*" Marni echoed, unable to comprehend Liysa's words. "Chris is *dead?*"

Marni was a sensible woman whose personality and profession didn't lend itself to hysteria. But if Chris was as bad as

Liysa said he was, she had often wondered why Liysa would keep her children in such a terrible environment. Still, Marni had never taken Liysa's emotional stories as gospel, and she hesitated to judge her because she didn't know the whole story.

Marni had once prosecuted domestic violence cases for the city of Walla Walla, and she had seen women afraid to testify for fear of retaliation. Now she was concerned that all of her information had come from Liysa. "I don't have the flip side of the story from Chris," she told the detectives. "There are two sides. I only have one. It's not black-and-white. There is a lot of gray."

Marni's biggest concern was what Liysa might have done. She didn't know what had really happened. She said that she knew Liysa made poor decisions and that her marriage to Chris had probably been one of them. "But she was crazy about him. He was handsome and she loved him. I'm not sure if he returned the love."

When Dennis Dinsmore asked Marni if Liysa's conversation and behavior were ever delusional, she shook her head: "No."

Of all Liysa's friends, Marni weighed information the most carefully. It was the lawyer in her. She acknowledged that she had seen Chris drunk and that Liysa would get tipsy once or twice a year. She recalled that Liysa had suffered from seizures as a child and that she had always hated taking medicine. However, she had occasionally smoked marijuana. She *had* gotten drunk at the Wa-Hi senior prom and her parents had grounded her for a long time. "I seem to remember that it was for a whole year," she said, looking back more than two decades.

Marni was troubled that Liysa hadn't demonstrated any remorse over Chris's death, saying only, "I had a private service for him in my mind." And, as an attorney, she had tried to block all of Liysa's attempts to tell her about the night Chris died. She warned her to speak only to her attorney. "Every time she tried to talk," Marni recalled, "I told her to shut up. 'Don't talk to me about it. We're not talking about this. I don't want to hear. . . .' "

Marni was figuratively putting her hands over her ears, but it wasn't because she was squeamish. She was an "officer of the court," and, ethically, she might have to repeat whatever Liysa confided. So she had ordered her friend to stop babbling things that might be used against her.

DR. BEN CLARK wasn't nearly as conflicted as his wife was on his thoughts about Liysa. Yes, she was Marni's closest friend, but he told Dinsmore and Montgomery that he wanted them and any future jury to know the truth. Even before the shooting at the campground, Liysa had become a disruptive factor in the Clarks' marriage with her surprise visits, her histrionic outbursts about Chris, and her apparently total inability to understand that other people had lives and problems of their own.

Ben Clark recalled his acquaintance with Liysa, dating back eleven years. When Marni was awarded her law degree and he became an M.D. in November 1989, they had taken a trip around the world to celebrate. They had stopped off in Hawaii and spent two weeks with Liysa and her then-husband, Nick Mattson. That visit was a happy time, but when they traveled to Hawaii again in January 1996, it was painfully obvious that Liysa and Nick were not getting along. Nick told Ben that he was afraid their marriage was ending.

"Liysa married Chris Northon that spring, right after she divorced Nick," Ben recalled.

Throughout both her second and third marriages, Liysa had spent ten to twenty days a year visiting the Clarks. After she married Chris, he came with her about a third of the time. Ben said he had liked Chris. And, like his wife, he found Liysa "bright and energetic," but when he viewed her personality in terms of a medical diagnosis, he thought she would best be described as "manic-depressive." He stressed, however, that he wouldn't presume to make that determination himself—not without referring her to a psychiatrist. Most of the time, she struck Ben as manic, "so upbeat and positive that she was not realistic. *Very* positive and fun, laughing, sincere, would confide in you, open, and honest."

Those were all fine characteristics, but there were warning signs. Ben remarked that Liysa seldom slept and had "a million things she was working on." He noted that she rarely appeared to have downtime, and when she did, she was subdued and slept heavily. "But most of the time," Ben said, "she was *going*. . . ."

Liysa had had trouble sleeping the first time Ben ever met her—back in 1989. She was working with Nick in the surf photography business, but she struck Ben as completely disorganized and very scattered. "She had a very nice car that was dirty, full of bills and receipts that were thrown all over." Of course, lack of neatness doesn't indicate a homicidal personality, and Ben knew that. What struck him most about Liysa was her exaggeration. "Her perspective may not always be one of reality," he said cautiously.

Ben had met Liysa's mother, Sharon, and he found her "very normal," not the abusive monster that Liysa had described. He felt a lot of the situations Liysa had gotten into might have been the result of her own bad judgment. As far as Ben knew, she had traveled extensively, including living for a time in the Caribbean.

He recalled that Nick Mattson had let Liysa have whatever she wanted—mostly property—but it was different with Chris. He wanted an equitable division of what they bought together. When Dinsmore asked Ben about the last time he'd seen Chris, the doctor remembered that "Chris was beside himself. He kept saying, 'This is just *crazy*, what she's doing.' She wanted two ranches—one in Hawaii and one in Bend. Chris was getting to where Nick was. He was having to work more and more to support her property needs."

As far as Chris constantly following Liysa, Ben Clark felt it was more that Chris was worried because she would take off without telling him where she was going or what she was going to do. He never knew where she or the boys were. Chris sometimes called the Clarks or Liysa's relatives in Joseph to get some idea of where his family was.

Liysa had frequently phoned the Clarks to tell them she would arrive in the coming week. "But she never specified a day or a time. Then she would just show up and expect people to readjust their schedules," Ben said, adding, "Usually, she traveled at night."

"Was Chris physically abusive to Liysa?" Dinsmore asked.

Ben said he'd never seen anything like that. "It might be true, but then she exaggerates without reality."

In a pattern Ben had seen before, Liysa had been the pursuer in her relationship with Chris, but as soon as he tried to put limits on her, she wanted out of the marriage. "Chris had a good life," Ben said, reflectively. "He loved life. He did not want to die. Chris wouldn't waste time if Liysa left him. He might hurt, but he wouldn't waste or wreck his life over her. . . . Chris wouldn't give up life, and he wouldn't waste his life on revenge."

Ben was frank about Chris's drinking. In his opinion, it was quite possible that he might have had a problem with alcohol, but he'd never seen Chris turn mean after drinking. He said that Chris always drank when the families got together. But Ben was firm when he said, "Alcohol and marijuana did not affect his work."

"I feel sorry for Chris," Ben Clark said slowly to Dinsmore and Montgomery. "Chris is *dead*. I feel bad for Liysa, too, but *Chris is dead*. . . . He didn't want to be dead. She did an awful thing and she should be punished. If she gets off free, she'll think she was justified. She has no remorse."

IF THERE WERE OTHERS among Liysa's friends and relatives who had doubts about her stability and her actions on the night Chris died, they didn't speak up. Instead, they continued to rally behind her. And the posters asking for money to support Liysa Northon, a tragic victim of domestic violence, proliferated around Walla Walla.

Oddly, Liysa wasn't as happy about the publicity backing her as one might think. She had had visits from women associated with Safe Harbors, a support group for victims of domestic violence. Now she wrote and asked them to tone down their efforts on her behalf. She feared becoming "too high-profile," which could result in a change of venue that might move her trial to a larger county in Oregon. She felt she would have a better chance for acquittal in Enterprise, and her attorneys agreed.

* * *

BOTH THE DEFENSE and prosecution teams were gearing up for a trial in June that would last at least two weeks *after* a jury was picked, a very *long* trial for Enterprise, Oregon. But this case was in no way a fait accompli for the State. There were pieces missing that no one in the prosecution team could find. They needed something solid to back their premise that Liysa had, indeed, planned Chris's murder for a long time—perhaps for at least two years. The defense was prepared to call innumerable well-spoken and believable witnesses who would testify that Liysa was a warm and loving woman who had only reluctantly confided her terror of her husband to them.

Dennis Dinsmore and Pat Montgomery interviewed two of Liysa's staunchest supporters—her brother, Tor, and her father,

Wayland. Neither of them could offer anything but hearsay descriptions about Chris and Liysa's relationship, information provided by Liysa herself.

Wayland DeWitt said that he and his daughter were very close and talked weekly. He believed her when she told him that Chris surrounded himself with drug dealers. Indeed, she'd told him she had compiled a drug sales record on Chris between 1991 and 1995, but someone had removed it from the Bend house before Wayland and Tor arrived to take away all the furniture and paperwork at her instruction. He said Liysa's friend Mia Rose had seen a bagful of marijuana in one of Chris's filing cabinets that day.

Wayland acknowledged that he had given Liysa a .38-caliber revolver loaded with five rounds, along with five extra rounds. He was aware that she kept it in her camera bag and estimated that he gave it to her in September, a month before Chris was shot. "I was afraid he would kill her," he said, "so I told her to use the gun to protect herself." Liysa had told her father that she'd fired off some rounds in the woods at the Maxwell Campgrounds so that she would know how the gun worked.

Dinsmore traced the revolver and found that Wayland had purchased the Brazil-manufactured weapon in August 1988 in Pittsburg, Texas.

Liysa's father complained that the justice system did not deal with domestic violence and that had only exacerbated Liysa's problems. "The laws must be changed," he said vehemently. "Liysa wants them changed so this never happens to another woman."

"How have the current laws hurt your daughter?" Dinsmore asked.

"Chris dragged her around by her hair—on her knees—and her knee got infected," Wayland said. "The doctor called the Bend police, and they took her statement and a statement from

Chris. So he was arrested—but *she* had to deal with him after he got out of jail and [was] angry at being arrested."

Presented with Wayland's devotion to Liysa, Dinsmore wondered about their past history together. "Was Liysa ever sexually abused while she was growing up?" he asked, abruptly changing the subject.

Wayland vehemently denied knowledge of any sexual abuse. He also denied physically abusing his daughter.

"What about her mother?"

There was a long silence. No one spoke. Wayland finally answered, "In her *mind*, Liysa was physically abused by her mother," explaining in the same breath that he worked long hours. "I would come home from work and see welts on Liysa. My wife and I contrasted each other in family discipline."

Wayland said he felt this was because there was stricter discipline in the very rural area of Joseph where his ex-wife had been raised, while his family had always had a more "laid-back" attitude about punishment. Further, he said he viewed discipline in Liysa's early years as "cyclic," which he felt was the reason Sharon was given to physical discipline. His reasoning was obscure; he could have been discussing his ex-wife's and daughter's moods during their menstrual cycles, or perhaps he was hinting that one or both of them suffered from a bipolar disorder.

Whatever he had tried to do to reach a middle ground they could live with, Wayland said that he and Sharon always seemed to revert to their very different child care methods. He said he'd learned that Liysa had sought counseling on Oahu to cope with her memories of childhood abuse.

"Did Liysa ever have to have medical care for her injuries when she was a child?" Dinsmore asked.

"No."

"Did she suffer broken bones?"

"That is not true."

Wayland said he understood his daughter's third marriage better than anyone—with the possible exception of his late son-in-law. "She realized after a year or two that it was not her who caused the abuse," he said firmly. His knowledge of psychology and his training, he explained, had taught him that victims tend to think *they* are wrong. "That's why they don't talk about the abuse. Liysa talked to *me*—she couldn't talk to her mother."

Wayland DeWitt was positive that records existed in Hawaiian police files that would substantiate incidents where Chris had assaulted Liysa. "Once with a rake . . . Chris hit her with a rake that time," he said.

Liysa's father was convinced that she had gone to several counselors on Oahu, while Chris always refused to go. All three of her marriages had been damaging to her, her father explained, but her marriage to Chris was the worst. "Everyone tried to talk her into divorcing Chris," he said, "but she was afraid. Chris told her, 'I will kill you and me.' "

Whatever the truth might be about Liysa's childhood, it was clear to Dinsmore and Montgomery that Wayland had taken everything she told him as absolute gospel. In his soft-spoken way, he was ferocious in his defense of Liysa. There was no gray area. It was all black and white to Wayland DeWitt; Chris was the devil.

* * *

DAN JONES, Chris's former flight student and longtime friend, traveled to Salem from his home in Utah on March 12, 2001. He came to the Criminal Justice Division of the Oregon Attorney General's Office to speak to Dennis Dinsmore and Steve Briggs, the assistant attorney general who would be assisting Dan Ousley in Liysa's trial. Dan said that Chris's career as a pilot had been phenomenal and that he was about to qualify as a DC-10 captain when he died. Dan had been one of the last people to speak with Chris. "I called to ask for some airline tickets on Hawaiian. It was on that last Friday—October sixth. Chris told me he'd be glad to arrange for some buddy passes," Dan said. "While we were talking, I heard someone in the background, and he asked me to wait a minute. When he came back on the line, Chris said, 'Liysa has some half-baked idea of going camping *right now*. I'm just the designated driver. . . .'"

Chris had been in a good mood, Dan remembered, but he mock-groaned when he said, "We *are* going camping this weekend—it's Liysa's idea. . . ."

"They took two vehicles," Dinsmore told Dan.

"I don't understand," Dan said. "That's why Chris was going—because Liysa wanted him to drive."

Dinsmore explained the complicated logistics of the trip and why Papako wasn't at the Lostine River campsite when Chris was killed.

Dan said he'd met Liysa about six months after Chris married her. He visited on Lanipo Street, staying in the eagle's nest three or four times a year. Liysa had told him that she left Nick because she couldn't stand having a husband who was gone two months at a time making movies. "But she always complained about Chris, too," Dan said. "I'd say, 'Liysa you knew Chris was a pilot—that he'd have to be gone, too. Look around—look what you have.'

"She always said, 'Yeah, I know, but . . .'"

Later, when Dan visited them in Bend, he found that Liysa was still complaining about how "miserable" her life was. Chris wouldn't help her enough with the children, even though it seemed to Dan that he was always rearranging his schedule to accommodate her trips. She told him that Chris kicked their new puppy, KoKo.

"The dog was skittish, but not with Chris," Dan said. "It ran to Chris to be petted. He was embarrassed that she said that. Later, he explained to me that the dog was digging up the new landscaping, and he'd run at it with his arms in the air, but he'd never kicked it."

"How was Chris's relationship with Papako?" Dinsmore asked.

"They didn't hug as much as Chris and Bjorn—but then Papako was older. Chris always included him in whatever they were doing. He taught him how to fish, things that Bjorn was still too young for. If Chris asked him to go to the beach, Papako was anxious to go and grabbed his beach gear. He sat on Chris's lap when he read to them at night."

"Was Chris violent?"

"Violent? *Never.* He was the type of person who would go a hundred miles to walk around trouble. One time, we met this hostile drunk on the beach. Chris immediately put his hands up, surrendering, and he said, 'Let's talk—what's the problem?' "

Dan Jones recalled when Liysa was flying to Los Angeles quite frequently in late 1999 and early 2000. Chris had obtained the plane tickets for her, and she'd been very excited. "She said she was going to meet Meg Ryan and she had to buy a new suit for that meeting. Later, she told me that some agent kept hitting on her, calling and showing up at her motel."

"Was Chris jealous?"

"I never saw anything like that. He trusted her."

Chris hadn't talked about his marital problems much, not even to Dan, whom he'd known for twenty years. "One time he did say she'd threatened to leave him and take the children," he told Dinsmore. "He said the talk about divorce was 'dumb,' and he told her he would want shared custody of the children and get half of their property together."

Liysa, Dan said, seemed to want to argue with Chris. "He would say, 'I don't want to talk right now,' and she would go on and on and on and wouldn't stop. Chris would try to leave and she would run after him and jump on his back. She'd claw at him, and he'd finally just have to leave the house."

As he had with Arne Arnesen, Chris had murmured to Dan Jones that Liysa was getting "psycho."

"When was that?" Dinsmore asked.

"During one of our last phone calls—sometime in late September or early October."

The marriage that began on a romantic Hawaiian beach by moonlight sounded as if it had become a nightmare. Even Chris's friends were feeling the fallout. Dan said that someone had made an anonymous call to Dave Story's airline, complaining that Dave was a drug user and dealer. A pilots' union rep had taken care of the spurious accusation.

"It happens a lot," Dan commented. "When pilots are involved in divorces or child custody issues, about half of them get anonymous complaints about drug use. It's a method of intimidation from ex-spouses. Even when the complaints prove to be unfounded, they remain in the pilots' files. Liysa knows that."

CHAPTER THIRTY

ALTHOUGH NONE OF Chris's friends had ever known him to take drugs, Pat Montgomery obtained copies of his medical records and claims made to Blue Cross and Blue Shield. There were claims for his numerous visits to Dr. Linda Carr for counseling in Hawaii and for prescriptions that included Augmentin (an antibiotic), Allegra (an antihistamine for allergies), MetroCream (a topical treatment for rosacea), and Trimox (a form of amoxicillin). There was no record of sleeping pill prescriptions or for any other habit-forming drugs. That didn't necessarily mean that Chris hadn't obtained such drugs illegally, but no one who knew him—save Liysa—had ever suggested that he had. And it was hard to picture a man so devoted to exercise and sports that demanded stamina as a drug user.

Interviews of both Liysa's and Chris's friends and relatives in Oregon had taken months. However, one thing was obvious to Pat Montgomery and Dennis Dinsmore. Even though they had talked to—and would continue to talk to—people in the Northwest, they had to reach out farther. Half of the couple's life together had been spent in Hawaii. They couldn't hope to find the answers they needed in Oregon alone.

Flying to Hawaii sounded like a really great assignment, and in other circumstances, it might have been. But the two detectives were going there to work, to try to retrace lives that had ended in tragedy. They knew they weren't going to be welcome visitors to a lot of people. But they were used to that. Homicide detectives become familiar with closed doors and suspicious minds.

It was April 28, 2001, when Dinsmore and Montgomery flew to Hawaii to continue their investigation. They checked into a hotel in Honolulu where all the other guests were on vacation. "We got there at two in the afternoon," Montgomery recalled with a laugh. "And we knew we probably wouldn't get another chance to see the beach. We each had a big cigar and ventured out on the beach, wearing T-shirts and shorts over our fish-belly-white skin we had from where it rains most of the time in the winter. We were strolling along in the sunshine, looking and walking. Then Dennis said, 'You notice anything strange?' and I said, 'No.' Then I looked again. It was all guys.

"We didn't know *which* beach to go to," Montgomery remembered. "We just picked one that was close, and we were walking along on the hot sand, looking and enjoying being in the tropics. We must have been halfway down the beach when we realized that it *was* all guys—wearing little tiny thongs and rubbing suntan lotion on each other. I guess we both figured it out at the same time. That was the only time we saw a beach while we were in Hawaii."

They would be teased mercilessly about their beach miscalculation by the detectives who hadn't been picked for the Hawaii trip. But they weren't on vacation anyway; they had dozens of possible witnesses to interview in the space of a few days.

Dinsmore and Montgomery drove their rented car less than twenty miles to Kailua, but they had to cross the Koolau Mountain Range that formed a ridge in the middle of Oahu. Honolulu had been hot, but now the air grew slightly cooler as they reached the windward side of Oahu and glimpsed the calm harbor where the beach was protected by a barrier reef. It *was* paradise, or close enough to it. Their destination was Lanipo Street, where Liysa and Chris had shared a house.

Neighbors tend to know what is going on—which couples are happy, which ones are always fighting—and the two Oregon detectives knew by now that the fortunes of many of the residents were braided together on Lanipo Street with past and present relationships. Nick Mattson lived there with his second wife, Lora Lee, their baby son, and, of course, Papako. Tim Sands, the man Liysa had once been engaged to lived there, too. There was also Chris's former landlady from his single days. And Cal and Kit Minton, Liysa's friends who were caring for Bjorn, weren't far away, nor were Debbie and Dave Story.

The temperature was in the low eighties when Montgomery and Dinsmore walked up the steep street where Chris had first glimpsed the "surfer/photographer" girl who would change his life forever. Back home in Oregon, it was undoubtedly raining or even snowing, and the first few daffodils and tulips would be tentatively poking out of the ground. On Lanipo Street, everything was shimmering green, the plumerias' leaves had fallen but their flowers were blooming, and they were two short blocks from a beach that looked like the photograph on a calendar. The two investigators accepted that they probably couldn't hope to find any more *physical* evidence to build a murder case against Liysa Northon, but it was possible that the very complex circumstantial case against her could be strengthened.

They found the house where Liysa and Chris had begun their marriage and knocked at the residence next door. Two army doctors and their children had lived there since June 1998. They said they had been shocked to hear about the fatal shooting in Oregon; on occasion, they had noticed tension between Chris and Liysa, but they had never heard any sounds of physical fighting. "And we could hear anything that went on because our houses are so close."

"Liysa took care of our children sometimes," the doctors said, "and she seemed like a really good mom. But then, Chris seemed like a really good dad. Liysa did complain that Chris was gone all the time."

As far as police coming to the Northons' house, they'd never seen that, nor had they ever noticed any bruising on Liysa. Chris and Liysa had been, to all outward appearances, a completely normal couple.

Pilots who had flown with Chris—but who were not particularly close friends—recalled to Montgomery and Dinsmore that Chris had been a nice guy who never complained about his marriage. When his family flew with him, he'd always let Liysa ride in the first-class section, while he sat with the boys in coach.

One pilot, who had been having marital problems himself, recalled only that Chris would sometimes commiserate and say, "I know what you mean." But he had never offered any details on his own marriage.

Marlene Figueroa, who was the senior director of human resources for Hawaiian Airlines, spoke with the Oregon detectives. She brought out Chris Northon's file, explaining that she was the one who dealt with any problems HAL employees might have.

"We heard a rumor that Chris had once slapped a flight attendant," Dinsmore said. "Any mention of that?"

Marlene shook her head. "He was never involved with any dispute that I've heard of. Hawaiian Air is small enough that anything like that would have been talked about by other employees."

She said that Chris had never been disciplined for any infraction by the airline. "Ken Reweick, our director of Flight Operations for Hawaiian, nominated Chris for the Ohono Hono Award," she added. "It's given to employees who go above and beyond the call of duty."

Pressing further, the two detectives talked with Jim Grymes, who was the Director of Occupational Safety and Health for the airline. He was in charge of its drug-testing program. Dick Northon had turned a cassette player with a tape in it over to Pat Montgomery, along with several of Liysa's journals. On that tape, according to Liysa, who had recorded it surreptitiously, Chris and another pilot were giggling and talking about outwitting the airline's drug tests. Liysa steadfastly insisted that Chris and his friends hid their marijuana use from the airlines. Now Montgomery asked Jim Grymes if that was possible.

"I don't see how," he answered. "We do testing on new employees, in post-accident situations, with reasonable cause—and *randomly*. All of our tests are done through a company in Maryland. We divide our employees into two groups. Pilots, crews, mechanics, and other essential personnel are given quarterly tests."

There were 1,545 essential personnel at Hawaiian, and four times a year the Maryland company randomly selected 25 percent of the names on the list for drug testing. Ten percent of those names were also picked arbitrarily for alcohol testing.

"Two years ago," Jim Grymes said, "it might have been possible to beat the tests by dilution or substitution—but not now. The labs in Maryland can spot it."

Pilots and crews picked for testing were notified while they were in the air, with only thirty to forty-five minutes warning. When they landed, urine samples were taken, and if the tests came back positive, the individual would be called in and asked for a plausible excuse. Thereafter, Jim Grymes was notified and a meeting would be set up with the suspect employee, the chief pilot, and himself. The employee would be offered two choices.

"They can quit or go through rehab," he said. "If they complete rehab satisfactorily, they can get a special certificate to return to work. Then they're tested routinely for five years. One more failed test—and they're terminated."

Jim Grymes validated what Dan Jones had said about those making complaints about pilots—only more so. "Nine out of every ten allegations against a pilot come from a disgruntled wife or girlfriend," he said.

Liysa's claim that Chris used every drug known to man and that he had tested himself at home for drugs before he reported for duty made little sense. She had said he called in sick if the test showed drugs, but both Chris and Dave Story had almost perfect attendance records at work; they never called in sick. If essential personnel were tested coming *back* from a flight, what good would it have done for Chris to do tests at home?

Despite Liysa's accusations, Chris had had a spotless reputation with Hawaiian Airlines.

* * *

LIYSA HAD BOTH HER FANS and foes along Lanipo Street. Jane Sands, who lived on the other side of her house, had a very long memory when it came to Liysa. After Liysa broke off with her son Tim, Jane had tried to be kind to the young woman who seemed to have suffered a nervous breakdown of some sort, but now Jane told Montgomery and Dinsmore about what an outrageous farce Liysa's "amnesia" had been.

"Do you still have the journal your nephew found—where Liysa outlined her plan to break off with Tim?" Montgomery asked.

Jane shook her head. The family had read Liysa's entries, realized that they had all been duped, and decided it wasn't important to keep the journal around. It was only a reminder of a bad time. No one had ever expected that Liysa would come back to Lanipo Street, and, of course, none of them had foreseen that Chris would end up dead or that Liysa would be facing murder charges.

Jane didn't recall that she'd ever seen noticeable bruises on Liysa, and it would have been easy to spot them. "She usually wore only a bikini or a short wrap." The woman who had once felt so sorry for Liysa warned the detectives that they were dealing with an extremely bright, ultimately manipulative woman. "Watch her—she's always thinking," Jane told them.

MONTGOMERY AND DINSMORE continued their canvass of the neighborhood and found that Liysa had had one good friend on Lanipo Street. A longtime resident of the area, Jane Pultz was nearing eighty, but she was a very young, very sharp eighty and nothing much slipped by her. She was a woman who had lived an exciting and fruitful life, succeeding at a number of careers. She told the detectives that she'd learned that Liysa was a photographer and said that she herself had spent many years in the newspaper business. By the late 1990s, Jane was involved with book publishing and that intrigued Liysa, who said that she was working on screenplays and a book.

"I offered to read anything that Liysa might want to share—and give her my opinion of its potential," Jane said. "Lots of people have told me they were writing a book, but I felt that Liysa was really serious about it."

Jane Pultz said she had known Chris both before and after

he met Liysa, and she had found the couple very neighborly people. "I saw them at least a dozen times a week, and occasionally they would have me over for a visit."

Ironically, one of Jane's many causes was the protection of women who had suffered harm at the hands of their husbands or boyfriends. In fact, she had volunteered at the local domestic violence shelter for more than five years, working in every aspect of the charity—answering the hot line, picking up frightened women off the street, and helping others to transition back into a safe world.

She recalled that Liysa often dropped off items of clothing with her to take to the shelter. "Our shelter gives battered women the opportunity to talk to one another about what they were going through, sharing experiences," Jane said. "We also assist women in getting restraining orders and finding jobs and housing. If the danger is strong enough, we even help some of our clients pay for transportation to the mainland, where they can start new lives without being afraid."

Not all of their cases ended happily. Jane admitted that some rescues didn't work because the women themselves blocked their efforts to help. She stressed that they had voluntarily returned to their abusers. "Some women seem incapable of making the emotional break. No one can find our shelter," she said. "Its location is absolutely secret. The only way their men found them is because the women gave them our address."

"Did Liysa ever ask you for help?" Montgomery asked. "Was she looking for a way to get away from her husband?"

Jane Pultz shook her head. Although Liysa had seemed curious about her work at the shelter, she never hinted that she herself was in trouble. Jane was adamant that Liysa had none of the indicators that she had long since learned to recognize in domestic abuse victims. "No, I did not see it in Liysa," she said firmly. "She was interested in the shelter, but I saw none of the qualities of abuse in Liysa. She was a very open person and not the quiet, shy, withdrawn, secretive personality that we normally see in abuse victims. I must say that, if she had a problem, I was totally unaware of it."

Liysa had never asked Jane Pultz for help. And, of all people, Jane felt that *she* would have spotted any bruises or cuts on her young neighbor, especially because Liysa usually wore shorts or a bathing suit. "I never saw a mark on her," she said, puzzled. "Never."

Montgomery and Dinsmore wondered how Liysa could have been beaten and terrorized on this street where doors and windows were open in the balmy climate, where houses were so close together, where everyone seemed to know everyone else. They both knew that households could maintain seamless facades of calm while all manner of horror went on behind closed doors—but there weren't many closed doors on Lanipo Street. And a police car parked in front of any house there would certainly have attracted attention.

MARY MATTSON was Nick's mother. She and Nick's father were people of substantial means and longtime residents of Oahu. She agreed to talk to Montgomery and Dinsmore, but it became obvious that she was nervous about this interview when she stopped short of answering most of their questions fully. She clearly adored her grandson Papako, and she didn't want to say anything that might make Liysa cut off her contact with him.

Mary recalled the woman who had been her daughter-in-law for almost a decade. She had known Liysa for about nine months before she married Nick and really liked her in the early years. "She was very sports-oriented," Nick's mother said, "and so was Nick. I always tried to get along with Liysa—stay neutral, you know, in their marriage—tried not to pry into their affairs, but I could see there was some tension when Nick had to travel."

She said she knew very little about Liysa's background, only that she'd been in Hawaii for some time before she met Nick. "I know she went to the University of Hawaii, and I think she lived on the Big Island for a while."

Still very hesitant, she admitted that she'd heard rumors and gossip about Liysa, but she'd paid little attention.

"Did you know that she was married before she married your son?" Dinsmore asked.

"No, I didn't. I do know that Liysa was a wonderful mother to Papako."

Yes, she had had some reservations about other aspects of Liysa's life, but she hastened to explain that was only because Liysa craved so much excitement and adventure. She also had a great hunger for property.

Montgomery and Dinsmore had heard that many times before.

Liysa's former mother-in-law said her obsession with land had caused trouble between Liysa and Nick, and put a great deal of pressure on him. She finally ventured the possibility that Liysa might be a "gold digger," but she quickly took that back, saying that she thought Liysa only wanted to be sure that Papako would be financially secure because he was the center of her life.

As far as Liysa's marriage to Chris, Mary didn't know much about that. She was sorry, of course, that Liysa had divorced Nick, but she'd kept her mouth shut so she could stay in touch with Papako. "I could still go to the house and get Papako because I had a good relationship with Liysa—even better after the divorce."

"Ever see bruises on her?" Dinsmore asked.

"Once—on the side of her face. She tried to hide it with her hair." And grudgingly, Mary admitted that she sometimes questioned whether Liysa always told the truth. Liysa tended to see things only from her own viewpoint and she was self-centered.

But again, Mary and her husband never outwardly questioned what she told them.

Finally, Mary offered her opinion that Liysa created a world of her own making, a world marked by her totally unrealistic expectations that she could afford everything she wanted. The Mattsons had helped Nick and Liysa finance property at first, but they had finally had to say no. Instead, they bought some rentals in Texas where their daughter lived. Liysa had been furious and accused them of wanting to be "slumlords" rather than invest in good, solid property in Oregon. "We finally had to tell Liysa that she and Nick needed to pay off what they already had," Mary said.

"Did Papako talk to you about Chris and Liysa fighting?" Montgomery asked.

"When they were first married—when he was four or five—he said they yelled. But he never said that Chris *hit* Liysa."

Mary stressed again that Liysa was always a good mother and never, ever struck Papako. "But then, he didn't ever pin her down, either."

Apparently, even Papako walked on tiptoes around his mother, aware that there were limits to her patience. One aspect of Liysa Northon's personality and effect on people was surfacing. The Oregon detectives realized that many people were actually *afraid* of her—not physically, but because of some control she had over their lives.

"She's only one little woman," Dinsmore said. "She probably doesn't weigh more than a hundred pounds—but she has a lot of power, and people are afraid to cross her. And I'm not even sure why."

"It's more than that," Montgomery said. "No one seems to know who she *really* is. . . ."

CHAPTER THIRTY-ONE

LIYSA HAD AS MANY loyal friends in Hawaii as she had doubters. Many of her women friends from the prenatal classes or the pool group peered suspiciously at Montgomery and Dinsmore through barely opened front doors, heard what they had come for, and immediately slammed the doors, locking themselves away from questions.

Others spoke up. One woman was positive that she had seen two sides to Chris's personality. "If he thought you were important, he could be very charming," she said. "Or he could be cold and not give you the time of day." She recalled being shocked when she went to Bjorn's first birthday party/"baby luau," caught a whiff of marijuana smoke, and saw airline pilots smoking pot. It didn't matter to her that they were not on duty and were not scheduled to fly for days. "That just wasn't right," she said. "They were *pilots*."

Several women discussed the bruises or marks on Liysa's throat and neck that she explained away by saying they were a reaction to antibiotics. Later, of course, Liysa had told them about how brutal her husband was. A surprising number of her Hawaiian girlfriends had known that she had a gun.

"The only thing I know is what Liysa and other people told me," one woman recalled. "I never saw any black eyes or bruises. Wait—one day I did see a small bruise on her stomach and she told me that Chris poked her with a rake. Chris was a tall, blond, smart pilot who could play the piano. I didn't really know him—I only saw him about ten times in the four years Liysa was married to him, but I never saw him drink or smoke marijuana. She told me she had a gun. I told her I wished she'd never let me know, and it was never mentioned again."

Neither Montgomery nor Dinsmore doubted that the

women they talked to were describing what they believed to be true. Either Liysa *was* a battered wife, or she had done a remarkable acting job in convincing any number of people that she lived a life of constant dread.

One acquaintance said Liysa characterized Chris as being unreasonably jealous. "She said he thought she was having an affair with David Kelley [the producer married to actress Michelle Pfeiffer whose vacation home was on the beach where Liysa once strolled]. She was afraid Chris was going to confront Kelley—but Liysa didn't even *know* Kelley. She said it was just because Chris was so jealous of her." Another familiar story.

One of the people Dinsmore and Montgomery really wanted to talk to was Makimo, the lifeguard on the eastern shore of Oahu whom Liysa had idolized for years. They found him and he was very open with them. Makimo was a firefighter, a handsome and powerfully built Hawaiian who acknowledged that he'd met Liysa about eighteen years before.

He said when he first saw her, she seemed to be tagging along with three or four other girls whom he knew were either strippers in private clubs or paid "escorts." She had come on very strong to him, and now he was embarrassed when he admitted having a very abbreviated affair with her. "But that was a long time ago," he said. "Later, we only saw each other on the beach. Both Nick and Liysa were surf photographers. If they needed help with something in the water, they would call me."

"Did you know her last husband—Chris Northon?" Dinsmore asked.

"Never met him—that was unusual, too, because Liysa usually introduced my family to her husbands or boyfriends. But then I've only seen her twice since she left Nick. The first time was at a surfing contest and I saw a ring on her finger. She told me she was married again. The last time I saw her was at the funeral of a friend—in 1996—and she didn't look like herself. She looked ragged and kind of drained."

Makimo was as confused about Liysa's background as everyone else who thought they knew her. "I didn't know she had a first husband," he said. "I thought Nick was her first husband. Then, when she was divorcing him, he told me she was once married to some guy named Kurt who was killed in a car wreck."

Makimo had never heard of Tim Sands. Or of Ray, her "fiancé" during college. He said he'd met Nick through a mutual friend and become closer to him after Nick started dating Liysa. Not positive that Makimo was being totally candid with them, Pat Montgomery showed him pages of Liysa's journal where she waxed erotic about her long affair with him. He was clearly upset with what he read and began to shake his head. "That's not right," he said. "We were only together for a night or two. I wouldn't want my family to read this—because it was way before either one of us was married. She must have fantasized most of this."

"Would you say that Liysa could be dangerous—that she could shoot someone?" Dinsmore asked.

"I can't even imagine Liysa holding a gun. She was a daredevil herself—she'd go out in a twenty-foot surf and she'd go hiking in remote areas, but she never put anyone else in danger."

"Did she drink—smoke pot?"

"A long time ago, she would drink a glass of wine or a beer. She'd smoke a joint."

Makimo recalled that Liysa had continued to be seductive with him, but he said he had never responded to her flirtations after he was married. He had listened to her secrets, though. "She told me she was going to write a book about her life, and I heard that she'd suffered from some kind of abuse when she was a child."

One of the most important interviews Dinsmore and Montgomery scheduled in Hawaii was with Kit Minton and her husband, Cal. Kit appeared to be as close to Liysa as Marni Clark and Ellen Duveaux, and it was the Mintons whom Liysa had chosen to entrust with Bjorn when she was first incarcerated. By the spring of 2001, the Mintons were packing to move to New England because Cal, a pilot for Northwest Airlines, was being transferred.

Kit said she'd known Liysa for four years—ever since they were both pregnant and attending prenatal classes, and they both belonged to the pool group. "We had children the same age," Kit explained, "and we talked on the phone, took the kids to the beach, had family barbecues, and Liysa came to dinner at Thanksgiving."

Fifteen months later, Kit had noted some bruises on Liysa's lower back and Liysa had admitted that Chris had "hurt her."

"She was missing a chunk of hair on her neck, and she had cuts on her wrist from a gold bracelet she wore. She said Chris pulled her hair and the cuts on her wrist were because he grabbed her there. She said they got in a fight and he got her down on the ground and sat on her chest and pinned her arms to the ground with his hands."

Kit had been fully apprised of the "Bend incident" by Liysa. She, too, noted that Liysa "was walking on eggshells most of the time."

"Did you ever see Chris drunk?" Dinsmore asked.

"No—but I saw him drinking," Kit said. "I really didn't see him that often—maybe a dozen times altogether."

She said that Bjorn had stayed with her family for more than five months. Both he and Papako were getting counseling for post-traumatic stress disorder.

The detectives said they'd heard that some rather bizarre photographs of Liysa existed, and Kit said it was true. She had received a letter containing a slide from Liysa in September 2000, a month before Chris died. In the letter, Liysa told her that Chris had forcibly raped her. To prove that, she had some-how managed—with the help of a mirror—to take photographs of her own pubic area to show bruising she alleged Chris had inflicted.

"She said she wanted it for evidence for 'custody reasons.' I don't have it anymore," Kit said, somewhat embarrassed. "I sent the slide to Liysa's attorney, Pat Birmingham, and I must have thrown the letter away, or maybe it was in the envelope with the slide I sent."

Kit recounted other stories Liysa had told her about Chris's cruelty. On their Tahiti vacation, she said Chris had locked her and Papako in their room in the hotel and given them only bread and cheese to eat. "And once when they were on vacation in Montana, he went to the airport to check his schedule, found out he needed to leave, and he just left Liysa and Papako in front of the airport."

Kit obviously believed Liysa, She described her as "funny, nice, very independent—and someone who would try to help someone else out. She had a lot of friends and she traveled all alone with the kids. She told me she was the main source of income for the family and that she paid for everything. Chris did his own thing with his money. She paid for the Hawaii house and he paid for the Bend house—she was so upset when he bought that without telling her."

Actually, Chris had bought that house long before he married Liysa, but the detectives said nothing.

The Mintons knew that Liysa had a gun. They believed that she got it to protect herself from Chris. "She said she bought it at a gun store in Oregon. She went to the store to buy Mace, she said, but the guys at the store talked her into buying the gun."

Liysa had sent numerous letters to Kit from jail, and they had talked on the phone. "The Liysa in jail is not the same Liysa I knew on the outside," Kit murmured. "Her voice doesn't sound like she is fun-loving anymore. I don't feel like I know the girl who is in jail."

Cal Minton offered a memory of his own—that he had once

seen Chris smoking a joint in the kitchen of the house on Lanipo Street.

The Mintons explained why they were not taking Bjorn to Connecticut with them. They had felt very sorry for the little boy, especially when Liysa told them that no one else would look after him. It was to have been an interim arrangement until Liysa was released from jail, but it had been six months and the trial was still three months away. They had three children of their own and they had finally made the wrenching decision that it would be better for Bjorn to stay in Kailua. He was going to be living with Nick Mattson, his half brother, Papako, Nick's new wife, Lora Lee, and their baby.

Nick was one of almost a dozen people who had offered to care for Bjorn, and, with him, the three "brothers" would be together. Dave and Debbie Story wanted Bjorn, too. Dave felt an allegiance to Chris and vowed to be another father figure to the little boy left behind. It was never the case that Bjorn had no place to go; many families were willing to open their arms to him.

* * *

WHEN PAT MONTGOMERY and Dennis Dinsmore boarded a plane for the mainland less than a week after they landed in Honolulu, they had a much better picture of Chris's and Liysa's lives in Hawaii. They had interviewed two dozen people, those whom Liysa had written to from jail, her old friends, her ex-lovers and ex-husband, her strong advocates and those who detested her. The characters in her journals and screenplays were now more identifiable and easier to understand.

While the State's detectives were checking out Liysa's background, investigators for her defense team were doing the same. There were various stances they could take, and depending on the reports that came back to them, Pat Birmingham and Wayne Mackeson would decide whether a straight self-defense position would be better than a "battered woman syndrome" approach.

It was a difficult call. If they went for the battered woman syndrome defense, it would be necessary for Liysa to undergo a psychiatric examination. If that happened, the State would also be allowed to have her examined by a psychiatrist of its choosing. It would be like reaching into a grab bag: they might get a classic battered woman syndrome report—or they might get something they didn't want to unwrap in open court. Even her own attorneys didn't know what really motivated Liysa, and they weren't willing to guess.

Both Birmingham and Mackeson journeyed to eastern Oregon to talk with their client in jail. The defense's investigators, Robin Karnes and Harold Nash, spoke with the counselors that Liysa had talked to over the four years leading up to Chris Northon's murder. One psychologist recalled that only four months after her marriage, Liysa had been disenchanted with Chris. She had commented that she would leave "if things didn't get better." Liysa had raved about the man named "Ray" to whom she'd been engaged before her first marriage. "He was killed in a car wreck two months before our wedding," Liysa had said sadly. "For years after that, I didn't care about anyone or respond emotionally."

She told the psychologist that Chris was the first man she'd been attracted to since Ray died. She wondered if she'd been suffering from post-traumatic stress disorder ever since Ray's death, and the doctor discussed the way the problem was diagnosed.

Pat Birmingham found this information interesting and possibly of value—until Liysa had difficulty remembering Ray's last name. During the time when she was supposed to be engaged to him, she had actually been on a South Sea island with the man who *did* become her first husband: Kurt Moran. Indeed, she hadn't learned of Ray's death until some friends told her about it months after his funeral. That made her honesty questionable and suggested she might have fantasized the whole "Ray persona."

There were other disturbing bits of information. Despite the research Liysa had undertaken on battered woman syndrome since 1996, she had feigned ignorance on the subject during her first days in the Union County Jail. Starla DuBois, a very caring worker/counselor from Safe Harbor, the domestic violence group in Enterprise, had visited Liysa and found a woman who seemed to know nothing about domestic violence. Liysa had asked Starla to explain what battered woman syndrome was.

Liysa's bouts with "amnesia" became known to the defense team. Besides the incident with Tim Sands, Karnes and Nash talked to one of her Hawaiian girlfriends, who said that Liysa had told her that she had lost her memory for a whole year when she was in grade school. They checked with her family and found that had never happened.

Birmingham and Mackeson had begun to have grave doubts about Liysa's credibility. After their own investigation and after they were made aware of the State's position, they opted to pursue a straight self-defense strategy. They could not fit Liysa into the parameters of the battered woman syndrome. Most abused women keep the violence a secret, too embarrassed or afraid to tell anyone. Liysa had discussed Chris's alleged abuse with *everyone,* including a lawyer and at least one mental health professional. Moreover, the majority of domestic violence victims are monitored by husbands who check the odometers on their cars, their phone bills, their grocery spending, and who manipulate situations to detach them from their families and friends. Chris had never objected to Liysa's worldwide travels, her spending (other than real estate), or her friends and family. He wasn't jealous or suspicious.

And notes made by counselors Liysa had visited said she had talked far more about how she needed to wait to divorce her husband until she would get the most financial benefits possible than she did about abuse or her fear of him.

To prove self-defense, Birmingham and Mackeson had only to convince a jury that Liysa Northon had suffered enough physical and emotional abuse that she had reason to fear for her life, and that she had used the amount of force needed to save herself and Bjorn. Not too much and not too little.

They thought they could do that—*if* they could keep their client off the witness stand.

CHAPTER THIRTY-TWO

THE HOT SUMMER of 2001 would see the most intriguing trial in Wallowa County legal history. There were rumors that Court TV was actually going to film the Northon trial and that the secrets revealed by witnesses would be shocking. Newswise, it was the biggest thing to hit Enterprise, Oregon. Elane Dickinson, reporter for the local paper, the *Wallowa County Chieftain,* would also be emailing coverage to the *Oregonian* in Portland. In terms of human tragedy, there were so many people grieving—either for Chris or for Liysa, and for the little boys left virtually orphaned.

Liysa packed to be moved to the Wallowa County Jail for her trial. It was a tiny facility, meant more to be a temporary holding cell than an actual jail. There was room for one prisoner at a time, or possibly two of the same sex. The jail had once served as the brig on a ship, although no one who knew its story was alive to describe how it was trundled from the sea to the mountains, a feat that seems almost impossible.

In the late spring of 2001, with the expectation of a prisoner who would be staying longer than a few hours, the jail was painted a soft green and a shower and combination toilet/sink were added. Two twin-sized leather-covered bunks could be folded down from the wall. There were no windows at all. And, like all jails, it smelled of pine-scented cleaning solution, sweat, cigarettes, and the acrid sting of tears.

The minuscule jail wasn't used often. There wasn't much violent crime in Wallowa County because most miscreants would have had to drive way out of their way to break the law. DUIs, bar fights, family beefs, and traffic offenses filled most of the court docket spaces. Dan Ousley had no assistant D.A.s because he could handle the cases that came his way easily. Although Liysa was officially a Wallowa County prisoner, it had been unthinkable to put her in the "brig" until now. Anyone walking up the worn courthouse steps and then into the hall in the old building would have been able to glance in through the woven steel door and see her captive there, unless she stayed cloistered deep in the bedroom part of the cell.

If Liysa was truly an unfortunate victim of years of spousal abuse, the last thing she had needed was to be all alone in a suffocating cell. Out of compassion, she had been housed in the Union County Jail.

When Liysa was transferred to the Wallowa County Jail, she entertained guests who sought her out. Women corrections officers and former prisoners from the Union County Jail often dropped by to sit on her "bed" and visit as if they were having a slumber party behind bars. She'd been so popular in the jail in La Grande—just as she was in her pool and prenatal groups in Kailua—that they'd hated to see her go. When Dan Ousley heard that Liysa was holding court in her jail cell, he ordered a more restrained editing of her visitors list.

* * *

LIYSA NORTHON'S TRIAL was set to begin on Monday, July 16, 2001, forty weeks to the day since Chris Northon died with a bullet in his brain. That had happened in early fall; now it was full summer, and so many lives had been ripped apart in the interim. Liysa, who had always been deeply tanned, was now pale and fragile-looking as she sat between Wayne Mackeson and Pat Birmingham at the defense table. "She looked like Anne of Green Gables," one court watcher sniffed.

The members of Liysa's family who were able to be in Enterprise were in the courtroom, but there were also eyes watching her from the row set aside for Chris's family and friends. Liysa's group wore "campaignlike" buttons with her picture on them.

The court operations specialists—Jary Homan, Klista Steinbeck, and Tracey Hall—had made small pink signs to mark off sections of the courtroom for families, interested townspeople, and prospective jurors. It probably wouldn't be a long trial—not more than two weeks at the most—but they were organized and ready for crowds and the emotional outbursts that would surely come when feelings ran so high.

It was a big courtroom, with a sense of history in the oak doors, benches, desks, and railings, burnished by thousands of hands over the years. The families and spectators would sit behind the rail on seven rows of long benches, divided by a center aisle. Unlike modern courtrooms, this one had tall windows where the sun could be muted with venetian blinds. The jurors' chairs, some of which swiveled, had caned backs and leather cushions. Judges from long ago peered down sternly from their sepia images on the wall.

Judge Philip Mendiguren presided from behind a huge old desk, and there were no newfangled electronic devices in his courtroom—only a corkboard on which to tack items of evidence and a slide projector. The twenty-first century had brought with it a tape recorder, rather than the Gregg shorthand method or a stenotype machine. And as a commentary on the times, everyone who came into the Northon trial had to pass through a metal detector.

Picking a jury for Liysa's trial would not be easy. Enterprise and the other towns in Wallowa County were so small that most people knew one another, and rumors proliferated. Dan Ousley was familiar to most of the county's voters, of course. Liysa's extended family were longtime residents, and Dick and Jeanne Northon had just bought property in Joseph. An exceptionally large jury pool of well over a hundred people had to be narrowed down to sixteen who would actually hear the case. There wasn't space for all of them in the courtroom, and they waited in the Oddfellows Hall and the Cloverleaf Hall, the only buildings large enough to house them during the laborious jury selection.

Klista Steinbeck stayed with the jury pool, communicating with the courtroom on a walkie-talkie. Jary Homan and Tracey Hall remained in the courthouse, shuffling witnesses, spectators, and families.

By July 17, all but forty-four of the potential jurors had been dismissed. It was a very hot day, and Judge Mendiguren suggested that they do the final winnowing in the courtroom itself, but Pat Birmingham said the defense would prefer to do it in the judge's chamber. He or Wayne Mackeson would step out of chambers to confer with Liysa about each selection, ensuring confidentiality.

Before the day was over a jury of two men and ten women was selected, along with four alternates—one male, three female. They would sit in chairs that weren't all of equal comfort; the first four in front were the newest, and Judge Mendiguren apologized for the others.

Although there were a few restaurants nearby, none was set

up to afford privacy to a party of sixteen. Judge Mendiguren observed that it would be too easy for jurors to overhear comments made by locals. Lunch would be brought in for them—to be eaten on the velvet lawn or in the gazebo as long as the sunny weather held. Mendiguren's bailiff, Dick Miller, a retired Oregon State policeman, would be nearby to be sure they were separated from the crowds.

Court TV had, indeed, sent two cameramen, who were ready to film testimony that would be dissected and discussed by anchors back in New York as soon as the trial was over.

Indeed, everything seemed to be in place for the commencement of trial. And yet something was going on behind the scenes that only the judge, the four attorneys, and a few trusted staff knew about. Only on television dramas like *Perry Mason* or *Murder She Wrote* does startling new evidence surface so close to trial, but something had been brewing for three weeks.

* * *

KIT AND CAL MINTON were now living in Connecticut and they had taken certain of Liysa's possessions with them for safekeeping. Although Liysa had told Chris and his friend John Gill that someone had stolen her computers in June 2000, at least one of those computers still existed and it had been given to Kit Minton. To protect her own secrets, Liysa had first deleted document after document.

Too late, Liysa—or someone with access to the Internet—had used a search engine to look for articles and/or websites about "computer forensics." Liysa realized that a forensics expert could dig below the blank surface of her "stolen" computers and bring up documents she never wanted anyone to see. In a letter smuggled out of the Union County Jail, she had written to Kit and asked her to get rid of her computer, saying, "Destroy it A.S.A.P. My Gateway could hang me because emails are forever on hard drive. Get it *away* A.S.A.P. Soon. Please. Before someone searches your place. Which probably wouldn't happen but just in case." Some time earlier, she also had instructed her father to destroy his computer with emails she had sent him, promising to buy him another one.

Up to this point Kit had done everything she could to help Liysa because she believed in her innocence, but she was troubled by Liysa's orders to destroy her laptop computer. Kit called Pat Birmingham and asked him what she should do. An ethical attorney, Birmingham told her that she should not destroy the computer or give it to Wayland DeWitt as it might contain potential evidence in a murder case.

"I'd suggest you contact your own attorney for advice," he told her.

After Kit Minton talked to a lawyer, she told Liysa that she could not comply with her wishes. Liysa had then instructed Birmingham to retrieve her computer and destroy it, saying that she feared there might be hidden files that could incriminate her—and possibly her father, too.

"I could not—and would not—do anything that might lead to the destruction of evidence in a murder investigation," Birmingham recalled a long time later. But he knew that at least one of his client's missing computers still existed, and it hung around his neck like a rotting albatross. What might be in that computer was anybody's guess. At some point, he would have to tell the State's prosecutors that it hadn't really been stolen, just as he would be ethically bound to tell them that Liysa's brother, Tor DeWitt, had picked up other possible evidence from Ellen Duveaux's house.

Around Valentine's Day, a package had been delivered to Birmingham's office by regular U.S. mail with no return address, although he assumed it had come from Liysa's brother. He asked his client if she owned the items contained in the package, and she acknowledged that she had once owned them but had not taken them to the Lostine River campground; she had purchased them only for self-defense. She thought her brother must have found the two sets of handcuffs and the stun guns in her home in Bend. After talking with the Oregon State Bar, a Multnomah County Circuit Court judge, and several attorneys, Birmingham deduced that he was not required ethically or legally to turn the cuffs and stun gun over to the prosecution, given the posture of the case at the time. Instead, he placed those items in a sealed envelope along with an affidavit.

As it turned out, Birmingham would not have to make the decision about when to reveal the information that had come to him. Someone else—someone unknown—was anonymously alerting the State about that missing computer.

Carol Terry was the legal assistant to Wallowa County District Attorney Dan Ousley. She was a smiling presence who greeted everyone who walked into the second-story D.A.'s office, and she fielded all phone calls. On June 26, Carol had spoken to a man who refused to give his name. She assumed it was a male, although it could have been someone calling through a machine that changes voices completely.

"Listen carefully," the voice said. "A woman named Kit Minton has possession of a computer that belongs to Liysa Northon."

The last time Pat Montgomery and Dennis Dinsmore talked to Kit, the Mintons were living in Kailua, Hawaii. There had been no mention of computers at that time. Now Dinsmore called every phone number he could find for the Mintons, finally homing in on their new number in New England. He left messages for them to call him at once, but there was no response. It was July 13 when Kit Minton called to say that her family had been on vacation and had just returned.

When Dinsmore asked her about the missing computer, she said she didn't want to comment until she conferred with someone. Later that day, Cal Minton called Dinsmore and verified that they *did* have the computer that Liysa had given them to keep "maybe four to eight months before Chris's death."

"Can you describe it?"

"It's a Gateway Solo laptop."

"Could you read me the model and serial numbers?" Dinsmore asked.

Cal Minton said he didn't feel comfortable in revealing that. He and his wife were caught between Liysa and the homicide investigators, and he wasn't sure what they should do. He asked to speak with an attorney to be sure that he and Kit wouldn't be held liable for giving Liysa's property away, especially if it damaged her criminal case.

"Would you honor a subpoena or a search warrant?" Dinsmore asked.

"Of course."

Liysa's problems and histrionics had disrupted the Mintons' lives just as they had the Duveauxs' and the Clarks'. Being her close friend was akin to stepping into a tornado with no easy way to escape. Cal said that when Liysa gave them the computer for safekeeping, they'd all been in Hawaii—not in Bend. She had explained that she feared Chris's sister would steal it from her because she'd robbed them before. Further, Liysa said that Chris was so jealous of her that she was afraid he would delete her work if he saw what was in there.

Cal Minton promised Dinsmore that he would be in touch as soon as he talked to a lawyer.

But time was growing short.

Dennis Dinsmore called the Bend Police Department and retrieved their report on the burglary case: 00-4179. Chris had been the complainant when the computers vanished, and even *he* thought that they'd been in the Bend house when they were "stolen." He told the investigating officer that his family had been away for the weekend, and when they returned, Liysa said her two computers, a 35-mm camera, and a watch were missing.

Early on Saturday morning, July 14, 2001—with the trial looming only two days away—Dennis Dinsmore had contacted Trooper Earl Rozman of the Connecticut State Police and asked him to have a trooper contact the Mintons in Salem, Connecticut, to check the serial number on the Gateway computer they were holding for Liysa. The Connecticut police did so and found that it matched the serial number in the Bend police report: #0015336775.

With the help of the Connecticut State Police, a subpoena was served on the Mintons' residence and Trooper Jon Holston recovered the long-missing laptop. Liysa's camera hadn't been stolen either; it was also with the Mintons. Holston called Dennis Dinsmore at 7:45 A.M. (Pacific Time) that same Saturday morning to tell him that a Federal Express plane was already carrying the computer west for delivery later in the day. Pat Montgomery was waiting on the tarmac at the Pendleton Airport when the plane landed.

Liysa hadn't lost her work or her email. There was a good chance that most of it was locked in disorganized clusters inside the computer. However, neither the prosecution nor the defense knew what secrets the computer might divulge. "If we had gotten the computers sooner, it would have been different," Montgomery said. "But we only got them a day before the trial started, and we couldn't possibly download everything that was in there."

Still, they had a pretty good idea about what they were looking for. During the course of the investigation, Montgomery and Dinsmore had learned from both Phil Hetz and screenwriter Craig Elliot about the story line of one of her screenplays. The detectives suspected that more of her screenplays, journals, and emails might well reveal premeditation and planning in her husband's murder. Perhaps there might even be some evidence of her thought processes regarding her marriage. But how to *find* this material, if, indeed, it existed?

As Liysa had learned, there *were* ways to unearth deleted files, and Special Agent Ariel Miller, working out of the FBI's Portland office, was one of its special agents trained in forensic computer analysis. The trial was going to start on Monday, July 16. They had perhaps two days—maybe three—before actual testimony began, and the technique to bring back files would be arduous.

Pat Montgomery had filed a search warrant to enable the FBI agent—or "any police officer in the state of Oregon"—to search Liysa's computer for "evidence of the crime of murder in the writings, emails, and screenplays stored on the hard drive or stored in the computer memory. The computer [is] to be examined by a forensic computer specialist and the computer may be shipped to the computer forensic laboratory for analysis. The writings, emails, and screenplays shall be reduced to printed documents to be analyzed for evidentiary value."

This was a new kind of forensic science, unimaginable even a few years earlier. Ariel Miller got to work. Most computer users know that they can type in a word or group of words in a "global search" mode and their computer will race to find it. It can then be deleted, replaced, or ignored. Using much more sophisticated software, Miller was armed with words and phrases that might be in the Gateway laptop. He would have to work around the clock, but Miller began to bring up documents that Liysa believed she had deleted.

The files didn't appear in the order most computer users have become familiar with. Instead, they came up as "Unallocated Space Text Fragments," bits and pieces of what Liysa had typed in a year or two earlier. There were garbled words, strange symbols, and missing segments, but there were also large chunks of text that left no doubt that a central theme had insinuated itself throughout her screenplays: a woman, usually named "Elise," is married to a pilot with a "dissociative" personality who "jumpseats around the world committing rape and murder." His new bride tries to cope with his bizarre behavior but places herself at risk as she gets closer to understanding him.

"The confusing thing," Liysa had written in the words of Elise, "is that he goes to so much trouble to appear to be doing the right thing, when, in fact, he is incapable of caring for another human being in any mature way."

The writer had given the "Chris" character three different personalities: "(1) the 'Charming Chris'—charismatic, handsome, friendly, talented; (2) 'Holden'—the rebellious adolescent—hates people, speaks in clichés, but is still somehow eager to please and even a bit naive, and (3) 'The Destroyer'—hurts people in any way he can—sadistic to the people close to him . . . the one who uses women and throws them away. . . ."

Working feverishly, Ariel Miller winnowed out what could only be Liysa's skillfully written but weirdly fictional view of her marriage. She envisioned child molestation, rapes, sex with animals, and the steady progression of the "wife's" peril as she comes closer to the secret of "The Destroyer."

In all of Liysa's screenplays, the husband character apparently dies in the last scene, when the wife kills him by a fatal blow or bullet to his temple. All her tales were, just as Pat Birmingham had found when he read the pages she had already given to him, consumed with the good and noble wife, the pathological husband, and the time, finally, when she kills him.

But there was more, a kind of miasmatic evil that seeped to the surface of the computer's brain. With the defense team's rights to discovery, Pat Birmingham and Wayne Mackeson would be made aware of how much violence and hatred was in Liysa's computer, and it was shocking—more shocking than the samples of her work that they had received from the State through discovery already. For now, the process continued while both the prosecution and the defense waited to hear what Special Agent Miller had found.

"Ariel Miller did a great job for us," Montgomery said. "He found what we hadn't been able to find."

The FBI expert unearthed fragmented files containing the emails Liysa had sent from late 1999 until June 2000. Just as she now sent letters written in her cramped handwriting out of jail, she had flooded the Internet with her feelings about Chris and her hopes to be with Craig Elliot as a lover *and* as a wealthy screenwriter, followed by her subsequent boredom with him. But most devastating of all were her emails that suggested Chris Northon's murder had been premeditated. Miller printed them out as the trial began.

CHAPTER THIRTY-THREE

NO ONE IN THE GALLERY of the courtroom knew that the computer even existed, and the principals were careful to debate its value as evidence only in chambers. But the defense team was antsy. The suggestion that Liysa's computer or her screenplays might be introduced into evidence had them between a rock and a hard place. They didn't know what else might be on the hard drive that was spitting out information. It might be a positive thing for Liysa's case, or it might be devastating. They leaned toward keeping this evidence out.

Wayne Mackeson argued that the contents of Liysa's computer—whatever might be in there—should be permanently excluded from the trial even before opening arguments began. How could the defense make an opening statement if they didn't know what the State had to offer?

Judge Mendiguren denied his request. "I'm not going to do

that. I still think that the opening is an outline of what you think the evidence is going to be, and what you think the case is going to be—with both sides. There may be other evidence that may come in. We'll cover that when it does. I make that decision at that point, whether it's coming in or not, and we live with it. And if I make a mistake on it, and certainly if it hurts the defense, then you guys can go back and appeal. If I screw up and it's a not-guilty verdict, the State has an option then, but it would be much more limited. I have no idea of what I'm looking at as coming in. He [Steve Briggs] said there's a computer. Maybe it's there, maybe it isn't. I cannot make a ruling on what is total speculation."

STEVE BRIGGS made the opening statement for the prosecution, explaining to the jurors the legal definition of self-defense.

"A person is justified in using physical force upon another person to defend herself from what she reasonably believes to be the use or the *imminent* use of unlawful physical force. A person may only use the degree of force which she reasonably believes to be necessary. I have to prove that she [Liysa Northon] did not comply with the law of self-defense. That's the burden of the State."

Had Liysa used more physical force against Chris than was necessary to protect herself and Bjorn? Briggs suggested that she had, telling the jury that they would hear incriminating information about her from the results of Chris's autopsy and blood tests. The assistant D.A. wondered why Liysa had driven through so many towns without reporting the shooting. And he beat the defense to the draw in bringing up the incident in Bend two years earlier when Liysa and Chris had, indeed, had a physical fight that ended with Chris's arrest. The Bend encounter was sure to be important to Birmingham and Mackeson's case, and Briggs wanted to defuse its effect before it could be built into something bigger than it was. "The charges were dropped," he said flatly.

The jurors were not familiar with the details of the fatal camping trip, and Briggs went through the sequence of events that Liysa had related to the staff in the Dayton hospital, to Deputy Keith Larkin, and to Deputy Dick Bobbitt.

Liysa had told them all that Chris drank a whole bottle of vodka at the campsite. "But she actually never *saw* him take a drink," Briggs said. "All she ever saw was him drinking out of a red cup." Liysa had told so many people that Chris was drunk on vodka the night he died, Briggs stressed, and then he turned to the jurors. "Remember I told you [that] at the autopsy they drew Chris Northon's blood, and they found Restoril, the sedative, in it? They also checked for blood alcohol. Did he have any alcohol in his blood?

"None."

That was a shock to the gallery and the jury. Briggs explained what he and Pat Birmingham both knew—something that seemed to war with the crime lab results. Chris Northon *had* had alcohol in his body, but not in his blood. It was residual alcohol in his urine. He'd died with a full bladder: ".03 or .04 percent of alcohol . . ."

Briggs didn't deny that Chris had had something to drink earlier in the day, or that his body had processed it, but for some reason, he had not urinated. What did that mean?

Briggs and Birmingham had come to the same conclusion. A human being with a massive overdose of a sedative is comatose, and therefore unable to empty his bladder. That is why hospital patients who are in comas have all manner of tubes and drains sprouting from their bodies.

The jurors would have to wait for expert witnesses in toxicology to explain that.

"At the crime scene, there was an open half-empty bottle of Kahlúa," Briggs continued. "There was a bottle of bourbon, only one eighth of it left. There was an empty wine bottle—but *no* vodka bottle lying around the crime scene."

What had happened to the missing vodka bottles? Or had they never been there at all?

There was also a problem with Liysa's version of the shooting, the assistant A.G. continued. The trajectory was at about seventy degrees, not quite straight down through Chris Northon's temple and out the other side after it destroyed his brain and penetrated farther into the sand. But the bullet could not have entered Chris's head at a horizontal angle as it would have if Liysa had been running by, firing wildly toward the sleeping bag.

"However, she said that she was running or walking by about eight feet of distance—which would put the trajectory much lower. She also told an inmate friend of hers that she was backing up when she shot him."

Viewed with a doubter's eye, there were too many details that didn't jibe, Briggs said. Liysa's injuries were slight—a moderate black eye, a few scrapes—but she'd had no marks on her neck to indicate she'd been strangled "two or three times." She had full range of motion in her extremities, even though weeks later she had written letters from jail saying she still couldn't dress herself.

Chris's injuries had also been slight, save for the fatal shot. His shoulder was scraped, too, and one toe was injured. There were also the odd scratches or burns on his chest.

Why, Briggs asked, had Lisa taken time to strap Bjorn in his car seat when she was so afraid that Chris was after them? Why had she said she wasn't familiar with the area in Wallowa County? She had family there—she vacationed there. She knew it very well, indeed.

Liysa had given three versions of her gun's misfiring. In one, she said the gun had gone off in the car while she was loading it, and to someone else she said it went off accidentally just after she'd shot Chris. She told her father she had fired it in the woods to see how the action went.

"As I told you," Briggs continued, "the defendant's a professional photographer. She likes to write. She has written a couple of screenplays. . . . One story she wrote for a screenplay was about a woman who was abused by her husband who then kills her husband with a speargun to his temple. . . ."

Briggs didn't know it all yet. Ariel Miller was still squeezing lost documents out of Liysa's computer. No one knew how much incriminating evidence might be extruded. But for now, they had the "speargun" murder.

PAT BIRMINGHAM, just as curious about what Miller might find, rose to make the opening statement for the defense. He offered the jurors a "preview" of what was to come. "It's just a big jigsaw puzzle to you right now to try to put it together so that you can more easily follow the evidence as it comes in.

"We feel that the evidence is going to show that this is a plain, simple case of self-defense and defense of another. And the other is her three-year-old child, Bjorn Northon. The evidence is going to show that she had every reason, justifiable reason, to be in fear of her life and the life of her child."

Birmingham had arranged for many of Liysa's women friends in Hawaii to testify to the "strange bruises on Ms. Northon's face, her neck, her back, missing hair." He said that at one time they had confronted her about it. "And she broke down and explained to them what had happened."

Pat Birmingham had an onerous job to do, and he did it with a cloak of apprehension on his shoulders, although the gallery couldn't see that. He did not bad-mouth the victim, describing Chris as a "confirmed bachelor . . . charming guy, a nice guy, an airline pilot, liked to do his own thing, liked to go out in the woods. That's when he was happiest. . . .

"Ms. Northon was the opposite. She was very much into children, family, child rearing, homeschooling. There was a clash and there was some violence—but nothing approaching what happened on October ninth."

Birmingham re-created the Sunday the Northons spent on the Lostine River. "They had been leaving the campsite from time to time, taking turns baby-sitting, a little hiking. He appeared to be getting drunk, and she confronted him. She said, 'You're an airline pilot. You shouldn't be drinking.' He was smoking marijuana and popping some pills. He became enraged and grabbed her and threw her in the river fully clothed and held her head underwater. . . . Once she got away from him; she just went limp. She didn't fight back. He put his sleeping bag between the tent and the campground, and she thought he was asleep—passed out. So when he was quiet, she tried to walk past him and he jumped up, grabbed her, tackled her, put his hands on her throat, pushed her down on the ground, and asked her what in the hell she was doing. And she told him, 'I want to take the baby and leave,' and he said, 'Do that and I'll kill you.'

"Then she waited and after he'd calmed down, she tried to decide what to do. She took the back way up to the car, got past him, retrieved a revolver that her father had given her several months before for self-defense. She was trying to load it in the dark, but somehow she cocked it and the gun went off. And she really panicked then, thinking that he was going to be enraged—ran down and got her child. As she was walking or running by, back up to the car, six to eight feet away, she fired the gun at him or at the bag. . . ."

Birmingham acknowledged that Liysa had driven all the way to the Walla Walla area, but he stressed that she had been terribly afraid, fearful that Chris was coming after her to assault her again.

And at the hospital, the defense attorney continued, things had begun to go awry. He suggested that Liysa, in shock, had been questioned too many times, virtually interrogated. The gathering of evidence had been flawed, items had been lost, and the witnesses who would testify would not remember details as well now—nine months after the crime.

Further, Birmingham said he would produce toxicologists who would contradict the State's experts.

THE GALLERY and the jurors settled back for what they fully expected would be weeks of witnesses. Liysa seemed very small as she sat between her attorneys, her shoulders hunched, her straight brown hair falling down her back, her face devoid of makeup. She was the picture of vulnerability as her chin quivered and her teeth chattered. How *could* such a fragile woman have fought off a two-hundred-pound man?

Testimony began, as it does in most homicide trials, with the first officer on the crime scene—Rich Stein, the undersheriff who had found Chris's body.

He was followed by Ellen Duveaux, the friend Liysa had run to, who was clearly not a friendly witness for the State. The prosecution called her to the witness stand on July 17, 2001. Both Pat Montgomery and Dennis Dinsmore had spoken to her before she took the stand, going over the statements she had given to them earlier in the investigation. She testified to those and to nothing else and appeared to be very ill at ease.

Ellen spoke of her close friendship with Liysa for twenty-three years. Although they had only actually *seen* each other about ten times in that period, they had always written letters.

"Her letters are beautiful letters," Ellen said softly. "I've kept many letters from her high school and college years."

She explained why Papako Mattson had stayed at her family's home on the weekend Chris Northon died. "In August, I taught a child's course in glassmaking at the community college in Walla Walla and Papako had wanted to come. So she [Liysa] was calling me to see if I could do a little special weekend session with him. I said, 'Of course.' Any time I could see Papako, I'd grab him if I could."

"What time on that Friday evening of October sixth did the defendant arrive?" Briggs asked.

"It was getting late, but I don't know if it was between seven and nine. We don't wear watches. We sort of just work from sunup to sundown."

Liysa had spent the night and then left at 11:00 on Saturday morning to meet Chris for their camping trip.

"When was the next time you saw her?"

"Monday morning—between seven and seven thirty. My husband was on his way out to go work."

"Tell us how she looked when you saw her."

"Awful. She was beaten up."

"What was it about her appearance that makes you say that?"

"Her cheekbone popping out of the skin and bruises on her arms after she took her coat off—"

"Okay. Was she wet?"

"I hugged her and I got wet. A damp wetness."

"What did she say happened?"

"Well, immediately we were more concerned about Bjorn in the car. Liysa couldn't use her right arm because it was sort of buggered up—"

"Is that what she told you?"

"No, I could see it was just dangling and then we took her wet clothes off. I could see her arms had bruises up and down and a lot of abrasions, and she couldn't use her shoulder properly to lift anything. So I picked Bjorn out of the car and brought him into my home."

Ellen said she drew a bath and Liysa got in with Bjorn.

As she testified, Ellen was very nervous and kept correcting herself.

"Her legs had big bruises—"

"Let me ask you about the arms first of all," Briggs interrupted. "You said she had bruises all up and down her arms?"

"Not bruises all up and down—she had some major things going on where her shoulder—I mean, I'm not a doctor. I don't know how—you know."

"Well, let me make it more clear then. Did you see bruises on her arms or not?"

"Maybe I was more upset about the open cuts. She had open cuts on her knees. And I don't know how many bruises she had on her arms, but I know she was bruised. I mean, I wasn't exactly in a great state either. Gosh, it all seems like a big blur now because, I mean—I know I saw the things I saw. I know she wasn't looking like Liysa looked Saturday morning when she left."

The witness said she'd washed Liysa's clothes for her while she took a bath with her son. Apparently, Ellen didn't realize that she had contradicted herself several times. She wasn't able to recall any particular bruises at all on Liysa—except for the one on her cheek.

"Did she tell you that morning anything about the use of a gun?" Briggs asked.

"Not until she came back from the police."

Ellen wasn't sure what had caused the fight at the campground. "He was upset—he was trying to drown her. I don't know how much of the beating happened then, but it had been a pretty nasty situation."

"Did she tell you anything about being in the tent?"

"Yes."

"And looking out and the moon was gone?"

"When she came out of the tent to go up to the car, the

moon was gone. I remember that. I don't know how many times she came out of the tent."

"Did she tell you whether she looked out and saw Chris at all?"

"One of those times—I don't know which—he was laying in the river facedown naked."

"Laying *in* the river?"

"Well, laying by the river."

"All I'm asking you is what she told you," Briggs pressed a little. "Did she tell you 'laying *by* the river?' Do you remember?"

"I don't remember."

"Did she say what she did with him when he was laying there?"

"She pulled him back up and put him in the sleeping bag."

Ellen said that it had been her idea for Liysa to call the domestic violence shelter and they told her to go to the hospital. "I insisted she call. . . ."

Liysa had been gone for a few hours at the hospital and Ellen said she had become a little concerned.

"What did she say when she returned?" Briggs asked.

"She said things weren't—didn't go so well."

"Did she say anything specifically?"

"Yeah . . . as far as that she was in trouble, and that she had some things to resolve."

Only then had Liysa told her old friend that she had shot at Chris's sleeping bag, and that the gun had gone off again—accidentally—on her way back to her vehicle.

"Did you ask the defendant if she knew whether he was lying there bleeding or not?"

"Yes. She said she shot at the dark image of the sleeping bag and then just took off."

"Did she say anything about whether anybody offered—anyone went to help him at all?"

"No."

"Did she tell you whether she stopped at her brother's house on her way to yours?"

"No."

PAT BIRMINGHAM CROSS-EXAMINED Ellen Duveaux, who was in most ways a defense witness. He didn't say it aloud, but Liysa hadn't told *him* that she'd stopped at her brother's house after she shot Chris either. He had long since discovered there were many things she hadn't shared with her attorneys.

"Ms. Duveaux, would you describe her emotional state when she showed up at your house?" Birmingham asked.

"I've never seen anyone hurt, ever. I mean, I've led a pretty sheltered life. But she was pretty disheveled. And, I mean, definitely a beaten-up woman wasn't something I wanted to see."

"Was she shaking?"

"Oh, yeah."

"Was she shivering?"

"Yes."

"Was she speaking clearly in a strong tone?"

"No, we really didn't—I sort of just took her in like a mother hen. We didn't really talk that much. I just knew something bad had happened to her."

"Okay. When this was happening, were you taking notes or writing everything she said down and what order she said it?"

"No—I was chewing my fingernails like crazy." Ellen's eyes flooded with tears.

"Are you absolutely certain that everything that you've told the court here happened in the same order that she told you, or—"

"No."

"Did the wounds look different before she got in the tub and after she got out of the tub?"

"Well, they were clean. There wasn't so much debris, gravel and stuff in her little legs."

"And you said you didn't discuss a whole lot because her other son woke up?"

"Oh, yeah—we were all doing our protective mode of just trying to keep it calm, I mean. I could have been screaming and running around."

"And," Birmingham continued, "she said she fired at the bag—she didn't say she actually hit him?"

"No . . . my concern was what happened, if he was laying there and needed help. That's what I asked Liysa—what we should do."

Ellen seemed so nervous that she wasn't helping either side very much. Birmingham soldiered on.

"Now, the firing of the two shots—do you know for sure whether she said she fired two shots, one before she shot him or one after she shot him?"

"From what I recollect, it was all the way back up after she'd shot at the sleeping bag that it went off when she was going up the trail to the car."

"Now, are you sure of that—or is that just to the best of your recollection?"

"That's the best of my recollection."

"Thank you, I have nothing further."

Ellen Duveaux asked Judge Mendiguren if she could hug Liysa and he shook his head, so she blew her a kiss instead as she walked by the defense table. And then she was *gone*. Although the investigators had asked her to remain in Enterprise so that they could speak to her further, she practically flew out of the courthouse to her car and was on her way home to Dayton before they could reach her.

They knew they could always find Ellen again. For the moment, the prosecutors and the detectives were more interested in what Liysa had left on her computer's hard drive.

* * *

THE TRIAL was barely under way, but in the inner workings of her computer, Liysa's carefully constructed facade as the innocent victim of domestic violence had begun to shatter and fall away. Neither the jury nor the defense team, however, knew about this devastating evidence yet. As the sun grew hot enough to make the petunias droop on the courthouse lawn and the bailiff closed the venetian blinds to cool the big oak courtroom, Deputy Kevin Larkin took the witness stand. He recalled the Monday in October when he was called to the Dayton General Hospital.

He identified the Polaroid photographs he took of Liysa Northon in the ER there. They showed a pale, freckled woman, her eyes closed, with a brownish bruise under her left eye. Her face was so devoid of expression that it looked like a death mask. Other photos showed a slight scrape on one shoulder and what appeared to be a small, healing cut on her knee.

"Now," Steve Briggs asked, "are these photographs whited out at all or are they pretty accurate?"

"Those look to be exactly the same Polaroid photos I took. They're not the best-quality pictures I've ever seen, but they're pretty close."

They did not depict the savagely beaten woman that Ellen Duveaux had described. Pat Birmingham suggested that Liysa's injuries and bruising had continued to darken as the day passed.

"Would it surprise you that there were photographs taken later where the injuries looked more distinct?"

Briggs objected. "Whether he's surprised doesn't matter."

Judge Mendiguren overruled the objection.

"Yeah," Larkin answered. "It would surprise me."

"So, in your experience, bruises don't get darker after a while?"

"Well, it's been my experience if a bruise is such and the

trauma to the skin is such—that it creates a dark bruise—there is usually evidence of it right away."

"So if there are photographs that show her eye darker than your photographs and show bruises darker than your photographs, you'd be surprised?"

"I wouldn't be surprised on her cheek injury, but I *would* be surprised on the neck injuries."

Pat Birmingham suggested that Liysa didn't have bruises on her neck from being strangled because her husband had simply pressed on her carotid artery, but it was a reach.

There were questions that stayed in the jurors' minds. Why had Liysa waited almost an hour into her interview with Deputy Larkin before she mentioned that she had shot at her husband? Why was she still so wet when she arrived at Ellen Duveaux's farm, when it had been hours, by her own reckoning, since she'd survived drowning?

If she had turned her SUV's heater on as she drove through the chilly October night—which she surely must have—it would seem that her clothes would have been almost dry by six or seven in the morning.

CHAPTER THIRTY-FOUR

JEFF DOVCI, now the laboratory supervisor of the Oregon State Police forensic lab in Pendleton, took the witness stand next. He recalled that it had been essential for him and criminalist Christine Ogilvie to get to the crime scene the night of October 9. "It was dark when we arrived . . . [but] there was a strong likelihood that it was going to rain the next day or even that night, so we couldn't wait—we proceeded."

The witness described the scene near the river; the camping gear spread out, the flashlight so new it still had a price sticker on it, fishing tackle, the chair in the Lostine River, two yellow rubber gloves that seemed oddly out of place as they floated in the river, the male clothing draped over a chair.

The man's clothes were soaked. "There were several items of clothing. . . . When we examined them, they were very damp. I believe there was a pair of sweatpants, and they seemed very heavy. The pockets were full of river sand."

One rubber glove had been tested, Dovci said, for signs of blood. "It was found to be negative."

"Was there a pot on the stove?" Briggs asked.

"Yes . . . there was about a half inch of water in it, but nothing else."

Photographs of the scene were introduced into evidence, all showing the campsite. One was of a plastic bag holding children's antibiotics.

"Did you find any other types of medication anywhere in the camp scene, any other type of prescription drugs?"

"No."

The impressions in the sand at the edge of the river had interested Dovci. "I'm a fairly stout person, and it took quite a bit of effort to push that sand around, so there was a depression and scuff marks and especially that series of impressions which led me to believe that somebody at least had fallen, or maybe been pushed and left the impressions there."

"And which direction would the person who was on the ground have been facing with the hand, knee, and footprints?" Briggs asked.

"They would have been facing toward the water . . . facing roughly north."

These were the small prints that Christine Ogilvie's hand and knees had fit into, prints of a person kneeling.

Dovci said that he had found three sets of shoe prints along the packed sand of the shore—large, small, and a child's—but the scuffed-up area was just south of the camp table. "It led me to believe that somebody had at least fallen there—or maybe been pushed down."

Moving on to photos of the trail directly above where Chris Northon's body lay, Briggs pointed to something black on the ground and asked what it was.

"This is a headlamp. It has an elastic band and then it has the flashlight which is attached to it. And basically it's for hands-free hiking—or whatever."

All in all, the items found near the Lostine River were what one would expect to find at a campsite. Tupperware with cookies in it, high-end camping gear owned by obviously experienced campers.

Steve Briggs moved on to the possible trajectories of the bullet that killed Chris Northon. The most likely angle would suggest that he had been lying on his left side when he was shot. However, he had been found with his face looking toward the sky, and his body was somewhat twisted where it was zipped up tight in the mummy bag.

Jeff Dovci said that he had found this position "odd. I was looking at the face and I saw basically two different blood flow patterns on the face—which led me to believe that either someone had moved him over or he had rolled at some point after being shot. . . . What brought my attention was there was evidence of blood flow which was going *toward* Mr. Northon's left [ear], and then there was this other streak of blood which was flowing toward his right. That supported my conclusion that he had slumped or rolled—or somebody had moved him."

"Could you explain that a little more? Why if there was blood flowing at one point *this* way—and at another point *that* way—why did that mean anything to you?" Briggs asked.

"Well, gravity is going to act on a liquid and it's going to drain to the lowest point. So at one point, the forward part of his face was lower than the temple area, and so it was flowing toward the eye. And then at some point, he changed positions . . . and the blood was able to flow backwards or to the right."

Both of the victim's ear canals had held pooled blood.

Why would Liysa have moved Chris's body? She had told everyone that she was so frightened that he was coming after her. All of her reminiscences of that dark night were of flight. Had someone else come upon Chris and lifted him? That didn't seem to make much sense either. Or was it possible that there were *three* adults present that night? Not likely.

Dovci testified that they had never found the keys to Chris's vehicle, even though they had gone over it carefully looking for a magnetic key holder like Liysa had. They hadn't found Chris's cell phone either. Even if he'd been conscious and able to call for help, the mountains would have blocked out the signal.

Pat Birmingham Stood to cross-examine the State Police criminalist. His best chance was to point out that some evidence might have been lost or not tested as it should have been. The defense position must always be to place a seed of doubt in the minds of jurors.

He now brought up the camping pillow found next to Chris's head. "Okay, what, if anything, did you do with that pillow that was next to the head?"

"I remember looking at it, but I didn't do anything with it."

"Was it ever sent to the crime lab to see if there was blood spatter on it or a bullet hole in it?"

"I do not believe it was submitted."

"Did you notice any sand on the body of Christopher Northon?"

"Yes, there was sand. I didn't examine the entire body

down to the toes, but there was sand visible on his face and the upper shoulder area. . . ."

"And did you dictate as you were going through the scene?"

"Yes, I did."

"And didn't you dictate the statement that apparently the body was moved at some point because there was a drip which 'runs across the brow ridge which appears to have traveled from the deceased's right brow ridge area across to the left brow ridge?' "

"If you're reading it verbatim, I probably did."

Birmingham pounced, saying that he had seen nothing in the report about blood running the other way, too.

Dovci stonewalled him, saying that he remembered strongly seeing two directions of flow, even though he hadn't noted it in his dictation.

It was a moot point. There were photographs showing the two flowing blood patterns. But this was a fair fight between two professionals. Pat Birmingham wanted the jury to know that Dovci had found a marijuana "smoking device" and some rolling papers on the picnic table.

"And did you find marijuana."

"No."

"And did you find a knife sheath with a missing knife?"

"Yes, we found a leather sheath—I used to have a knife similar to it. The sheath looked like it went with a fish knife that you use for scaling and opening up fish. They're fairly long and slender blades. The sheath was there, but the knife we never found."

"Did you or anyone shine a light into the water the next day trying to see whether there were car keys in the river or there was a knife in the river?"

"I did. Basically, I stood at the water's edge and I had a

bright flashlight and looked through the water. At night, you don't have the sun bouncing off the water, so I looked for something that would be shiny as would a knife or keys, and I could not see anything."

Birmingham knew that the sleeping pad Chris was found on had slipped outside the chain of evidence when it was accidentally given to Dick Northon. Birmingham was merciless with Jeff Dovci as he informed the jury of the temporarily missing evidence through the criminalist's answers. He had every right to do so; it was a strong point for the defense, even though, in reality, Dick had never touched the pad.

Birmingham did his best to denigrate the crime lab's tests or failure to test certain items. He suggested that the criminalists' triangulation measurements to allow reconstruction of the placement of objects at the scene were faulty. He raised his eyebrows because the witness had found no powder burns on Chris Northon's face or the sleeping bag, and moved on to a very complicated series of questions on blood spatter patterns.

Birmingham's questions were cleverly esoteric, good fodder to confuse some jurors and convince those who may have watched television's *CSI* that Dovci and the other investigators had not done everything they should have. But the State had never claimed that Liysa had held a gun close enough to her husband's head to leave the stippling of gun barrel debris behind. And no one could be sure exactly *where* Liysa had been standing when she fired her gun, but she still claimed she had been running and firing blindly into the night at a dark lump in a sleeping bag. And she had heard a grunt or some exclamation from the target, and kept running all the way to Dayton, Washington.

At one point, to respond to Pat Birmingham, Jeff Dovci had to get on his hands and knees in the courtroom to demonstrate his theory on the position of the person who was trying to drown the other person. For Dovci, at 240 pounds, it was a rigorous cross-examination.

On redirect, Steve Briggs elicited answers that a blood spatter examination at the scene wouldn't have made much difference in Dovci's opinion that Chris Northon's body had been moved. Nor would an examination of the camping pillow.

"You also testified that there was sand in the man's wet pants that were slung over that chair? How much sand was in the pockets?"

"About a handful, maybe a one- or two-inch diameter ball of sand."

"Do you have any idea of how that sand might have gotten in those pants?"

"I have a real elementary idea."

"Tell me what you think."

"When I was a boy, I learned to swim in a freshwater lake that had sand on the bottom. And I remember when I used to dive down to the bottom and I was just messing around, I'd come up with sand in my pockets in my swim trunks. I think if someone was to roll around on the bottom of the water there, especially if they were moving, a kind of friction or motion—where the sand could get into the pockets. . . . Somehow it got scooped up as he was moving along the bottom of the river."

"When you were a boy," Briggs responded, "and you were swimming on the *top* of the lake, you didn't get any sand in your pockets, right?"

"No."

Pat Birmingham asked Jeff Dovci on recross: "When you were a boy, if you were rolling around with somebody in the water, in fairly shallow water, you'd probably get some sand in your pockets?"

"Sure."

"Perhaps you'd stir up sand from the bottom?"

"It's not so much what you're doing at the time, it's just the action of being on the bottom and scooping it up into the pockets."

Finally, Jeff Dovci was excused.

What did sand in Chris's pockets have to do with this case? According to Liysa's version of that night, she and Chris *had* struggled on the beach of the Lostine River, and it was *he* who had held *her* underwater.

If the jurors were as puzzled as the gallery was, no one knew. Like all jurors, their expressions were bland masks.

ELLEN DUVEAUX had left Enterprise, but before she could even cross over into Washington State, Dennis Dinsmore received an anonymous message on his voice mail. It was virtually impossible to identify the voice, although it sounded male. The information that was imparted, however, was electrifying—and probably explained why Ellen had been nervous about being cross-examined any further.

According to the informant, Ellen knew many things that she had not mentioned. He said that Liysa had called Ellen a few weeks before Chris was killed and reportedly, had asked her for some poison. Ellen had told her that they didn't have any poison. She then had been concerned enough to call Chris and tell him not to go on a camping trip with Liysa.

Pat Montgomery located Ellen and asked her about the allegations made in the anonymous call. The look on her face was half stricken and half relieved, but finally, Ellen sighed and admitted to Montgomery that it had become so difficult for her to protect Liysa. Obviously a conflicted woman, she was very sad as she finally opened up to the State Police detective.

"We didn't realize that Liysa was so mentally sick," Ellen said. "We had no idea until after she shot Chris. But she doesn't need to go to prison—she needs help."

It was true, she said, that Liysa had asked for poison and reacted in disbelief when Ellen said there wasn't any on their farm. Liysa had said, "You *have* to have something to kill rats and mice."

It was either during that phone call or one shortly thereafter when Ellen talked to Liysa again. "I wish Chris would just go up onto that mountain and never come back," she had hissed. "I'd drown him, but I'd probably be the one who got drowned. . . ."

Ellen said she hadn't warned Chris not to go camping then, however. She didn't really think Liysa was serious. She had complained about Chris for such a long time that her friends didn't believe how serious she was about getting rid of him.

Liysa had willingly given her gun and bullets to Deputy Kevin Larkin, but until now the investigators hadn't known that Liysa had arrived at Ellen's house the morning after Chris's murder with a backpack. In her concern for Liysa's condition, Ellen had completely forgotten about it until after Liysa was arrested later in the day.

It had looked like something any camper would carry, and Ellen said she had put it in her basement with some of Liysa's other belongings for a while. Sometime later she looked into it and found a purple Crown Royal whiskey sack inside and figured that Liysa must have some expensive liquor. But there was no bottle. Instead, there were two strange-looking black metal objects that resembled guns, only they had prongs on them. She'd shown them to her husband, Francois, and he didn't know what they were either, but he warned Ellen, "Don't push the buttons on them."

When Ellen described the objects to a friend, he said they sounded like "stun guns"—TASERs that police sometimes used to drop someone with electrical shocks but without killing them.

Ellen said that Liysa had also left a 35-mm camera in the pack. But then she never went anywhere without a camera or two.

Ellen admitted that she had decided not to tell the police about the backpack; her first thought had been, as always, to protect Liysa. She put the pack in her basement until, sometime later, when Tor DeWitt came to her house and said that Liysa wanted her camera. Ellen gave the whole backpack to him, and neither of them had discussed the stun guns.

"Why didn't you testify to all of this?" Pat Montgomery asked.

"I was confused," Ellen said, "and I didn't know what to do at first because Liysa was my friend. I just wanted her to get some mental help. I was willing to answer the questions when I testified—but nobody asked me about poison or a backpack."

Liysa's requests had seemed so frightening that Ellen hadn't wanted to believe her, or perhaps she'd been in denial. Beyond looking for poison, Liysa had asked Ellen if she knew how to get Valium, sleeping pills, or other "hard drugs," only a few weeks before Chris died. And, strangely, she had also asked her old friend if she knew of any swift-running rivers.

"And you didn't volunteer any information, did you?" Montgomery asked. "Will you come back and testify now?"

Ellen Duveaux nodded. When the State called her, she would drive back to Enterprise and tell the whole truth, as painful as it was.

CHAPTER THIRTY-FIVE

WITNESSES FOLLOWED one another to the stand. Court TV cameras focused on them—carefully avoiding the jurors. The cameras revealed a battered old door behind the witness chair, its oak panels the shade of honey from decades of varnish brushed over dents and scars in the wood.

Liysa's brother, Tor, now sat in the witness chair. He looked much like her and their father Wayland, except that he had the thick neck and shoulders of a bodybuilder. He testified about seeing Liysa's bruises and her wet clothes very early on the morning of Monday, October 9.

Dr. Khalil Helou explained Chris Northon's postmortem exam to the jurors, many of whom winced at his description. Jeanne and Dick Northon could not stand to be in the courtroom as the photographs of their son's body were shown and waited nervously in the court offices.

Deputy Dick Bobbitt testified about seeing Liysa at the Umatilla County sheriff's substation. He appeared to be sympathetic toward her as he related how afraid she had been that day. She had repeated to him her story of her terror when her husband had tried to drown her and take her baby away from her.

"Could you describe for us how she looked?" Steve Briggs asked.

"She looked beat. She had a bruise on the left—I *believe*—the left side of her face, I guess. She looked like she was fifty instead of in her thirties is the best way I can think of to describe it."

"Did she look tired?"

"She looked tired."

And Liysa had voiced the mantra to Bobbitt that was now so familiar: "At least my kids are safe."

Michelle Hooper and Patty Gallaher, the nurses on duty at the small hospital in Dayton, Washington, testified about their impressions of Liysa when they treated her in the ER. They repeated what she had said to them about being attacked by her husband. Neither nurse characterized her injuries as serious.

In the formal setting of the courtroom, Patty Gallaher was only slightly less sardonic about Liysa's demeanor in the ER than she had been when she talked to Sheriff Ron Jett the day after the shooting.

"Did she [Liysa] say whether or not her husband was a light sleeper?" Steve Briggs asked Gallaher.

"Yes."

"What did she say?"

"She just threw out that he was a light sleeper and occasionally took sleeping pills to sleep."

"Did she say if he took sleeping pills that night?"

"No."

"Did you examine the defendant at all for any marks or anything on her body?"

"I looked at her neck because she asked us to—to see if there were any. She said, 'There's got to be some bruising on my neck. My neck's really sore, you know.' So I got up and looked at her neck, but there was no visible bruising at the time."

On cross-examination, Pat Birmingham strove to elicit testimony from Patty Gallaher that would indicate that Liysa was disoriented and unable to connect her thoughts in the proper sequence as Deputy Kevin Larkin questioned her. But this was not a friendly witness for the defense, and it was hard-going for him.

"Was it fair to say that this was more of a cross-examination than a straight interview—when she would say something, the officer would then question her about it?" Birmingham asked. "Well, for example, about the drug usage. Didn't she tell the officer that her husband was an airline pilot and was drinking and using drugs? Didn't the officer make her justify what she was saying?"

"That's a yes and a no. I would say he would ask the question, but he wasn't trying to get justification in my impression. He was just trying to get a clear statement because it was fragmented."

* * *

LATE ON TUESDAY NIGHT, July 17, the State had handed over the first pages of material that Special Agent Ariel Miller had printed from a search of Liysa's "stolen" computer. Wayne Mackeson and Pat Birmingham hadn't had time to read the printouts before court. On Wednesday, Mackeson argued outside the jurors' presence that it could take a long time for the defense team to evaluate what were probably thousands of pages, much less interview people mentioned in those pages. The defense moved to have *all* of the computer-generated pages absolutely excluded from the trial *immediately*.

There was a little war going on between the prosecutors and the defense attorneys, a war over discovery. Mackeson didn't feel that the State had handed over the computer files in an expedient manner. The prosecution team groused that the defense was holding back, too. Probably they both were. Pat Birmingham had known the computer was in the Mintons' possession a few days before the investigators learned of its existence. He hadn't told them, but he *had* insisted to the Mintons that it must not be destroyed. And he was still holding the package sent to him anonymously that contained the stun guns, although now the prosecutors knew about their existence.

Both sides were edgy, all of them aware that a back story was taking place even as they proceeded with the public trial. Each side had strategies they intended to employ in the the trial they had expected. Would they still work? No one could be sure. Pat Birmingham was sticking to his straight self-defense position, and Steve Briggs was homing in on the many versions Liysa had given about the night of October 9. While those two attorneys asked questions of the witnesses, Dan Ousley and Wayne Mackeson were dealing with the problems that might or might not erupt if Judge Mendiguren allowed Liysa's computer material into evidence.

Robert Swanson, Ph.D., took the stand on Wednesday afternoon. Dr. Swanson was the director of the laboratory at the

Oregon Health & Science University in Portland that did the toxicology analysis in death investigations for the Oregon State Medical Examiners Office. Much had been said about Chris Northon's alleged drunkenness on the night he died, and Swanson could address that subject by explaining the results of tests performed on vials of blood preserved after Chris's autopsy.

"Let's start with the blood alcohol," Steve Briggs said. "What was the result of the blood alcohol test on the blood of Chris Northon?"

"Actually, we did two assays on the blood," Swanson said. "The first one was negative. Some time later, we were asked by the medical examiner to repeat the assay. That was negative also."

"What does negative mean?"

"It means that there was no detectable alcohol in his blood."

Swanson explained that in the state of Oregon, motorists with 0.08 percent blood alcohol were considered under the influence and too impaired to drive safely. The lowest reportable level of blood alcohol would be 0.01 percent. Chris hadn't even had that percentage in his blood.

Swanson said that his lab had gone further. After some discussion, samples of Chris's blood and urine were sent to the National Medical Services lab near Philadelphia. This was done, he explained, because of six Oregon screening tests they had performed on Chris's blood and urine. There were no amphetamines, opiates, cocaine metabolites, or barbiturates in Chris's blood. But they had come up with two positive results—one for benzodiazepines (tranquilizers) and one for THC (marijuana). To determine the finite level of those two positives would require the East Coast lab's validation.

Dr. Robert Middleberg, from the National Medical Services lab, was the next witness. "I'm a forensic toxicologist," he explained to the jury, "from Willow Grove, Pennsylvania. It's a small town just a little bit north and a little bit west of Philadelphia. We are generally used by almost every state for performing analyses that they may not have the capabilities to perform. [In this case] we were asked to both screen and confirm, to specifically look for compounds related to marijuana and a group of compounds known as benzodiazepines."

Dr. Middleberg said that the latter were commonly known as "the Valium family of drugs." More specifically, these were the calming drugs and some sleeping pills (Valium, Serax, Ativan, Librium, and some otherss).

"Let's start with the test for THC," Steve Briggs said.

The witness was obviously comfortable in testifying and had a folksy air about him as he discussed his findings in layman's terms. He said there were three components related to cannabinoid compounds (marijuana) and that the major psychoactive ingredient in marijuana was known as Delta-9-Carboxyl THC. "That was present at eleven nanograms per milliliter."

"What does that mean?" Briggs asked.

"The compound is inactive in the body. It has no effect on us. It's not a very high value—it may reflect a recent exposure to a very low dose of marijuana. Marijuana stays in the body for a long time—it may reflect some concentration from up to five or six days ago."

Briggs asked how much 11 nanograms was, and Middleberg said that one joint—a typical cigarette—would leave about 25 to 50 nanograms per milliliter of blood. In essence, there had been a negligible amount of marijuana in Chris Northon's blood.

However, there had been a great deal of Temazepam—the sleeping pill commonly known as Restoril—in the blood sample sent to Middleberg's lab.

"How much was there?" Briggs asked.

"Twenty-nine hundred nanograms per milliliter."

"Can you give us an idea about how much twenty-nine hundred nanograms of Temazepam is?"

"We kind of—pardon the expression—break these down in toxicology into 'a little bit,' 'some,' 'a lot,' or 'a hell of a lot.' And this one would kind of fall into bordering between 'a lot' and 'a hell of a lot.' "

The jurors smiled faintly. They understood this less-than-scientific but crystalline explanation. Somehow, Chris had ingested an overdose of sleeping pills—"a hell of a lot" of sleeping pills. Restoril was available in capsules of 7.5 to 30 milligrams and, because it was a Schedule 4 controlled substance, only by prescription.

"Can you give us an idea, based on the twenty-nine hundred nanograms, of approximately what type of dosage might have been involved?" Steve Briggs asked Dr. Middleberg.

"We're talking about the upper dosage units of thirty-milligram capsules—the highest you can get—of somewhere between three and five capsules if they were all consumed at the same time . . . for the seven-and-a-half-milligram capsules—twelve to twenty."

"Can you tell us what the impact on a person approximately six foot, a hundred ninety pounds, would be?"

"I would expect this person to be in a rather significant sleep."

PAT BIRMINGHAM ROSE to cross-examine Dr. Middleberg. He had to try to defuse the impact of his testimony and suggested that an individual who had taken a Valium-like compound over a period of time would develop a tolerance to the drug and not be affected by such a large dose. Middleberg agreed that some people did develop tolerances.

"[But] tolerance kind of works both ways. They may take

more to get the desired effect. And the desired effect with this particular compound generally is to induce sleep. . . . But if someone is taking enough to get twenty-nine hundred nanograms per milliliter, they're getting to that level, ahh, it is within that realm at which we have found that people die. As a forensic toxicologist, I would expect untoward effects from this amount."

That approach from the defense hadn't worked well, so Birmingham moved on to ask what side effects were associated with Restoril.

"Typically," Dr. Middleberg answered, "what you would expect to find is drowsiness, dizziness, lethargy, sleep, potentially coma, and death. In a very small percentage of people— probably less than 0.5 percent has been recorded—you will see some people become stimulated to a point where they become agitated. And there are self-reports of anger where people realized from taking this particular compound they became angry."

"This is referred to in the *Physicians' Desk Reference* as a 'rage reaction'?"

"Yes—"

"Thank you. I have nothing further."

It was a small victory, soon mitigated when Briggs elicited the information from the toxicologist that he had never heard of any studies where people who took Restoril had actually become violent—only the .05 percent who were agitated, and a much smaller percentage who'd *felt* angry.

Temazepam/Restoril was one of very few sleeping medications to be dispensed in gel capsules. They were filled with a very small amount of white powder. For someone with sinister intentions, it would have been an easy matter to twist open the capsules and release the contents. The powder alone dissolved very easily in water and alcohol.

What Dr. Middleberg's testimony meant was that if Chris Northon had not been shot, he probably would have succumbed to an overdose of Restoril. Scores of deliberate suicides have been accomplished with far fewer capsules than Chris had ingested.

_____ CHAPTER THIRTY-SIX _____

THE TRIAL was barely halfway through its third day when Dick Northon took the stand to testify about finding the sleeping pad and the tarp, both stained with his son's blood. They had been inadvertently left in Chris's Chevrolet when Dick picked it up. He had returned both to the investigators.

Sadly, Dick identified a picture of Chris and Bjorn, father and son, red-cheeked blonds smiling into the camera.

Ex-sheriff Ron Jett testified next. Steve Briggs had no choice but to focus on the retrieval of physical evidence in this case. It was Jett who had traveled to the Columbia Country Sheriff's Office to retrieve Liysa's gun and bullets. There was no problem with that. But the tarp and sleeping pad that Dick Northon had returned to Dan Ousley's office were problematic. Anything that falls outside the chain of evidence is, of course, leapt upon eagerly by defense attorneys, and Pat Birmingham made sure that the jurors were aware that the pad and tarp and an audio tape had fallen through the cracks. Who knew any longer if the bullet holes in the pad and tarp were still in the same place they originally were?

It would be well nigh impossible to distort that evidence, and Dick Northon hadn't touched it. He wished he'd never seen the items with dark dried blood on them.

The audiotape was a piece of evidence Liysa was vehement about. She insisted that she had surreptitiously taped Chris and another pilot giggling about adulterating drug tests so they could fool their airline. The tape had been in the sheriff's evidence room since it was found in the Northons' Bend home. It had nothing on it but some innocuous conversations with Liysa at their breakfast table. She, however, felt sure that the Wallowa County sheriff's investigators had deliberately erased the sections that validated her claims that Chris smoked marijuana before flying.

Had that been true—and there was no indication that the tape had been tampered with—it seemed to have nothing to do with Chris's death. He'd had such minimal residue of marijuana in his system when he died that it should have had no impact on the jury's decision.

It was so early in the trial that virtually no evidence had been introduced. Still, the ferocious struggle to block inflammatory evidence was going on outside the jurors' hearing. They ate the lunches sent over from the little shop across the street from the courthouse—Cloud Nine—while Judge Mendiguren jousted with the prosecutors and the defense attorneys.

Dan Ousley and Steve Briggs wanted Liysa's screenplays and the contents of her stolen computer *in*, and, naturally, Wayne Mackeson and Pat Birmingham wanted it all *out*.

Craig Elliot was on the witness list for the prosecution, but calls to his California home went unanswered. The screenplay he and Liysa had collaborated on was a virtual master plan for the way Chris Northon had been killed. No one suggested that the Hollywood screenwriter had played any part in the plan; Liysa had written the entire screenplay and Craig had only done some fine tuning and introduced her to production companies. Dennis Dinsmore's and Pat Montgomery's interviews with him had convinced them that Craig was an innocent dupe, totally unaware that Liysa was writing anything but fiction. It was understandable that he wasn't enthusiastic about testifying.

But the manuscript itself was too close to reality. "Elise" was the main character, obviously similar to "Liysa." The murdered husband in the screenplay was named "Ted," and Liysa had often characterized Chris as so evil that he reminded her of the real-life serial killer Ted Bundy. Liysa's best friend in Walla Walla, Marni Clark, was nicknamed "Bear," and so was "Elise's" best friend. Chris had been shot in the temple, and "Ted" in the screenplay had died of a wound to the temple. The small child was called "Bjorn." The similarities went on and on, too striking to be ignored. The screenplay involved insurance payoffs, and "Elise" was portrayed as heroic and selfless.

It might well have been Liysa Northon's life as she wished it to be and much too easy to mine for dangerous comparisons for the defense to accept.

The other entries on the hard drive of the computer Liysa had falsely reported as stolen were proving to be even more destructive to her. FBI Special Agent Ariel Miller had followed a dark trail through the files of Liysa's laptop. And he was still holed up in a motel room, working around the clock, locating and printing out emails and notes, chunks of screenplays.

Some of the most damning evidence Miller had found thus far was a batch of emails that warred with Liysa's claim that Chris's shooting was unplanned. She had maintained from the beginning that she had been forced to kill him only as a last resort. However, she had written a shocking email which appeared to have been to her father:

"It has *been worse lately*. I'm going to have to end it one way or another soon. There have been some really ugly public scenes, and my friends at the pool look at my bruises and don't know what to say. Drowning is the best in terms of detection—but I want a gun for back up, and then will have to get a sure fire disposal method. Both of us will have to throw the computers away because I just read they can trace email on hard drives. But I would replace yours with a new one. . . ."

Liysa went on to say that "there's more of this going on than anyone knows," and that she had found many other women who were being abused as she was. "Many people have stories—like Barb* and the fire, my friend of two years—I never knew beating was the reason she ended her marriage. Her dad beat her mother, too. My friend was one of only 2 women to escape the "beauty queen serial killer" and after the kidnap/rape/torture, all she could talk about to the FBI shrink was her dad. The shrink said seeing her mom cope with him all those years is probably what saved her life. She did the Stepford thing until she had a chance to make her move."

Was there ever a "Beauty Queen Serial Killer"? The detectives who read this unearthed email had never heard of him. In this email, Liysa moved easily from writing about her plans for drowning and/or shooting her husband to stating: "Randall Edwards is running for state treasurer, my old prom date/tennis partner. He's asked me to write a letter of endorsement for him for Bend."

But Liysa's narrative slipped quickly back to her main topic. "I would consider any relevant help from [a relative] more than adequate compensation for Papako's check. Silencer. Assistance. Anything. But it's not required. Just in case you thought I'd changed my mind, I thought I'd reassure you that I haven't."

In another email to her father, Liysa was scornful of both Craig and Chris: "I hope they like the script. I personally like the one I started with. I honestly think Craig just wanted a way to get in on this one, but I think we've turned it into a fairly good story, just not a great one. . . . Basically, I'm just doing anything I can to be enough of a commercial success so that I can get rid of Chris and not lose my house. But even if I did, he might still go off. It's so strange to watch someone turn from a semi-normal person into virtually a demon in the span of a few seconds. . . . I miss you. I dreamed we were ice skating the other night. We'd taken a sleigh ride under a full moon to a pond, and when we got there, there was a bonfire and an orchestra. And Christmas lights. It was a wonderful dream. I love you."

SHE WROTE TO A FRIEND in a lighter vein, but still discussing her desire to be rid of Chris. "Sorry about babbling. I keep so bottled up and I haven't even been writing lately so my way of lettin' off steam has been gone, and I'm about to lose it. . . . Can't someone beam him up and away in a beautiful balloon?"

There was no question at all that she wanted to be free of her husband, and that she wanted it to happen in a way in which she came out as financially enhanced as possible.

OUTSIDE THE JURY'S PRESENCE, Wayne Mackeson and Pat Birmingham suggested to Judge Mendiguren that the State must have known all along about Liysa's computers, as far back as January 2001, six months before the present trial, and had deliberately held them back to spring as a surprise at the last possible minute, essentially hog-tying himself and Birmingham with what might be *thousands* of pages of Liysa's writings that the defense couldn't begin to read thoroughly.

In truth, the only computer the prosecutors and their investigators had known about was the Apple *replacement* computer that Liysa had in the Bend house. And it had been clean as a whistle, with nothing that might link her to a premeditated murder.

Dennis Dinsmore and then Pat Montgomery were called to the witness stand. Dinsmore agreed that he and Montgomery *had* talked to Cal and Kit Minton in Hawaii in April. They had not asked about a computer because they believed both Liysa's laptop and the desktop model had been stolen almost a year before. They had asked about Liysa, and especially about the photo or slide of her crotch and inner thighs that she had reportedly sent to Kit.

"Did Kit Minton volunteer to you that she had a computer of the defendant's?" Steve Briggs asked.

"No."

"Did you ask for anything else, any other writings or letters from the defendant?"

"We talked about the fact that she received other letters, writings, but they were in the process of moving from Hawaii to Connecticut so they were just not around."

It wasn't until June 26—less than three weeks before—when Carol Terry, Dan Ousley's assistant, received the anonymous call in which the investigators learned the Mintons had Liysa's computer, Dinsmore explained. As for the ten spiral notebooks that Chris's friends had found in his Bend house and in the Kailua house, Dinsmore said it would have been very difficult to read through the more than three thousand pages of scribblings Liysa had jotted down.

One note among the many the detectives hadn't had access to was a note Liysa sent to Kit Minton, and it had already been forwarded to Pat Birmingham: "Hello, Kit, Thought I'd better send these while I can. Please stash the one slide with the receipt from one of Chris's drug tests with my computer. When I get the other shots, I'll send them along. Love and miss you, Liysa."

Birmingham hammered at Dennis Dinsmore, insisting that he and Pat Montgomery, along with Steve Briggs and Dan Ousley, must have known about the missing computers all along, and were now trying to sneak the laptop's contents into evidence.

Dinsmore wouldn't buckle. His demeanor was always calm, and he had testified in scores of murder cases. He explained to Judge Mendiguren that there had actually been *three* computers—one in the Bend house that had been purchased after the "theft," the laptop given to the Mintons, and a third.

Neither side was going to budge, and the judge finally decided to call the jury in that Wednesday afternoon just long enough to tell them to go home. No one could be sure just when testimony might resume. There was even the possibility that the trial would have to be split, stalled for weeks or months, and then begun again. If everyone involved had to read every word of Liysa's writings and, as the defense suggested, interview who knew how many more witnesses, the time-out could stretch on endlessly.

After the jurors left, Pat Montgomery took the stand. He verified that he and Dennis Dinsmore had not known about the missing computer until Carol Terry got the anonymous tip. Further, it was not the police investigators who took Liysa's journals from her homes; it had been Chris's friends. Montgomery had not suggested that they do that—it had already been done when he learned about it. He was too savvy a cop to suggest such a thing. Private citizens can remove items if they have access to property; sworn police officers cannot—not without a search warrant. If either Montgomery or Dinsmore had done that, the material would be useless as evidence. Illegally seized, it would be considered "fruit of the poisonous tree," in legal parlance.

Indeed, Montgomery had warned the Storys not to take any more journals, but they had already made that decision themselves. The recovered material had been stored in the Wallowa County Sheriff's Office, and Detective Matt Cross, the original case supervisor, had read some of it.

Carol Terry took the stand to testify about the call from the unknown man.

"How many anonymous phone calls have you received about this case?" Steve Briggs asked.

"Just one—on June twenty-sixth."

"Do you recall what time of day it was?"

"It was right after lunch—1:10, 1:05—something like that."

"And could you tell the judge how the conversation went?"

"Yes. As always, I answered the phone, 'District Attorney's Office—this is Carol.' And a gentleman said, 'I want to make an anonymous call,' and at first I kind of thought it was a joke. And I said, 'Sure, go ahead.' "

Carol Terry took notes on what he said and then she typed them up. "I'm not saying this verbatim, but somebody said that a computer was given to Kit Minton and she was told to destroy it by Liysa—that it had been reported stolen earlier in the year."

That was all. She hadn't thought to punch *69. She didn't think Wallowa County phones had that capability. She didn't know if the call was local or long-distance.

After much discussion and arguments from both Dan Ousley and Steve Briggs and Wayne Mackeson and Pat Birmingham, Judge Mendiguren ruled that the prosecution had *not* known about the location of Liysa's computer until the weekend before the trial, and therefore they had broken no discovery rules. As to what had been retrieved from the inner workings of that computer, it remained to be seen whether the judge would allow it in as evidence. It was still coughing up files that Liysa believed she'd erased.

Birmingham and Mackeson knew their client had lied to them before, and they shared a sinking sensation about what might be on the few hundred pages that Steve Briggs had just handed them. They agreed that Birmingham would read as fast as he could on this warm evening of July 18, 2001, while Wayne Mackeson would talk to Liysa.

Liysa had fourteen potential visitors waiting to see her, and the judge granted permission to those who had already testified. However, since Wayland DeWitt's time on the witness stand still lay ahead, he would not be permitted to visit his daughter.

As it turned out, it would be a very long night for everyone, Liysa included.

CHAPTER THIRTY-SEVEN

WAYNE MACKESON and Pat Birmingham read with apprehension the emails that FBI Special Agent Ariel Miller had culled from Liysa's long lost computer. When they'd begun preparing her defense, there were some positives; they had found Liysa's enthusiastic friends who were ready to testify to her good character, her perfection as a mother and as a friend, and her brilliance. These witnesses would also describe her bruises and the way hair had been ripped from her scalp. The defense team had even found one Hawaiian Airlines pilot who recalled that he'd once seen Chris Northon speaking unkindly to his wife.

Even with Liysa's compulsive talking and letter writing, her attorneys had had reason to believe they could win an acquittal with their self-defense game plan. Certainly, their trust in their client had eroded in the nine-plus months of trial preparation. And now they were certain that the emails would be devastating when a jury read them—*if* a jury read them. Judge Mendiguren hadn't ruled yet on which evidence would be admitted, but that was only because he himself hadn't read Miller's reports.

When Liysa wrote to Kit Minton, saying, "Destroy it A.S.A.P. My Gateway could hang me," she was figuratively on target, although the death penalty was not an option in her case. But if she should be convicted of the murder of her husband, the sentence range was twenty-five years to life in prison.

Liysa's emails to Wayland DeWitt would be even harder to explain away. She had wanted a gun with a silencer and she assured her father she hadn't changed her mind. Add this correspondence to the strong possibility that jurors would read her "Let's kill my husband" screenplay, and the situation looked bleak.

When they see a conviction lying in wait, defense attorneys have no choice left but to practice damage control. The Portland attorneys had to consider other pitfalls. A motive—or motives—for Liysa to want Chris dead was obvious. Her own financial worth had shrunk markedly during 2000, she'd lost her movie deal, given up on Craig Elliot, and she wasn't doing many photo shoots. But with Chris dead, Liysa would be first in line to collect his insurance, his pilot's benefits—including free flights on Hawaiian as a pilot's widow—and his property in Bend. Either way, Bjorn would have free tickets until he was eighteen. Chris also had a 401(k) plan to which money would be added—whether he was living or dead—until he would have been sixty. She had told her counselors that she had to wait to leave Chris until he made captain so she would get more money in a divorce settlement.

When the time was right, it now seemed, Liysa planned to divorce Chris, but she didn't want to share custody of her sons, and she knew that Chris would never give up visitations with Bjorn. "If I hadn't had Bjorn," she'd told her friends, "I might get away from him with Papako, but he'll follow me all over the world because of Bjorn."

But if Chris died, she could avoid a divorce and everything would be hers, including Bjorn. Liysa didn't love Chris any longer and her own witnesses would verify that. "I hope he goes up the mountain and never comes back," she'd told them vehemently. "I wish he'd drown."

It was all too apparent that Liysa had wanted to erase Chris from her life, just as she had done to so many men before him, and move on without hassles.

Birmingham and Mackeson had other problems to consider. Defense attorneys have to think like prosecutors to be ready for any surprise assault. Now they had to digest a number of unpalatable possibilities, aware that their client had hidden a lot from them. Ellen Duveaux was prepared to testify about the stun guns that she'd found in Liysa's backpack. They still existed; they were in the sealed evidence package along with Pat Birmingham's affidavit. At some point in the trial, he knew they would be offered into evidence. Chris Northon had had those strange marks on his chest, which Dr. Khalil Helou hadn't been able to identify during the postmortem exam, although he was quite sure they weren't fingernail scratches. Oddly, they looked more like burns.

As they prepared for trial, the defense team had shown the autopsy photos to Dr. William Brady, the former chief medical examiner for the state of Oregon—who had investigated thousands of homicides. Brady tended to agree with Dr. Helou that the marks looked more like burns than scratches.

It was quite possible that Chris Northon had sustained searing flash burns from a TASER weapon. Stun guns must be held to a person's skin to be effective. A novice would be likely to assume that if an electric charge from a stun gun zapped someone in a bathtub—or a river—they would be rendered helpless or dead.

There was another concern about the package that Pat Birmingham had received in the mail. There were two sets of handcuffs inside, along with the TASER weapons. Tor DeWitt had told Birmingham he had retrieved the stun guns and the handcuffs from Liysa's vehicle the morning after the murder. Ellen Duveaux said the TASER weapons were in the backpack—which Tor had picked up from her—and Liysa denied ever having the items with her at all on the camping trip.

If the trial continued, the jury would hear that, too.

Pat Birmingham went over a number of scenarios in his mind about what might have happened on the night of October 8. One possibility troubled him the most. When Chris's body was found, more than twelve hours after his death, it was in full rigor, his muscles frozen in place. His hands and wrists were almost touching, as if he'd tucked them under his chin to use as a pillow. But Chris had had a good camping pillow, so why would his hands have been in that position?

Birmingham wondered if it was possible that Chris had been rendered helpless enough by an overdose of Restoril for someone to slip handcuffs on his wrists. A man in a drug-induced coma, zipped up to his chin in a mummy sleeping bag, his hands trapped by cuffs, would have been brutally easy to shoot in the temple. He could have done nothing to save himself, and he certainly wouldn't have been a threat to anyone. Even without the cuffs, he would have been a sitting duck.

Was it even possible that Liysa had had an accomplice who joined her at the Lostine River campground and helped her overpower her husband? Birmingham didn't think so, but sometimes he wondered about it. If someone had gone back to the campground later to remove a pair of handcuffs, they would have had to move the body slightly. That would account for the odd pattern of blood that had coursed in two different directions on Chris's face.

Why had Liysa lied for so long about stopping at her brother's house the morning after the shooting? On the surface, it didn't seem to make a difference one way or another, but it was months before she admitted it to Birmingham, Nash, and Karnes. Tor DeWitt hadn't helped her; he'd sent her off to Ellen's house and gone to work. Hours later, of course, he had taken her to discuss her situation with his friend Deputy Dick Bobbitt.

And it troubled Pat Birmingham just as it puzzled Pat Montgomery that Liysa had been so wet when she arrived at Ellen Duveaux's house such a long time after she raced away from the Lostine River. Each of them wondered if she had stopped somewhere to drench herself again, thinking that would make her story of being nearly drowned more believable.

Ironically, much of the information that the defense investigators discovered—at Liysa's request—was more damaging to her than to the victim. She had demanded that they look through police files in Hawaii and Bend to find domestic violence reports naming Chris. Instead, they had found an inordinate number of thefts and burglaries that *she* had reported. Following that up, the defense was suspicious about the missing computers even before the state investigators were.

Initially, the revelation by the State that Chris Northon had a minuscule amount of alcohol in his urine seemed to substantiate Liysa's claim that her drunken husband drove her to shoot him. However, there were inferences that could be drawn from that which were *not* favorable. After drinking alcohol, most people have to urinate, but Chris's bladder had been very full at autopsy; the fact that any alcohol he had imbibed would have taken hours to metabolize from his blood to his urine suggested that he had not been *able* to empty his bladder, probably because he had lain unconscious that long.

MOST OF THE EVIDENCE that was likely to sabotage Liysa's self-defense and defense of another plea had come in at the last hour—almost the way it does in fictional trials. But it *had* popped to the surface—computers and poisons, stun guns and handcuffs. As intelligent as Liysa Northon was, she hadn't researched procedures performed after a homicide nearly as well as she validated insurance procedures for her screenplays. How could she not have known that crime labs did blood tests on murder victims? She had made so many mistakes and told so many lies that she'd virtually hog-tied her attorneys.

Pat Birmingham weighed the possibility of going for a plea

bargain rather than continuing the trial. The multiple areas of damaging information convinced him and Wayne Mackeson that they had no other choice. The State would have a field day demonstrating that Liysa Northon had been planning her husband's death for a long time, probably more than a year.

The only other way to go would be to try to convince the jury that Liysa was suffering from extreme emotional disturbance when she shot Chris, but even if that worked, she would still be convicted of manslaughter in the first degree.

Wayne Mackeson went to Liysa's cell on the first floor of the courthouse, braced for her resistance. Despite everything, she was still convinced she would be acquitted and had no intention of pleading guilty.

Mackeson explained that she would not have to plead guilty; she might be able to offer an Alford plea, where she would plead neither innocent nor guilty but that she believed there was strong chance she would be convicted of murder if the trial continued. If she agreed, Mackeson would meet with Steve Briggs to barter over what sentence she might receive.

Liysa had spent much of the early evening entertaining a number of visitors. Although being in jail was onerous for her, she had never really doubted that she would walk free at the end of this trial. But now she huddled with Mackeson as he explained what was, for Liysa, ridiculous. She had long since believed that the legal process was "not logical."

At first, she was resistant to Wayne Mackeson's arguments. She wanted to go on with the trial, to testify, to prove to the jury that it was Chris who was the sociopath. It was Chris who had been "Ted Bundy."

Liysa had never lost before.

Patiently, Mackeson pointed out that she didn't have many options. In her attorneys' opinion, the most she could hope for if the trial continued would be a conviction of manslaughter in the first degree. And that was only if the jurors believed that she was a battered woman. If she went for a plea bargain, she might be able to have the manslaughter sentence guaranteed, and she wouldn't risk being convicted of murder and the possibility of going to prison for life.

Grudgingly, Liysa agreed to let her attorneys make the best deal they could for her, although she was very angry.

Steve Briggs said that the State was willing to entertain a guilty plea to a charge of manslaughter in the first degree. But the chess game wasn't over by a long shot. Wayne Mackeson spent most of the night going up and down the long flight of stairs between Liysa's pale green jail cell and Dan Ousley's office. The woman who had once had everything and wanted *more* now paced in her tiny cell, unable to accept that her own written words had come back to trap her.

CHAPTER THIRTY-EIGHT

NO ONE INVOLVED had had much sleep. The principals filed into Judge Mendiguren's courtroom on Thursday morning, July 19. Informed that an agreement was in progress, the judge excused the jury for the morning so that plea negotiations could continue. Confused, the jurors filed out, and those in the gallery began to murmur. The Court TV representatives waited, too, perturbed. This small-town trial that had promised two weeks of interesting testimony seemed to have stalled.

Dan Ousley and Steve Briggs waited in the D.A.'s office while Pat Birmingham and Wayne Mackeson shuttled back and forth between discussions with Liysa. Sharon Fisher waited nervously outside her daughter's cell and conferred with Liysa several times as negotiations took place.

Liysa knew now that she was going to prison, but she didn't know for how long. The prosecutors wanted her to agree to serve an eighteen-year sentence. She listened, stunned, as each step of the legal bargaining was explained to her, and her attorneys waited for her response. Eighteen years was unthinkable. She was thirty-seven and she would be fifty-five in eighteen years. By then, her sons would be grown men and her career would be ashes. All she had wanted was to be free and to live her life on her own terms with enough money to enjoy it. But if she had any secret regrets about shooting Chris, she certainly didn't voice them.

The bartering in terms of years in prison continued, with Liysa's input at every stage. Her defense attorneys had saved her from a mandatory life sentence. With her vigorous good health, that could have been forty or fifty—or even sixty—years. At the very least, they had gotten twenty-five years down to eighteen.

In the end, both sides agreed that Liysa's sentence would be twelve and a half years. It seemed like æons to her, but it was negligible to Jeanne and Dick Northon and the scores of friends still grieving for Chris, who had no more years at all after the age of forty-four.

Ariel Miller was still mining Liysa's computer for more evidence that Chris's murder had been a carefully calculated, premeditated act of fatal violence. Although Liysa had the right to wait forty-eight hours to be sentenced, her attorneys were anxious to proceed with sentencing. They were very concerned that something might turn up in her computer that would make the judge deny their request for some sentencing concessions—such as credit for time served.

For all intents and purposes, Wallowa County Case #0101788 was over. Judge Mendiguren looked down upon the State's and the defense team's tables at 2:00 P.M. on that sunny Thursday afternoon.

It was very tense in the courtroom as the families and friends in the front row benches, one for each side, waited.

Liysa was almost hidden between her two attorneys. Ironically, now that the evidence suggesting her as a murderess had come to light, she looked more demure and frightened than ever, the very picture of a battered woman.

Too late.

Judge Mendiguren asked her if she understood her petition to plead guilty to manslaughter in the first degree. She did.

"Okay, and in here they spell out various rights that you have. Did you go over those rights?"

Liysa said she had read them and they had been read to her, but the judge went over them again. She still had the right to continue the trial and take her chances with the jury.

"Do you understand that . . . by entering this plea you'd be giving up that right?"

"Yes."

Someone's cell phone shrilled and everyone jumped. Judge Mendiguren was not amused and said he would confiscate any cell phone that wasn't turned off.

"[You have] the right to face in open court the witnesses called against you, and to have your counsel, either of them, examine those witnesses. Do you understand that?"

"Yes."

Judge Mendiguren moved on to mention that Liysa had the right to submit evidence, call defense witnesses, even to testify in her own defense if she chose to continue. Did she know that she was presumed innocent until she was proven guilty beyond a reasonable doubt. "Do you understand that?"

"Yes," Liysa said as her jaw tensed.

It seemed to be taking forever, and occasionally Liysa nodded rather than answering, forcing the judge to repeat his words. Finally, he came to the charges she faced.

"It's alleged that you, Liysa Ann Northon, on or about October ninth of the year 2000, in Wallowa County, did intentionally cause the death of Christopher James Northon by shooting him with a firearm while you were under the influence of extreme emotional disturbance. Do you understand?"

"Yes."

"And to that allegation, do you plead guilty or not guilty?"

"Guilty."

Liysa's chin wobbled now as if she could not hold her face together. After the endless hours of negotiation, her sentencing was dry and full of legalese. However, Liysa suddenly balked when Judge Mendiguren asked her, "And are you doing this today—that is, agreeing to plead guilty to manslaughter—freely and voluntarily without trick or coercion by anyone?"

The seconds ticked off and she said nothing, although her thoughts seemed palpable. People in the courtroom appeared to suspend breathing. Finally, having made her point, Liysa said, "Yes."

But it was clear she didn't mean it. She didn't want this sentence or this plea, or, at least, she wanted to leave that impression. Her attorneys slowly expelled the breath they'd held, too.

Before Liysa's actual sentencing, Judge Mendiguren now asked if everyone would wait while he called in the jurors and told them that the trial had ended. He thanked them and explained that they could sit in the courtroom and listen if they liked. Their notebooks would be shredded. They would not have to make any decisions. It had all been done.

Dick Northon asked to speak before Liysa was sentenced. Judge Mendiguren nodded. This was, perhaps, the last time Dick could speak for his son. "I can say that Chris was an extraordinary young man in an ordinary world," he said. "He was a superb pilot, a wonderful musician. He loved the out-of-doors. His whole life was his son. He loved his family, and had more best friends than anyone I've ever known, and only a few of the people who loved him are here.

"I grew up without a father. I admonished him [Chris] to be

the best father he could. And so he stayed in a difficult situation. He also loved Papako. We recall the day Papako had fallen off a log in Tumalo Creek, and Chris jumped in and pulled him out when he would have surely drowned under those logs—and saved his life. In fact, Papako's father wanted to bring Papako to Chris's funeral because Papako was so fond of Chris. . . ." Dick's voice quavered, but he kept on.

"My heart is broken. I feel a terrible sadness."

Liysa listened to her former father-in-law's words with a look of annoyed skepticism on her face.

Her turn to make a statement came next. She rose, still trembling, to say the words she had voiced many times before.

"Your Honor, I would like to go on the record saying that I did what I had to do in order to save myself and my children. My children's well-being is the paramount thing in my life. And it's too bad that this is what it takes to protect them. Thank you."

"The sentence," Judge Mendiguren began, "is stipulated to and based on the sentencing guidelines of the 120 months—ten years—to the stipulation to the aggravating factors involved . . . to make it 150 months."

He gazed at Liysa with an almost benevolent look. The corners of her mouth pulled up into a shy smile.

"I agree with Mr. Birmingham that financially you're not in a position to pay a large fine," the judge continued. "However, I would also make the finding that puts in there the $500 fine and the $105 unitary assessment and the other fees."

Liysa's sentence of 120 months was mandatory and would not be reduced for any reason, so there would be no time off for good behavior.

The judge remarked that Liysa looked young and healthy and that she probably could earn enough in prison over the years to pay those fines. Whether he actually felt sorry for her, or was making an effort to end the somber proceedings on a semi-upbeat note, he reminded her that she would be younger than he was now when she got out of prison.

Further, Liysa was declared a "slayer" under Oregon law, which meant that she could never profit financially by writing about the crime for which she'd been convicted. Most convicted killers couldn't care less, but Liysa was an *author,* and one who had always based her manuscripts on her own life and experiences.

She smiled bravely, her tremulous smile. She had used that smile to enchant many men in her life.

Outside the courthouse in the late July afternoon, Court TV cameras captured interviews with Dick Northon, Wayland De-Witt, and his former wife, Sharon Fisher. They looked into the bright sun, squinting as they spoke. Anger and pain etched their faces. This was a situation where nobody really won. Neither family could believe what their oldest child's life had come to.

"Liysa was a most gentle child, and she still is," Sharon Fisher said. "She's not an evil person, she's not a killer, and she's not a criminal. She was just trying to survive."

Wayland DeWitt was angry as he always was when he defended Liysa.

And so was Dick Northon, so angry that his son was gone. "Liysa killed the only person who knew the truth," he said flatly.

Chapter Thirty-Nine

WITH HER TRIAL ENDING so abruptly, Liysa was moved to the Oregon Women's Correctional Center in Salem on July 26, 2001, to undergo orientation. On August 9, she was transferred to Eastern Oregon Correctional Institute (EOCI) near Pendleton to begin serving her sentence. She was now Prisoner

#13948511, a sea change from her heady days in Hawaii and Hollywood. Her projected release date was April 10, 2013. When she was admitted, she weighed 112 pounds, very thin for her five feet, four inches. Because she had been convicted of a Class A felony and her victim had died, she was considered a "dangerous offender."

Wayland DeWitt moved to eastern Oregon so that he could be close by, an emotional support for her. Sharon Fisher returned to her home in Wood County, Texas.

Court TV broadcast the testimony and interviews its cameraman had filmed, interspersed with comments from experts, defense attorneys, and prosecutors who had no inside knowledge of the Northon case. The program counted votes from the "audience jury." At one point in the posttrial coverage, 44 percent of the viewing audience found Liysa guilty while 56 percent would have voted for her innocence. They had heard only a portion of the trial and the evidence, but Liysa's vulnerable image on camera had persuaded a number of viewers that she was the poster girl for battered wives.

UNTIL SHE COULD APPEAL her sentence, Liysa had to accept that someone else would be raising Papako and Bjorn. Almost any mother would agree that the worst punishment possible is separation from her children during the years when they need her the most. Liysa had striven to make herself indispensable to her sons, particularly Papako, who would be turning ten in four months. He had one natural parent left—his father, Nick. And he had been with Nick continually since shortly after Chris's murder. There was no question that Papako would miss the mother who had cosseted him and catered to him as she raised him to be the perfect son. Their bond was extremely close, but at least he had his father.

Bjorn had turned four two months before his mother's trial

began, and he was the child whose life had been totally turned upside down. Liysa had sometimes complained to her friends that Bjorn was too high-spirited, "too much like Chris." She'd resented the time Chris spent with Bjorn because she felt it kept Bjorn from being as attached to her as Papako was, although there was no question that she loved Bjorn. And she had been breast-feeding him until she was sent to jail on October 9. Although it was unlikely that he had been awake when his father was shot, too many changes were foisted upon Bjorn in a very short period.

Right after Liysa's arrest, Tor DeWitt had taken Bjorn to Marni and Ben Clark's house in Walla Walla, and they had cared for him for a few weeks. When Liysa learned she was not going to be released on bail, her brother flew with Bjorn to Kailua to deliver him to Kit and Cal Minton, the couple she had chosen to care for him until she was free. But the Mintons had moved on without Bjorn when Cal was reassigned to the East Coast. Bjorn then went to live with Nick Mattson and his wife, where he was often visited by Dave Story, Chris's good friend. As the Mattson family adjusted to their transition from a childless couple and then to a new baby in the house—followed by the addition of two more little boys—Bjorn was sent to spend a month with Nick's parents. Bjorn no longer had a father, and his mother was in prison. Between October 8, 2000, and July 18, 2001, he'd lived in five different homes. He'd been welcome in each and was much loved, but no child should have to undergo such losses and endless upheaval.

Given Liysa's sentence, Papako would be twenty when she walked out of prison and Bjorn would be sixteen. Liysa had planned to free herself from Chris, but it may not have occurred to her that her scenario might end the way it did. Now her boys were left without a mother. A few visits a year and letters and stories written in her prison cell couldn't begin to make up for her absence.

Liysa was responsible for taking away the man whom Bjorn had patterned himself after, the man he called "Mydad" so proudly, but she brushed that aside as she began another campaign. She wanted to control how her sons were raised, albeit from a distance.

One thing was certain. Bjorn shouldn't have to face any more interim solutions to custody questions. In evaluating where he should go, Dr. Barbara Rutter, who was counseling Bjorn in Hawaii, wrote: "Based on what I have seen, I would recommend that he not be placed anywhere temporarily and that no changes occur until a court is satisfied that the change will be permanent."

No one involved disagreed. Bjorn's placement was in the hands of Deschutes County, Oregon, because his parents had last lived in Bend. There were still many families who would welcome Bjorn. The question was, which home would be the best for him? Liysa's family and friends resented anyone who had cared about Chris. And, of course, vice versa. It was vitally important that the enmity between the two sides didn't affect Bjorn and Papako, but emotions spilled over.

Deschutes County retained Billie Bell of Portland, who had a master's degree in social work, to begin a custody evaluation in the case of Bjorn Northon. Should he stay with Nick Mattson's family or live with Debbie and Dave Story?

Bell sent out questionnaires to be completed by all the parties involved so she could look at their initial hopes for Bjorn. Jeanne and Dick Northon weren't asking for custody of Bjorn, as dearly as they loved him. They were nearing seventy, and they knew it wouldn't be fair for them to try raising a child when they might not be around to see him through his teenage years. Neither Mary nor Sally, Chris's sisters, were currently married or in a position to take him.

The Northons worried about what Liysa might be saying to Bjorn in visits and letters. All he had left of his father would be what other people told him or wrote to him. They didn't want to see the precious—but frail—memories of a four-year-old erased forever by his mother's denigrating comments about his father. Liysa and *her* allies voiced their objections to the Northons' having any opportunity to criticize *her*.

When his grandparents went to Hawaii to visit him in the Mattsons' home, Bjorn came running to Jeanne, shouting, "Take me home!" And then he said, "My mommy shooted my daddy . . . and my daddy's an angel. Can he come over here and play again?"

They had to turn away to hide the tears that suddenly stung their eyes. Bjorn looked just like Chris had when *he* was four. But they realized that he seemed happy where he was and that he didn't really want to go home with them.

Liysa detested the Northons and didn't want them to have any say at all over Bjorn. For the moment, she could not prevent Bjorn or Papako from seeing them, but she assumed there must be some kind of legal ruling that would block Dick and Jeanne from any visitation with the boys. So far, she hadn't been able to accomplish that.

* * *

JEANNE AND DICK had moved from Bend to the house in Joseph that Chris had wanted to help finance. Although they were very close to the campsite where their son died, they couldn't bring themselves to visit it. Still, it helped a little to leave Bend and the heartache there behind. Their new home was on Wallowa Lake, a big rustic place with plenty of room for their grandchildren to visit, along with guest rooms for Chris's friends, who had apparently decided to be substitute sons whenever they could. Arne Arnesen and Dan Jones showed up to cut wood for winter and to help Dick with other chores. One of Chris's old friends insisted on leaping into the icy waters of Wallowa Lake that first winter, "because Chris would have done that, and it would make him laugh to see me do it."

Liysa had a Christmas visit with Papako and Bjorn and then Dave Story took Bjorn up to Joseph to see his grandparents. The winter of 2001–2002 brought snow to Wallowa Lake and Arne, Dave, Bjorn, and Sally's and Mary's three boys were all with the Northons. Dick gave Bjorn a child's saw and he cut his own small Christmas tree, a spruce. The snow was deep and the little boys shouted with excitement as they rode their grandad's toboggan.

Bjorn walked downstairs, where he found pictures of Chris, and Jeanne's heart stopped. But he only said a cheerful, "Hi, Daddy." He liked looking at Chris's picture, and he carefully examined his father's flight bag and his pilot's hat that Dick and Jeanne had kept.

One day he would be old enough to read the scrapbook with letters from every pilot who had ever flown with Chris Northon. Could he understand what had happened? He was still living with Nick Mattson's family where he was completely welcome, but Dave Story was his special pal. He didn't have his own father any longer, but he had two father figures who loved him—Nick and Dave.

Where Bjorn would live permanently was still undecided. Nick had been kind to Liysa after Chris was killed, and that was difficult for Dick and Jeanne to accept, but as the months passed, they found him more sympathetic. "He's a nice man," Jeanne commented, "and we came to realize that. He was kind to us and let us visit with Bjorn."

Still, the ideal situation, as far as the Northons were concerned, and one that they were sure Chris would have approved of, was to accept Dave and Debbie's wish to have Bjorn in their home until he was grown.

Liysa wanted Nick to have "guardianship"—not "custody"—of Bjorn. Nick had usually respected her wishes and she assumed she could have a lot of input on the way Bjorn was raised if he lived with the Mattsons. But Nick had no blood ties to Bjorn and he hadn't been at all close to Chris. Dave Story had been Chris's loyal friend.

It seemed a decision that only Solomon could make.

Liysa's fallback position for custody was to have her brother named Bjorn's guardian. Tor DeWitt had custody of his own two children during the week, but his divorce from his ex-wife had apparently been bitter. Each of them had summoned police on several occasions when their weekend plans for custody erupted into arguments.

* * *

IN EARLY 2002, Liysa was gathering her strength for battle. She would appeal her sentence, of course, and seek a new trial. Her strategy began with attacks on the reputations of those she blamed for her conviction. Dan Ousley was one of her early targets. She wrote several letters to the Oregon State Bar to tell them that he had "erased evidence and lied about it." She continued to insist that the Wallowa County District Attorney had knowingly deleted part of the cassette tape she claimed she had made to prove that Chris was using drug tests to deceive Hawaiian Airlines. It wasn't true, but Ousley had to respond to each letter to the Bar Disciplinary Counsel until, finally, the counsel wrote to Liysa to say that they would entertain no more of her accusations.

She corresponded furiously with Ousley and Steve Briggs in her tight little printing. She realized that some of her writings were part of the official police investigation files. "That is a violation of my constitutional rights," Liysa wrote. "I must ask you to return my computers, papers, diaries, etc., to me. You can ship them certified to my brother, Dr. Jon Tor DeWitt.

"The Northons have made threats against my children. I

wish to seek a restraining order to keep them from my children. I plan to ask the FBI to investigate the Northons' activities and you will be held accountable for aiding and abetting their illegal activities."

She gave no specifics as to how the Northons meant to harm Papako and Bjorn. Locked away, Liysa was becoming unhinged. As she once wrote to Chris, travel had always been "huge" to her, and now she was hemmed in by walls everywhere she turned and her comings and goings were decided by the prison administration. But she worked in the kitchen, participated in her unit's sweat lodge, clerked in the library, and took a number of self-improvement classes offered to inmates. She joined a therapy group. Outwardly, Liysa was an ideal prisoner.

Still, the custody of Bjorn remained an unresolved problem. Dave and Debbie Story wanted very much to raise Bjorn. They loved him, and Dave had always been a big part of his life. With them, Bjorn would be living close to his half brother, Papako, so they could see each other as often as they wanted. The Storys' home was Jeanne and Dick Northon's choice of a safe and caring home for their grandson.

But Liysa was furious at that suggestion. She wanted Nick Mattson to have guardianship of both boys—until she was released. It wouldn't be that long. She was confident that she would be acquitted in a second trial, which she would see in her PCR (Post-Conviction Relief) hearing.

As far as Liysa was concerned, it wasn't over. She went through her days in the Pendleton prison quietly, but her mind worked feverishly with the details of battles she proposed to fight. She still hated Dick and Jeanne Northon bitterly, and she had particular enmity toward Dave and Debbie Story. This wasn't surprising in light of the fact that they had turned her journals over to the police after Chris's death. Now she wrote to the Honolulu Police Department to "file a report" that the Storys were "involved heavily in drug trafficking" and said that she would gladly take a polygraph test about her information, or "a hair sample or anything else."

When they didn't respond, she said that was because Honolulu police officers were Dave Story's best drug customers and they were covering for one another.

Dick Northon was the conservator of Bjorn's estate, his inheritance from his father. Although Dick was prevented from writing a check or spending any of those assets even if he wanted to, Liysa prepared to sue to have him removed, voicing her belief that Dick was somehow draining Bjorn's funds.

And she now insisted that she had only pleaded guilty to manslaughter because the State had threatened to charge members of her family as accomplices to Chris's murder. She had sacrificed herself not only to save Bjorn—but to save her father and perhaps her brother.

CHAPTER FORTY

ON APRIL 18, 2002, Liysa was moved back across the mountains to the new Oregon women's prison: the Coffee Creek Correctional Facility in Wilsonville, just south of Portland. Her father moved back to the Oregon coast, too, and remained totally supportive of her.

Without mentioning that he had a special interest in the early release of first-time offenders, Wayland wrote a letter to the editorial page of the *Oregonian*.

"As a former community college president who has endured the agonizing process of terminating excellent faculty members and college programs because of fiscal constraints, I am deeply saddened to see what is happening to our K–12 schools, community colleges, and university programs and budgets. How shameful!"

He went on to say he blamed Measure 11, an Oregon statute voted in to construct "$1 billion for warehouses that serve as prisons, along with a cost of $30,000 per inmate per year. . . . We need to reduce to 36 months (from 70 months) Measure 11 sentences for first-time offenders. We would save nearly $100,000 per inmate." The letter was signed, "Wayland DeWitt."

* * *

THE PAIN THAT ACCOMPANIED Chris Northon's death didn't subside as the months passed. Nor did the courtroom battles or the anonymous messages.

The first letter, postmarked in Seattle, was addressed to Lora Lee Mattson, Nick's wife. It was undated.

"We are a group of people that have sat back patiently watching the proceedings since our friend Chris Northon was murdered by your husbands [sic] ex-wife. Up until now we have seen no reason to make our presence known. Recently, you and your husband have made a decision that has altered our position. We have spent the last year compiling data that will change both of your lives and those of your children forever. Information that you do not want to ever have to know or have the rest of the world know. We have pictorial proof of this information. We would like for you to consider the two sons you have now as enough. We would like for you to consider the fact that neither of those boys will grow up mentally damaged if you and your husband quietly walk away from your fight for Bjorn Northon. They will see him, they will know him. Please concentrate on Bjorn's last name. We would like for you to consider that Bjorn will not grow up damaged if he leaves your care tomorrow or in a couple of months. We especially would like for you to consider the damage you will do to certain lives (especially yours) if you continue to try to get permanent custody of Bjorn Northon. Papako deserves to be left alone with regards to the information we have. He does not need to be traumatized. You deserve to be left alone with regards to the information we have. You deserve to have a normal life and raise your two sons and any more children you and Nick decide to have (except for Bjorn). You deserve to have a normal life. The drama that we could (and will, should you continue on this path) bring into your lives will destroy your family, your marriage and any hope of a normal existence. Please imagine your family totally fragmented. Imagine you and Nick being divorced. Believe us when we tell you, your marriage is not strong enough to withstand the data we have compiled. Please do NOT doubt our sincerity or resolve. And last but not least you need to know that NOBODY knows what is best for Bjorn Northon. All we know is that he will know who his father was, good or bad, and that he will be surrounded by good, loving people, people who are not greedy, people who have loved and known Bjorn long before you and Nick. You have enough. Be satisfied that you got Bjorn through last year. Feel good about that. Let him go to where he will finish the most important years of his life. You will see him often. You will be protected. Bjorn will always be safe, we will see to that. Do not self-appoint yourself as his keeper. You may win Bjorn but you will never know happiness."

THE SECOND, similar letter—postmarked in Spokane—went to Billie Bell.

"DEAR MS. BELL,

"We are a group of concerned people who knew and loved Chris Northon. Ever since his murder we have been studying the woman who killed him and all the people she knew. Her ex-husband, Nick Mattson, got his start in his chosen field by helping to film child pornography abroad. He also has a penchant, or at least did at the time that he and his ex-wife were to-gether, for little boys. She knew this. She knows exactly what he was doing. She holds it over him. Since Bjorn is now in his keep, we would like to ask you to investigate what we have discovered and please not allow him to be placed in a home that would subject him to any more trauma than he has already had to endure."

The letters were venomous and frightening, quite clearly the work of a devious mind. Billie Bell immediately asked that polygraph tests be given to Liysa, Tor DeWitt, Dave and Debbie Story, Nick and Lora Lee Mattson, and Jeanne and Dick Northon.

The vital questions would be: (1) Did you contribute to or write any of the letter received by Lora Lee Mattson? (2) Did you write or type the letter? (3) Did you read or see the letter before it was mailed? (4) Do you know for sure who wrote or typed the letter that was sent?

Perhaps somewhat naively, Jeanne and Dick Northon

agreed to fly to Hawaii to take lie-detector tests on January 30, 2002. They never had a doubt that they would pass. They were horrified to learn that the polygrapher had found their responses deceptive.

"He told us before the test what he was going to ask," Jeanne recalled. "Afterward, he kept telling me that if I would just tell him the truth, we could work things out. I *had* answered truthfully, but every time I referred to myself and Dick as 'We,' he would say, "*There*, you said *we*," and tell me again that I wasn't telling the truth."

It was unbelievable to them and they flew home, stunned. The idyllic life they hoped to enjoy had betrayed them. In the past sixteen months, they had lost Chris and it seemed they were about to lose Bjorn, too. A few days later, they asked to take another polygraph test. In the second tests, Jeanne was deemed truthful, and Dick, whose blood pressure had soared since Chris's murder, had inconclusive results. Jeanne began to fear she would lose him, too.

The others tested—Liysa, Tor, the Mattsons, and the Storys—were all deemed to be truthful. Wayland DeWitt wasn't asked to take a lie-detector test, nor was Sharon Fisher or any of Liysa's or Chris's friends.

Who sent those letters? No one knew. *Who* caused them to be sent? No one knew. Any expert on polygraph tests will explain that the results depend upon the skill and subjective opinions of the operator, and the health and emotional reactions of those tested. Those without consciences are not threatened by the sight of the polygraph leads and pens. Some have trained themselves to beat a polygraph. And, of course, many lie-detector results are right on the mark.

Since the Northons hoped to see their grandson raised in the home of their son's close friends, one could argue that they might have sent such letters to Lora Lee Mattson and Billie Bell. However, someone who wanted to make it *look* as though

Chris's parents were capable of sending such cruel letters might also have been responsible.

Whatever the mysterious "secrets" were that would ruin the Mattsons' marriage, they never surfaced.

* * *

BEFORE BJORN'S CUSTODY HEARING, the Northons, the Storys, and the Mattsons talked with one another about what would be best for him. They were all in agreement and had informed their attorneys of their meeting of minds as they prepared to appear before a judge in Bend, Oregon, on May 28, 2002. Liysa, of course, would have input, too.

Seana McMann Ash, once Chris's attorney, now represented the Northons; Joel Kent, the Storys; and Maxwell Merrill, the Mattsons. Liysa Northon represented herself. In Oregon, prisoners may participate in such hearings *if* they have the funds to pay for their own transportation and the expenses of an armed guard who will accompany them. Liysa appeared at the hearing in her blue prison scrubs, handcuffs on her wrists and shackles on her ankles, and with sheaves of records. Once she was in the courtroom, her armed guard removed her restraints.

This time, Liysa intended to do the questioning and cross-examining. Her former in-laws were appalled to see her in this role, and after all that had happened, they wondered who she would strike out at next.

Judge Stephen Tiktin of the Eleventh Judicial District of the Circuit Court of Oregon would render his judgment after hearing all sides of the custody issue. Dave Story, the Northons, and Liysa sat in the courtroom with the attorneys. It was an almost psychedelic scene for Chris's parents. They had expected the custody hearing to last less than a day, and they had not expected—ever again—to be in the same room with Liysa. Now they would be in Bend for more than three days for an agonizing confrontation with the woman who had killed their only son.

Judge Tiktin explained to Liysa early on that she had to stand when she addressed the court. She apologized in her sweet, chirpy voice, explaining that she was not an attorney so she might need some help from time to time. Tiktin nodded, but he became exasperated as he had to remind her of proper court-room procedure many times.

The first fact that had to be established in this hearing was that Bjorn Northon's father was deceased and his mother would not—or could not—adequately care for him. Since she was in-carcerated, Liysa clearly could not care for him.

The next decisions to be made were the most difficult. Everyone in this courtroom was there to discuss what solution would be in the best interests of the child.

Jeanne and Dick had already told Nick and Lora Lee Matt-son that they knew Bjorn was in a safe, happy home. Debbie and Dave Story concurred, and Nick and Lora Lee were quite willing to have Dave Story see Bjorn at least twice a month. They all agreed that the little boy should be able to visit with his grandparents both in Hawaii and in Oregon.

Attorneys Seana Ash, Joel Kent, and Maxwell Merrill each made short opening statements to tell Judge Tiktin that three of the parties were in accord. The only person who didn't concur was Liysa. She had other thoughts and requests.

Her opening statement wandered and rambled, but she sounded very confident, almost triumphant, to be able to speak in this venue. While she said that *she* had selected her second husband's home as the best placement for Bjorn, she wanted no court-ordered visitation with the Storys. She stressed that any visits should be unhampered by legal rulings. "The Mattsons should decide who Bjorn sees," she explained, pointing out that

Dave Story hadn't really been Chris's best friend at all. "John Gill was his best friend."

As for Chris's parents, she wouldn't object to their having visits with Bjorn. But first, she would have to insist that Dick take the same tests that "his letter" had asked of Nick Mattson. She mentioned the mystery letters several times, always attributing them to Dick, when there had been no proof that he had anything to do with them. She had made that judgment herself. And the letters had never mentioned Nick Mattson taking any tests.

Now Liysa played what she obviously considered her trump cards. She announced that Chris had told her that his father had sexually molested him when he was eight. How could she let her small child visit with a grandfather who was pedophile? She said that Chris had also told her that his mother was once a prostitute.

While Dick and Jeanne stared at her, poleaxed by these bizarre and false accusations, Liysa demanded that Dick submit to "penile excitation" tests before he ever be allowed visitation with either of her sons.

Not then, but later, Jeanne could almost laugh at such an outrageous denunciation of herself, but her heart was breaking for Dick, who was still struggling with the almost overwhelming loss of his son. There probably was nothing worse anyone could say about Dick, whose whole adult life had been dedicated to children, both as a teacher for thirty-one years and as a father, than to call him a child molester. It didn't matter that there wasn't a word of truth in what Liysa was saying; even the thought was humiliating.

Liysa was in her element, and in this arena she obviously intended to have the trial she felt she'd been denied. Although she accused the Storys of making this hearing "a theatrical event," she would be the one onstage.

She explained that she wanted Bjorn to know *her* friends,

too, people who could tell him about "the other side" of Chris. When attorney Seana Ash asked her if she had written a letter to three-year-old Bjorn a month after Chris's death telling him that his father had threatened her and him, too, Liysa said, "Yes," and offered to read it to the judge.

Proudly, she read it aloud: "It *is* okay to save your life and your baby's life. *That's what I did.* It's *not* okay to hit, choke, or try to kill anyone. That is what your dad did. It will just take some time for everything to get sorted out."

Liysa explained to Ash that she saw nothing wrong with giving a small child that blunt description. As she recalled, Bjorn had been asking questions and having bad dreams. So she'd given him what seemed to her a gentle explanation.

She then proceeded to tell the judge that the Storys were drug dealers, an old and familiar accusation of hers. It was patently obvious that Liysa meant to do everything she could to keep Bjorn away from Dave Story and Jeanne and Dick Northon. But *if* Dick would agree to take all the tests she wanted, Liysa said she would consider letting the Northons have Bjorn in their home for two days and one night twice a year.

Seana Ash, speaking for the Northons, said that her clients only wanted Bjorn in a good, safe, loving environment. During their visits to Kailua, they had found the Mattsons' home embodied all those things. Still, their wish was to have Bjorn visit them in Joseph for a week each summer when his three cousins were there on their vacations. That would be for the next three years. After that, they thought a two-week visit wouldn't be out of line.

As the hearing continued, Liysa's arguments wandered far afield. She wanted Judge Tiktin to know that she was having Dan Ousley investigated by the Oregon State Bar and that the Storys had perjured themselves "time after time after time."

Liysa's questioning often seemed quite skilled for a layperson, but it was also cruel. Her voice snarled with sarcasm as she cross-examined her former father-in-law. She was confrontational and demeaning, continually referring to his alleged "pedophilia." She tried to skewer Jeanne Northon, too. There was no longer any vestige of the "sweet young woman" who had come to Chris's door in Kailua.

Nick Mattson testified telephonically in this custody hearing. Liysa had fully expected that he would agree to "co-parent" Bjorn and only to assume guardianship of the little boy. She didn't want him to have custody. She intended to bring Bjorn to live with her when she got out of prison, although "not right away."

If Nick had custody, their reunion would be more difficult. Legally, Liysa might even find herself in the position of an unrelated party seeking custody. But Nick, who had almost always deferred to Liysa in the past, had changed and she seemed shocked. Until now, she had sent the Mattsons a barrage of directives about how Bjorn should be raised, what he should eat, his schoolwork, his bedtimes.

Bjorn had begun to call Nick "Dad," and that was fine with everyone but Liysa. He described Bjorn as "active and affectionate," and Nick angered Liysa when he said that Bjorn should spend time with Dave Story as well as himself.

Nick explained to the court that there would be far less stress and fewer arguments if his family didn't have to deal with Liysa directly. When she was released from prison, he hoped to have a fixed visitation schedule because they didn't want any surprise drop-in visits.

It was important, he testified, that Liysa not talk to Bjorn about money or his father's insurance. If she should decide to write any books in the future, he asked that his family not be mentioned.

Liysa asked Nick incredulously, a tinge of anger in her voice, "Don't you think that I'm capable of acting in Bjorn's best interest?"

"No," he said quietly.

But she wanted visitations in prison—more than two weeks a year, which would require that Bjorn travel to Oregon—and although Nick said he wouldn't rule out more visiting time, he had to balance prison visits with all the other people in Bjorn's life. "I don't want him to have too many obligations."

"But *I'm* his mother," Liysa said. "I'm his only blood parent. Aren't I the *most* important?"

"Yes—but it's harder when you're in prison for ten years."

Her voice tight, Liysa reminded Nick that she had sold him the Lanipo Street house below market value, saying she'd turned down an offer of $850,000 just so he could have the house for the boys.

"I saved the realtors' fees. That's all, Liysa," Nick said with some irony. "It's the second time I've bought this house without selling it."

Liysa either didn't catch his meaning or chose not to acknowledge that comment. Instead, she began to hammer Nick with questions, trying to get him to say something negative about Debbie and Dave Story. She reminded Nick that they had taken her journals and asked, "Should the Storys be *rewarded* for being annoying?"

Nick said only that, at times, it was more difficult to share Bjorn with Dave Story, but he said, "Bjorn has a good time with Dave, Liysa."

Despite her increasingly angry questions, Nick would not say what she wanted him to say—that he didn't want any court orders requiring him to let Bjorn spend time with the Storys. Liysa insisted that she could work things out with him, just as they'd always done.

"Have the Storys said anything negative about me?" she persisted.

"No—not for a long time. Just some facts about the case. We told them we didn't want to know the details."

This was a new Nick, one who wasn't trying to appease Liysa, and it seemed to baffle her. Why couldn't they have joint custody of Bjorn, just as they did with Papako? she asked him.

"We'll see in ten years," Nick answered. "You have a different bond with Papako than you have with Bjorn. Bjorn was only three and a half when he had to be separated from you."

"You always said I was a good parent," Liysa reminded him again. "Aren't I *still*?"

There was a long pause on the line, and finally Nick said, "You have some mental health issues that you need to deal with in therapy, Liysa. On one hand, you're a very good parent in so many ways. But if you thought Papako's life was in danger, you should have asked me to take him."

It was obvious that Liysa wanted him to tell her that she *was* a good parent, but Nick would say only that he wanted peace among the people who loved Bjorn.

"Do you believe that killing Chris was in Bjorn's best interest?" she pleaded.

"Only God knows. I don't want to make that judgment."

WHEN THE HEARING CONTINUED the next day, it was obvious that Liysa *did* intend to hold her own murder trial in this venue, but Judge Tiktin would not have it. Time after time he reminded her that her efforts to impugn Chris with witnesses and exhibits had nothing whatsoever to do with the present hearing. She had the right to offer proof that she had been afraid of her husband and that he did beat her—if she could do that—but not to present the entirely extraneous material she was trying to bring in.

Liysa was alternately aggressive and contrite. She smiled girlishly as she said to the judge, "Let me ask a question so I don't screw it up. At the end [of the hearing] can I bring up things not mentioned before?"

"No."

Tor DeWitt testified for his sister, identifying himself as "a physician." Mia Rose, perhaps her newest friend before the shooting, spoke of Liysa's utter terror. A handful of her women friends appeared, but many on her witness list hadn't come to Bend at all.

Liysa focused on four topics: her plans to oversee her sons' lives from prison and to "reintegrate" herself into their lives when she was free; Chris's alleged cruelty and use of marijuana; her own image as an exceptional mother; and her opinion that Dick Northon was a pedophile.

Jeanne Northon had watched her husband anxiously as Liysa went after him, jabbing at him with ugly questions. She did the same with Jeanne, and then, after three days, mercifully, the hearing was over.

ON SEPTEMBER 20, 2002, nineteen days before the second anniversary of Chris's death, Judge Stephen Tiktin wrote his decision on Bjorn's custody. The little boy would remain with Nick and Lora Lee Mattson, and with his two "brothers."

"To foster stability for Bjorn," Tiktin explained, "the Storys need the degree of authority and control over Bjorn's life to make the small day-to-day decisions and the larger more consequential decisions that parents would have without delay or uncertainty about who is in charge. To foster Bjorn's sense of permanency, the Mattsons and Bjorn need the kind of legal relationship that cannot easily be undone, readily challenged, or continually reviewed. The Mattsons will raise Bjorn for most, if not all, of his youth. They will be his 'parents.' They and Bjorn need the attributes of custody."

Judge Tiktin spelled out the rules: Liysa would be entitled to at least the minimum contact recommended by Billie Bell; her boys would be brought to whatever prison she was in. When he traveled to Oregon to visit Jeanne and Dick Northon, Bjorn would have a visit with his mother first. She could write to him and call him, but Nick and Lora Lee would monitor the content of her calls. She could write letters to the Mattsons, but they would be under no obligation to respond to or follow her recommendations. She could not contact Bjorn's teachers or his schools directly.

Four times a year, the Mattsons would keep Liysa advised of Bjorn's progress in school and his health and would send her a current photo. If he should have a serious medical problem, she had the right to be notified at once.

There would be *no* mention to Bjorn about his inheritance from his father or any other financial matters. His father had made sure that he would be well provided for, but the details shouldn't matter to a little boy. Liysa was forbidden to make negative comments about Chris or his relatives to Bjorn. Someday, with the approval of Bjorn's therapist, Liysa might be allowed to discuss his father's death with him.

Perhaps most important to his peace of mind, Liysa was ordered not to tell Bjorn that she might be released early. False expectations and promises she couldn't keep would be so cruel.

Finally, Judge Tiktin found that it had not been proven that Dick Northon had ever committed any act of sexual abuse against anyone. But the accusation had been made and it ate at Dick like acid.

After the custody hearing, Liysa's paid guard drove her back to Coffee Creek, and Dick and Jeanne headed home for Joseph. Another October lay ahead. It would always be a hard month for them, but the Northons hoped that it might at last be over. A terrible wound cannot begin to heal when it is continually ripped apart.

AFTERWORD

IN OCTOBER 2002, the Shady Campground looked virtually the same as it had two years earlier, but now there was no yellow crime scene tape fluttering in the wind, no trace at all of what had happened there. The air smelled of evergreen needles and dust because it hadn't rained in a long time. The road in was just as much a risky washboard as it must have been then.

I was there because I realized that it was essential that I see for myself what had once been a crime scene in order to understand the testimony of the Northon trial. I walked past the first picnic table, the logs that marked off the parking area, and then took the longer, less steep trail to the narrow sandy beach.

The sun was shining and the tall firs seemed more protective than lowering. Some of them had lost their purchase in the sandy loam and had collapsed into the Lostine, pale gray skeletons of dead wood with gnarled branches that might have caught the camp chair someone tossed into the river two years earlier.

The place where Chris Northon's body had once lain

couldn't have been blocking the entrance to either the steep path or the sloping path. His sleeping bag had been several feet away, his head closer to the logs that separated the beach from a thicket of vegetation. Now, wild flowers—daisies and purple asters—burst from the wild grass just beyond the sand line.

I could see that Liysa Northon should have been able to reach either their tent or her vehicle without stepping over her husband in the sleeping bag—or even coming very close to him. The tent where Bjorn slept had been *between* Chris and their vehicles. Liysa could have grabbed him and driven off at any time. Why didn't she?

And there were even more obvious questions that never really had answers: Why did Liysa plan a weekend in the wilderness with the husband she feared so much? Why *didn't* Liysa go for help in Wallowa County? She said she wasn't familiar with the area, but that wasn't true; she had spent all her summers there and had many relatives a short distance away from their campsite. Indeed, she drove right by the phone booth in Lostine, and the billboard behind it that promised help for victims of domestic violence—the billboard featured a counter that was frequently updated to say, "247 [or whatever the newest number was] Women Saved!"

I wish that I could have asked Liysa these questions in an interview, and she did contact me, communicating through one of her friends. She at first suggested—and then declined—talking with me or writing to me. Nor had she agreed to interviews with either Oregon State Detective Pat Montgomery or Attorney General's Investigator Dennis Dinsmore. She had talked continually to her friends and family, to fellow prisoners, to sympathetic domestic violence counselors, and yet she held back from anyone who had hard questions to ask her—including her own attorneys.

And so I have had to write this book from the view of those who knew her, those who knew Chris, from investigators and prosecutors, spectators in the courtroom, signed letters and emails, and, yes, anonymous correspondents. I have relied heavily on forensic evidence and the public record. My last four books have been about women who *were* abused, killed or nearly killed by someone who promised to love them and care for them, and I have long been a strong advocate and contributor to domestic violence support groups. So I had to struggle with my own preconceptions and prejudices as I began my research. In the end, I found that I could not explain the gaping inconsistencies in Liysa's recounting of her marriage and the way her husband died.

It is still unfathomable to me that a woman who seemed to have the whole world in her hands could not have simply walked away from a marriage that no longer fulfilled her needs. Liysa was well educated, had her own career, and almost unlimited emotional support from loyal friends and relatives. That she chose not to divorce Chris as she had Kurt Moran and Nick Mattson created an ever-spreading wave of tragedies that have yet to end. I believe that Liysa spent two years creating a monstrous persona for Chris, one cunningly designed to make her actions appear justifiable when she lured him to a lonely place, far from help, and shot him in the head.

An exhaustive review of the preparations Liysa made for this deadly weekend casts an appalling picture across the screen of one's mind. Chris wasn't expecting to go camping on October 6; he was just home from weeks of flying, planning to paint his storage shed, when Liysa told him she wanted to spend the weekend in the Wallowa Mountains. Apparently, he thought he was going to be the driver. He told this to Dan Jones during Dan's call on that Friday afternoon. It's plausible that Chris went along with Liysa's plans because, as Dave Story said, "Chris was always looking for solutions." Chris may have seen the camping trip as away to help save his marriage.

They could have gone camping near Bend, but Liysa chose

a county with a small population where murder investigations were rare. If, however, she expected that lawmen in Wallowa County were too inexperienced to consider the possibility of deliberate homicide, she was woefully mistaken. Every detective knows the progression of suspicion they must take in cases of sudden death. First murder, next suicide, then accidental, and, finally, natural.

It's unlikely that Liysa ever intended to take Papako on the Lostine River trip. He would have enjoyed camping, but instead she chose to leave him hundreds of miles away, a detour which meant she had at least sixteen hours of grueling driving. Was it because Papako was old enough to recognize what was going to happen and would surely remember it?

No one alive except Liysa knows what really happened from the time she joined Chris on Saturday afternoon, October 7, until the early hours of Monday morning. Bjorn was too young at the time to be a credible witness, and he was sleeping soundly after Liysa gave him his cold medicine. And Chris is dead.

Apparently, the three of them spent Saturday night and Sunday morning together at the campsite without incident. Liysa herself had told Deputy Kevin Larkin that she left Bjorn alone with Chris while she hiked on Sunday. That wars with her description of Chris a few hours later. The thought of Chris holding a knife to the throat of the child he cherished is suspect—and highly unlikely.

But Liysa maintained that had happened and that she drove away from the campsite Sunday afternoon. And, even though she was afraid for her life and Bjorn's life, she went back. *Why?* To fix supper for a man who terrified her? I think she went back to trick Chris into swallowing an overdose of Restoril. Or perhaps she had already slipped the sleeping pills into his lunch and she came back to see if he was unconscious.

The autopsy findings showed no food remained in Chris's stomach, so he probably didn't eat supper. (His stomach lining, however, was ulcerated and inflamed which raises the question: Had Chris been given slow poison even *before* their deadly camping trip?)

Liysa recalled, however, that they had eaten Sunday evening, and that she and Chris were sitting in chairs beside the river when she chided him about his drinking. That makes no sense. She knew they were far away from any help. If Chris was truly a wife beater, why would she have waved a red flag in his face in such an isolated spot?

It seems more likely that something like the following occurred. Believing that Chris was almost comatose, Liysa somehow maneuvered him so that most of his body was in the Lostine River, while she knelt in the sand over him, holding his head underwater. She had emailed her father months earlier to say that "drowning is the best in terms of detection" but she wanted a gun "for backup."

Now, for good measure, Liysa zapped Chris's chest with one of the stun guns. He was burned, but was not electrocuted as she had planned. And the water was frigid, rousing Chris enough to struggle instinctively with Liysa to get to the surface where he could breathe. This might well have been when she suffered a black eye. It's also quite possible that Liysa struck her own cheekbone with a rock to bolster her story that she'd been fighting for her life.

Chris would have had just enough strength to crawl out of the water. As he lay on the sandy beach, Liysa must have taken off his soaked clothing (with the pockets full of sand from the struggle in the river) and removed his sodden shoes, hanging his clothes on the remaining camp chair. If he were found naked, it would support her frequent claims that he raped her.

There probably *were* moments where Chris rose up from

the sand, confused and arms flailing, but the sedative in his blood wouldn't have allowed him to think clearly. As he rolled on the beach, his wet body was dusted completely with sand.

At this point, Liysa must have resorted to an alternative plan. Somehow, she coaxed Chris into his mummy sleeping bag. She certainly could not have lifted a two-hundred-pound man herself and dragged him into it. She may even have whispered comforting words to him, telling him that she didn't want him to catch cold. He would have been too disoriented at this point to weigh her words or what was happening to him.

And then she must have zipped it up to his chin. Chris couldn't get out of the bag.

Now Liysa waited. How long she waited only Liysa knows. Although Chris's brain function was so heavily compromised, his kidneys were still working and his bladder filled to the point where he would have been very uncomfortable if he were in a state of awareness. But he couldn't urinate in his comatose state.

Liysa went up to her vehicle and loaded her gun—accidentally firing one chamber in the process. The loud crack of a shot in the night air didn't wake Chris up because he *couldn't* wake up.

Once her gun was loaded, Liysa returned to a spot above where Chris lay immobilized in his sleeping bag. It's not likely that she shot blindly in the dark, running by with the gun in one hand and their little boy in her other arm, as she claimed initially. The Petzel miner's light on the headband would have focused a cone of bright white through the darkest night. Did she shout "I'm taking the baby and leaving?" Probably not. Why would she? Bjorn was still asleep in their tent beyond Chris's body.

She probably had rubber gloves on, perhaps to keep her fingerprints off the gun. She clearly prepared for this last camping trip with far more than camping gear and picnic food. Although detectives, criminalists, and lawyers still disagree on where she actually stood as she shot Chris, they agree on one thing. Liysa took careful aim—either from the knoll above Chris, from the side, or from a position at his feet. There were no powder burns or gun barrel debris around Chris's head wound, so she was more than twenty-four inches away. But she was close enough so that not even a novice could miss as she used the gun her father had given her to protect herself. But it doesn't appear that she was "protecting" either herself or Bjorn; she was getting rid of Chris and moving on with her life with her widow's windfall and all the privileges Hawaiian Airlines afford families of deceased pilots.

She likely had plenty of time to rouse Bjorn and fasten him in his car seat because Chris was either unconscious or fatally wounded. Just in case, Liysa probably took Chris's cell phone and his car keys with her, and tossed them out into the brush or down the mountain as she headed north.

When she raced away from the Shady Campground, Liysa's long hair and her clothing probably *were* wet from the struggle in the river, but it's doubtful they stayed wet over the next four hours as she turned up the heat in her Ford Explorer. Apparently, she felt her story would have more impact if she was not only bruised, but wet, too. Undoubtedly, she stopped somewhere along the way to douse herself with water before she reached Ellen Duveaux's house. She wanted Ellen to see how damp and cold she was.

There were a number of gas stations and travelers' rest stops between the campgrounds and the Walla Walla Area. It wouldn't have been at all difficult for Liysa to splash herself at a sink along the way to add credence to her story. There were also streams, irrigation ditches, huge sprinklers swirling in the produce fields, fountains and bottled water at convenience stores. I think that Liysa refreshed her "drowned rat" look somewhere along the way.

But for all her two years of groundwork setting Chris up as a wife beater and her meticulous plans, Liysa had made stupid mistakes. She told everyone that he had been drinking vodka, but crime scene investigators found no vodka bottles among the liquor bottles scattered around the campsite. Actually, these looked like the contents of someone's liquor cabinet, mostly liqueurs and wines that Chris didn't even like. I think that Liysa brought them from home to bolster her claim that Chris was drunk.

However, despite the fact that she was an avid reader of the mystery genre, Liysa apparently didn't expect blood alcohol and drug tests to be done on Chris's blood. She seemed completely ignorant of how much can be determined through postmortem examinations and blood and urine tests. She obviously thought the shooting would appear so cut and dried to the authorities that she wouldn't even spend a night in jail.

Chris's life was snuffed out with one shot, ending it when it was, statistically, only half lived. Hundreds of people would miss Chris, but none so much as his little boy, Bjorn. And for all intents and purposes *two* little boys were left without a mother. Liysa considered herself, above all, a wonderful mother, and it may never have occurred to her that her carefully premeditated plans to kill Chris wouldn't work out—and that she would not only destroy Chris but the serenity and joy of Papako's and Bjorn's lives. She is extremely intelligent, but her ability to connect cause and effect is flawed. Because she appears to see her life in "episodes," she probably didn't realize that clever and stubborn detectives would be able to string all the times of her life together until they found a repetitive pattern of deceit and destruction.

Liysa's own explanations and recollections simply did not fit, and she changed her versions of Chris's shooting often enough to make investigators blink. More devastating to her,

her screenplays and musings were *not* swallowed up forever in her computers; they lay there in wait to trap her with their searing similarities to the scenario she acted out in real life. She would have been wise to throw those computers into the Pacific Ocean or the Columbia River—or even in a garbage dump.

* * *

PAPAKO AND BJORN are doing as well as it's possible for two children whose family was ripped away to do. Nick Mattson is a loving and gentle man and he and his wife, Lora Lee, have welcomed both boys into their home. They are happy and cherished there.

Liysa writes to them once a week, perhaps picturing them suspended in time awaiting her return. When she gets out of prison, her sons will no longer be little boys who are comfortable with the constant attention and control of a mother who wants to shape and mold them to her image of what they should be. It's difficult enough for adults to keep a firm picture of someone in mind when there is no personal contact for months and months, and when what there is takes place in prison visiting rooms. It's even harder for children. Liysa, who prided herself on always being there for her boys, may never have considered how she was robbing them to get what *she* wanted. All the letters and stories in the world can't begin to make up for an act of violence that took not only Chris away from Papako and Bjorn but also removed *her* from their lives.

Papako had more time to bond with Liysa and she encouraged his dependence upon her. Of her two sons, he probably misses her the most. Bjorn was so like his father. There is no more cheerful "Mydad" bragging for him, no hikes, swims, bicycle riding, fishing, sports with his dad. He has two wonderful substitute "dads," but neither is his own father. Fortunately,

Liysa failed in her attempt to keep Bjorn from seeing his paternal grandparents, the cousins close to him in age, and the man he calls "My best friend": Dave Story.

With Nick Mattson's full approval, Dave Story tries to spend time every week with Bjorn, and Bjorn often sleeps over at the Storys' house on weekends. Dave is with Bjorn "as kind of a tribute to Chris," but it fills an empty place for Story, too. He often takes Bjorn down to the beach.

Once, when they were playing there, one of the women from the "pool group" recognized them and came down to speak to Story. "She said that she—and many of the other women in the group—realized now that Chris wasn't the one who was causing trouble in the marriage," Dave Story recalled. "She said she was sorry. *They* were sorry."

Although her regrets came far too late to save Chris, it helped to know that his reputation would not be tarnished forever.

"Chris would never hurt anything," Story said. "The thought of Liysa trying to drown him was ridiculous. If he'd been conscious, he would have laughed at her for trying such a thing. He would have thought she was kidding around. And if he had ever hit Liysa, she would have had terrible bruises and broken bones. Chris was *very* strong."

Dave bought a bike for Bjorn and often takes him out riding. Although a court order forbids anyone saying negative things about Liysa or her family to Bjorn, he knows what happened. Liysa herself told him—before she was forbidden to do so. She'd told both her sons, first waking Papako up at Ellen Duveaux's house with the news, and later writing to Bjorn.

Dave had occasion to see how vocal Bjorn is about the circumstances of his life. "We were talking to a grandmother who was in the park with her daughter and her grandchild. She asked Bjorn if I was his father. Bjorn shook his head and said, 'Oh no. My dad is dead. My mommy shot him and she's in jail.'

"I can't describe the look on that lady's face," Story recalled.

*　*　*

DAVE STORY IS CAREFUL to keep his conversations with Bjorn away from the subject of Liysa Northon. Story doesn't like her, but he knows it's important for Bjorn to believe in his mother until he's old enough to deal with all he has lost.

"Liysa draws people into her web," Story says slowly. "It's not that she's charismatic; it's far more dangerous than that. The thing about really good liars is that they know to put a grain of truth in their stories and then they interweave them with fiction. Liysa does that."

In his opinion, Liysa traveled constantly because she believed that "the grass was always greener someplace else."

It may have been that Liysa was seeking a geographical solution to the depression and anxiety that sometimes bubbled up to the surface of her mind. In her own view, she never got enough of anything: love, property, money, respect, excitement, or sex. Only Papako was perfect in her eyes, and even he had learned "to walk on tiptoe" around her as he grew older.

Liysa has not slowed down her efforts to walk free, or her vendettas against those people who, she feels, helped put her in prison.

On November 11, 2002, she painstakingly filled out an Executive Clemency application to send to Oregon Governor John Kitzhaber. She explained that she could not file an appeal because she had been "forced" to accept a plea bargain. She intended to file for post-conviction relief as soon as she could, but because Kitzhaber's term of office was almost over, she wanted to get her application in in time for him to review it. She was asking to have her entire sentence commuted.

With no computer any longer, she printed the answers to the questions, but her story was the same scenario. She had shot her husband because he was a murderous ogre intent on killing her and her child. She had done it so that "at least my children would be safe." She has proclaimed this so many, many times that it's probable that she believes it now.

Answering a question on her plans for future employment, Liysa wrote, "I plan to resume photography and writing and to open a 'Recovery Center' for families destroyed by domestic violence. This will be a place where those families can heal emotionally and physically, learn 'non-violent' communication, job skills, balance health, art therapy and pet therapy—a place to stay for at least a year or two to rebuild. This will stop the cycle of abuse from being perpetuated in the children who've been subjected to domestic violence, save the taxpayers thousands of dollars down the road. I plan to dedicate my life to helping prevent domestic violence."

In essence, it would still be her "Chrysalis," the sheltering ranch she had always wanted. Liysa has not lost her facility in letter writing. Her plea for clemency was a model of self-sacrifice and the terrible pain of a true victim—herself. When she finished filling out the form, Liysa added several more pages to drive her point home.

"My husband promised me that if he killed me, they would not find my body. I admit to having fantasies about my husband's death. However, this is 100% normal for victims of abuse. Despite having a gun, I did not use it for over a year and only when my husband tried to kill me."

Liysa blamed her attorneys, "prosecutorial misconduct," and Court TV for her imprisonment. She ended her impassioned plea, "I am sincerely hoping that you commute my sentence before you leave office, as it is a rare opportunity. I beg that you show mercy and allow me to return to my children. I did not take a life for sport or greed or lust. I did it to spare my own and the lives of my children. Not a day goes by that I don't grieve that it came to this—a choice between handcuffs or a headstone."

It was the first time Liysa had ever mentioned grieving, but was it for Chris or for herself?

Liysa's list of character references began with Randall Edwards, the Oregon State treasurer. Whether she told Edwards about this is questionable. She listed Deputy Dick Bobbitt; her old screenwriting partner, Craig Elliot; and Marni Clark—but most of the sixteen references were people who were relatively new in her life. Her champions of the past have mostly fallen away, disillusioned and full of doubt now.

Her plea reached Kitzhaber so late that his staff passed Liysa's clemency request on to his successor, Governor Ted Kulongoski.

Liysa's plea for clemency, citing the same old issues, was too much for District Attorney Dan Ousley and Dick and Jeanne Northon. Ousley fired off a letter to the governor explaining what had really happened, and noting that Liysa had had experienced and well-respected defense attorneys, who "did not even raise the defense of battered woman syndrome. Any and all claims of domestic violence were examined and rejected by both sides."

Liysa had agreed to a plea bargain and been sentenced according to that agreement, Ousley said. "Since that resolution of the murder charge, the Defendant has made life a living hell for the victim's family and friends. In the court cases involving guardianship and conservatorship of the couple's son, the Defendant has repeatedly made ugly, false, and unsubstantiated claims against the family, including claims of pedophilia, drug use and dealing, and financial fraud, all of which have been rejected by the Court in Deschutes County."

Dick Northon's letter argued with Liysa's claim that Chris's murder had not been motivated by "greed." "Chris's estate is valued at $1.2 million and this was her third marriage (his first).

She would have inherited all of his estate had she been successful in her attempts to drug and drown him."

Liysa mentioned in her clemency form that she helped support her sons with the royalties from her book and photographs. Dick hastened to correct that. "Chris and Liysa's son, Bjorn, is supported by Chris's Social Security and through Bjorn's conservatorship. Nick and Lora Lee Mattson were awarded *Legal Custody* of Bjorn, and not guardianship as she tried to infer."

There were other cogent arguments for keeping Liysa in prison, all of them part of the public record now. In May 2003, Governor Kulongoski denied Liysa's clemency plea.

Next, Liysa filed suit against Dave and Debbie Story, citing the theft of her journals and other written material. That suit has been rejected by the Court. She is also suing her own trial attorneys, Pat Birmingham and Wayne Mackeson, alleging that they were incompetent and claiming in her post-conviction relief hearing that she was forced to plead guilty to manslaughter because she had an inadequate legal defense.

If she should prevail and be granted a new trial, Liysa Northon will be taking a terrible chance. She doesn't need to fear the death penalty, but another conviction might not bring with it the comparatively short 150-month sentence that Birmingham and Mackeson negotiated for her. If she lost, she would lose big and quite possibly face a sentence of twenty-five years to life.

* * *

PARTIALLY DUE to her own depictions of her actual life *and* her fantasy world, no one really knows what Liysa's childhood was like. The mother who spoke out on her behalf after Chris's murder is the same mother that Liysa called "irrational" and "an agent from hell." A thorough search of hospital records in every town where the DeWitts lived failed to show even one notation of Liysa's suffering a broken bone—much less twenty-six broken bones.

Her high school years appear to be as normal and uneventful as any other student at Wa-Hi, although Liysa was more popular than most. She didn't leave home at sixteen as she claims, and it's questionable that she was grounded for an entire year for getting drunk at her prom. That would have kept her from beginning college in the fall.

Her bizarre claims seem to have begun after she left home. There are gaps of months—even years—in the eighties when it is impossible to validate where Liysa was or what she was doing.

Her life from then on has been lived in a very compartmentalized fashion, as if she sealed off the secrets of one relationship from the next. Like a dragonfly, Liysa never lit long on one spot.

Liysa doesn't appear to be insane—either medically, or legally under the McNaughton Rule. She certainly planned the trip to the Lostine River, and made every effort to cover up the premeditation of her crime afterward. She knew the difference between right and wrong, although it may not have mattered to her.

And yet Liysa can hardly be characterized as having no mental illness. Her behavior falls within the parameters of several personality disorders. Those suffering from personality disorders behave and think quite rationally, and yet they view the world from a different angle than the normal person does.

Personality disorders are tenacious and almost impossible to treat, mostly because the sociopathic subject doesn't *want* to be treated. They *like* the way they are. I've often said that treatment for an entrenched personality disorder would be like trying to peel ivy off the lobes and fissures of a brain. While you are extricating it from one side, it is growing back on the other.

Personality disorders tend to come in clusters, and it isn't unusual for a subject to have three or four. Those with antisocial personalities have virtually no empathy for others and no conscience. They will take what they want without the pangs of guilt most people would suffer, and never look back.

Liysa also seems to be histrionic, acting out dramatic scenes and delighting in calling attention to herself. Those with histrionic personality disorder enjoy being onstage so much that sometimes they don't care if they're eliciting positive or negative attention. The most important thing is to have an audience focused on themselves.

Both antisocial and histrionic disorders seem to manifest themselves in Liysa Northon's erratic behavior, but, most of all, she appears to be suffering from bipolar disorder. Dr. Ben Clark, her high school friend's husband, noted this early in his friendship with Liysa, although he acknowledged he was not a psychiatrist. Bipolar personalities may almost always be *up* in the manic phase of the disorder, or as he described Liysa, "always going." Some patients are depressed most of the time. More to be expected, most bipolar subjects soar up, only to crash into bleak depression—and then the cycle begins again.

Those in the grip of the manic phase are full of emotions, excessive joy, excitement, overactivity, tremendous energy, and they make grandiose plans. They seldom need to sleep and they often have unrealistic goals. But as they come to the top of the roller coaster and start down, they are sad and lonely and exhausted. Where they once felt powerful and brilliant, they suddenly feel worthless and anxious.

Liysa had such ambitious plans for her chain of re-energizing ranches and spas, which none of the men she married could afford to give her. When she was convinced of that, she moved on to someone else—"marrying up" as some who knew her said. Her screenwriting career sent her into free flight and the belief that she really needed no one—not even Craig Elliot, who was willing to share his fame and expertise with her. When their first project wasn't picked up by a studio, Liysa dropped Elliot and plunged into such depression that she didn't comb her hair or change her clothes, and remained locked behind her blinds.

Nick Mattson took care of Liysa the longest, sharing all of his skills with her and encouraging her. But she came to a place where she felt that even he was trying to booby-trap her career.

Of all aspects of her life, Liysa seemed to be the most conflicted about sex. She delighted in telling anyone who would listen that she *had* to have sex every day, and she often said that she stayed with Chris because their physical intimacy was perfect. At the same time, she accused him of rape, just as her past was riddled with accounts of men who allegedly raped or molested her—from the nameless ship captain to the navy Seal instructor. She accused Chris of being addicted to pornography and his father of being a pedophile. Her sexual obsession and, perhaps, *fear* of the males she seduces seems to color everything she does.

The natural assumption would be that Liysa suffered sexual abuse at some time in her life, possibly when she was a child. But, oddly, she has never spoken of that.

While Liysa serves her term at the new women's prison at Coffee Creek, the world goes on without her. The world goes on without Chris, too. Papako and Bjorn still live with Nick and Lora Lee Mattson. Liysa's first child is growing tall as he and his two brothers live in the paradise that is Kailua, the first home he knew.

Bjorn has a scrapbook of pictures of his father, but it's hard for him to remember Chris in action. He is eager to see videotapes of his dad, and the Northons, Mattsons, and Storys are hoping that there are some still in existence. Perhaps someone reading this may have tapes with Chris's image moving and talking. When Bjorn is older, he will get the book with letters from every pilot flying for Hawaiian Airlines with his father. They took it upon themselves to write their remembrances of Chris to help his son know him.

In the summer of 2003, Chris's friend Dan Jones flew with Bjorn to Portland. Wayland DeWitt then took Bjorn to a picnic at the Coffee Creek Correctional Facility where children can visit with their mothers in an outdoor setting that seems less like a prison than the visiting area inside. Papako, traveling separately, also attended the Coffee Creek picnic.

After Bjorn visited with Liysa, Dan flew him to Joseph for a week's visit with his Northon grandparents.

It isn't easy for all of Papako's and Bjorn's relatives to carry out court orders and be sure that the boys travel thousands of miles without an excess of fatigue and emotional upset. Liysa's parents and Chris's parents see the boys on separate occasions and their transfers are handled tactfully with a great deal of help from Nick Mattson, Dave Story, Dan Jones, and others.

Joe and Maggie Wilson moved to eastern Pennsylvania when he was transferred. They had their third child in 2002.

Pat Montgomery is still stationed in La Grande, Oregon, where he is often assigned to cases of child abuse, still making a difference in young lives.

Dennis Dinsmore has been working back-to-back high-profile homicide cases in Oregon, and running in marathons when he has rare moments off.

Steve Briggs is now head of the Organized Crime Section of the Oregon Attorney General's office. He recently prosecuted Christian Longo, who was convicted of killing his wife and three young children on the Oregon coast just before Christmas 2002. Longo received the death penalty.

Dan Ousley was reelected to the office of District Attorney of Wallowa County. Crime in his county has returned to its usual, more predictable patterns.

Dr. Jon "Tor" DeWitt's chiropractic office is no longer listed in the Walla Walla phone book.

Wayland DeWitt has married for the second time. His bride is Ukranian, a woman close to Liysa's age. Wayland had to wade through a year's paperwork before he could bring his new wife to America. She speaks no English, but is reportedly learning.

Jeanne and Dick Northon lived almost seventy years facing the normal problems that most humans do. No one who loves and raises children ever glides through life without disappointments, anxiety, regrets, and their share of emotional pain. But those who lose a child to murder cannot describe the agony, except perhaps to others who have suffered the same loss. They have filed a civil suit against Liysa for their son's wrongful death.

The Northons plant as many flowers as their deck can hold, and watch the deer eat those plants they prefer, and thus they learn what not to plant again. They take long walks every morning, and stop to talk with their neighbors. They attend potluck suppers and live *almost* the kind of life they hoped for in their retirement years. When the lake is calm, they go kayaking, finding a serenity that is mostly elusive for them. On some nights, they eat out at the big lodge in Joseph, where Gail Swart, a kind woman who plays the piano there, turns to some of Chris's favorites, particularly "Für Elise" and "Somewhere in Time."

When Jeanne shops in Joseph, strangers sometimes say, "Northon? I know that name," and then stammer with embarrassment when they realize where they heard it. Jeanne has learned to say, "Don't feel bad—it's okay."

They still have two beloved daughters and five grandchildren, and their lives go on, but the tragedy of losing their only son will never go away from their thoughts.

Every so often, I get a letter or an email from someone who

knew Chris. Too often, those who write are apprehensive and say, "I know this couldn't be the Chris Northon I knew. The guy I knew was a pilot and he got along with everyone."

And I have to tell them that, yes, this is the Chris Northon they knew.

There are also communiqués from those who knew Liysa. And they are mixed. Some are angry that I might write about her and "make her look guilty," and then I got an email this week:

"I was supposed to testify on Liysa's behalf at her trial. After seeing the prosecution's evidence on Court TV, I am convinced that she is guilty."

Acknowledgments

I AM GRATEFUL to so many people who led me through the mazes of this very complex case. In most instances, it was painful for them to relive blighted friendships and tragic family ties. I appreciate their willingness to speak once again about what seemed too devastating to be true. In terms of human misery and regret, it didn't really matter which side they supported. Those who believed in the killer are just as bereft as those who cherished the victim. While I am confident that this book will resonate with many of those involved in this story, I am keenly aware that some others will disagree with my conclusions.

My thanks go to Detective Patric Montgomery, Oregon State Police; Criminal Investigator Dennis Dinsmore, Oregon Attorney General's Office; Wallowa County District Attorney Dan Ousley; Carol Terry, Assistant to Dan Ousley; Jary Homan, Klista Steinbeck, and Tracey Hall, Wallowa County Court Operations Specialists; Oregon Assistant Attorney General Steven Briggs; Detective Matt Cross, Wallowa County Sheriff's Office; Sheriff Ron Jett, Wallowa County; Undersheriff

Rich Stein, Wallowa County; Deputy Kevin Larkin, Columbia County Washington Sheriff's Office; Detective Rob Ringsage, Oregon State Police; Detective Mike Wilson, Oregon State Police; Detective Jim Van Atta, Oregon State Police; Oregon Circuit Judge Philip Mendiguren, Anita Wilson (his assistant); Lucinda Heitmansk, Court Reporter; Dr. Karen Gunson, Oregon State Medical Examiner; FBI Special Agent Ariel Miller; Dr. Lowell Euhus, Medical Examiner, Wallowa County; Dr. Khalil Helou, pathologist; Jody Williamson, United States Forest Service.

And more thanks to a large number of private citizens in Oregon, Hawaii, Colorado, Idaho, and Washington State: Seana McMann Ash; Gay Bradshaw; Steve Brown; Amy Cross; Starla Dubois; Eva and John Gill; Mary Hetz; Kris Olsen; Becky Jones; Maggie and Joe Rhys-Wilson; Dan Jones; Debbie and Dave Story; Sharon Leighty; Betsy Haygood; Kay Teel; Jane and Allen Lipp; Jeanne and Dick Northon; Randy Ore; Sally Byers, Dr. David R. Jones; Marge Seidelman; Carol Ware; Ann Brower; Mari; Darla Sunderman; Jane Pultz; Dakota S. Smith; Doris Steiger; Ram's Head Inn, Joseph, Oregon; Elane Dickenson; Warren Kitchell; Carrie and Arnie Arnesen; Dr. Corrie Allen; Holly and Lori Lucas; Barbara Chitwood; Kathy Lepper; Tom Hutchinson; Kathleen Erskine; Patty Ousley; Lisa Sater; Lisa Ousley; Rick Northon; John Saul; Michael Sack; and the Maui Writers Conference.

To my friends and mentors at Simon & Schuster/Free Press, all the publishers, editors, production people, copy editors, proofreaders, attorneys, the team that I count on to take a manuscript from my computer and transform it into an actual book: Carolyn Reidy, who has always encouraged me; Martha Levin, Fred Hills, and Burton Beals (Our *eighth* book together!); Andrea Au, Hilda Koparanian, Isolde Sauer, Suzanne Anderson, Betty Harris, Alese Pickering, and Jennifer Weidman. Any author who believes she can do it *all* is fooling herself, and I am more appreciative with each book for all the suggestions, edits, and cuts (even though I may not show it at the time!).

To my literary agents of thirty-three years, Joan and Joe Foley of the Foley Agency; and my theatrical agent, Ron Bernstein, vice president, ICM.

And, always, thank you to my *first reader,* Gerry Brittingham Hay, my home-grown proofreader; Leslie Rule, my best friend and fellow author; Donna Anders; "Head Cheerleader" Shirley Hickman; and my gratitude to my family, who sometimes wonder if I *ever* come out from in front of my computer: Laura Harris; Matt Harris; Rebecca Harris; Kevin Wagner; Andy Rule; Mike Rule; Marni Campbell; Bruce, Machel, Olivia, and Tyra Sherles; Ugo, Nancy, and Lucas Fiorante; Freda Sampson Grunwald; Jim and Mary Sampson; Karen and Jim Hudson; Donna and Stuart Basom; Jan and Ebbe Schubert; Bruce and Dianne Basom; Chris and Linda McKenney; Maxine, Christa, and Terry Hansen; Sara Jane and Larry Plushnik; Glenna Longwell; Lucetta May Bartley; Sherman Stackhouse; and David Stackhouse.

And, finally, in loving memory of two of my dearest friends whom I lost in 2003: my neighbor, Jenny Everson; and my fellow detective Joyce Johnson (retired), Seattle Police Department.

About the Author

Ann Rule came to her career with a solid background in law enforcement and the criminal justice system. Both her grandfather and her uncle were Michigan sheriffs, and she was once a Seattle police officer herself. Ann has been a full-time true-crime author since 1969. She has published 22 books, all still in print, and 1,400 articles in such publications as *Cosmopolitan, Ladies' Home Journal, Good Housekeeping, The Chicago Tribune,* and *True Detective.* Ann Rule serves as executive producer of the miniseries of her books. She is a certified instructor for police training seminars in the thirteen western states, lecturing on serial murder, women who kill, and high-profile offenders. She has presented papers three times for the National Academy of Forensic Science, and has lectured at the FBI Academy, and to the National Association of District Attorneys. She has testified twice before Senate judicial sub committees on victims' rights and serial murder. She worked on the U.S. Justice Department Task Force to set up VICAP, the Violent Criminals Apprehension Program. Ann now lives near Seattle, Washington, on the shores of Puget Sound.

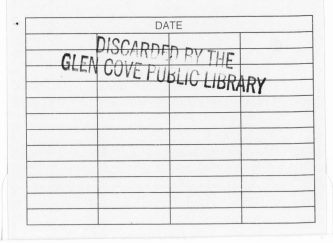